SHOP IMPROVEMENTS

GREAT DESIGNS FROM FINE WOODWORKING
SHOP IMPROVEMENTS

The Editors of Fine Woodworking

The Taunton Press

The Taunton Press
Inspiration for hands-on living®

The Taunton Press, Inc., 63 South Main Street, PO Box 5506, Newtown, CT 06470-5506
e-mail: tp@taunton.com

EDITOR: MATTHEW TEAGUE
JACKET/COVER DESIGN: RENATO STANISIC
INTERIOR DESIGN: RENATO STANISIC
LAYOUT: LAURA LIND DESIGN
FRONT COVER PHOTOGRAPHERS: MATT BERGER, ©THE TAUNTON PRESS, INC.;
INSET: ALEC WATERS, ©THE TAUNTON PRESS, INC.
BACK COVER PHOTOGRAPHER: STROTHER PURDY, ©THE TAUNTON PRESS, INC.;
DRAWING: DAVID DANN, ©THE TAUNTON PRESS, INC.

Library of Congress Cataloging-in-Publication Data

Shop improvements : great designs from Fine woodworking.
p. cm.
ISBN-13: 978-1-56158-891-6
ISBN-10: 1-56158-891-1
1. Workshops. 2. Woodwork--Equipment and supplies. 3. Jigs and fixtures. I. Fine woodworking.

TT153.S465 2007
684'.08--dc22

2006103141

Printed in the United States of America
10 9 8 7 6

ACKNOWLEDGMENTS

Special thanks to the authors, editors, art directors, copy editors, and other staff members of *Fine Woodworking* who contributed to the development of the articles in this book.

CONTENTS

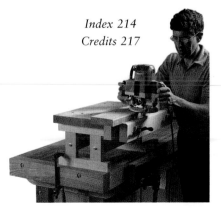

INTRODUCTION

The end product—furniture—is what draws most people to woodworking. You see a cabinet you'd like to replicate, or a table you wish were a foot narrower, or you are simply out of shelves and set out to build a bookcase. But I'm convinced that most woodworkers stick with the craft because of what happens in the workshop—not what comes out of it.

This book—compiled from years' worth of articles from *Fine Woodworking* magazine—offers a peek inside the shops of some of the world's finest craftsmen. Whether it's an elaborate workbench designed for cutting dovetails or a simple jig used to cut tapered legs, woodworkers have come up with smart, efficient aids for

storing, surfacing and shaping wood. And the smartest ones I've seen are all featured here.

The workstations, jigs, fixtures, and storage units in this book are presented with detailed exploded drawings—all the information woodworkers need to build their own. But the ingenious creations here also serve as a launching point for designing jigs, fixtures and shop improvements for your own workshop. This book is a celebration of what goes on behind the scenes in the woodshop—studied closely, it's as mesmerizing as the furniture that leaves the shop.

— MATTHEW TEAGUE

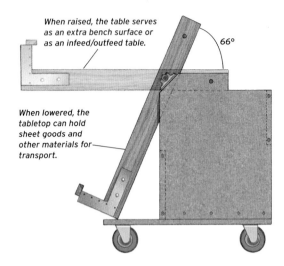

When raised, the table serves as an extra bench surface or as an infeed/outfeed table.

66°

When lowered, the tabletop can hold sheet goods and other materials for transport.

TILT-TOP SHOP CART HANDLES PLYWOOD

By Fred Sotcher

The first time I manhandled a sheet of 1-in.-thick medium-density fiberboard (MDF) onto my tablesaw, I realized that I needed something to assist with this backbreaking task. My wish list required this shop aid to do the following tasks:

1. Assist with feeding large boards and sheet goods onto the tablesaw
2. Transport sheet goods and other materials from my truck to the shop
3. Double as an additional bench surface when needed
4. Act as a tablesaw infeed/outfeed table
5. Store conveniently out of the way

It's safe to say that this cart meets all of those requirements. The tilting top makes it easy to load and feed sheet goods onto the tablesaw. Heavy-duty casters allow me to wheel it around the shop. It also works as an independent bench or as an outfeed table extension to my tablesaw.

I wanted a top that remained flat yet was light in weight, so I chose torsion-box construction. The interior is made up of 3-in.-wide pine strips stapled and glued into 5-in. squares. The box then is framed with a thicker hardwood, and the two sides are covered with Masonite®. Pressure laminate is applied over the Masonite on the top. Two 1/8-in. by 12-in. by 12-in. metal angles (Simpson® 1212L), with one leg cut off each at 7 in., support the shelf, which is constructed of hardwood.

The base of the cart is built using 1-in.-thick MDF and connected with 1/4-20 knockdown fasteners. (You could probably get by with 3/4-in.-thick MDF.) A 3/4-in.-dia. shaft extends through the table and terminates in pillow blocks at both ends, forming the pivot point for the table. With the pivot point near the center of gravity of the sheet goods, you can pivot several hundred pounds of material with little effort. At the opposite end of the table, a 3/8-in.-dia. locking pin is used to lock the top in the horizontal position.

I made the cart the same height as my tablesaw. When I'm not using it to feed stock, it fits behind the saw, where it acts as an outfeed table extension.

Fred Sotcher is a retired electrical engineer and an avid woodworker who lives in San Jose, California.

The L-shaped tilting top holds several sheets of plywood. A pin locks the tabletop in the horizontal position. Large locking casters can handle bumps in the concrete without stalling. Pillow blocks make for a smooth pivoting action.

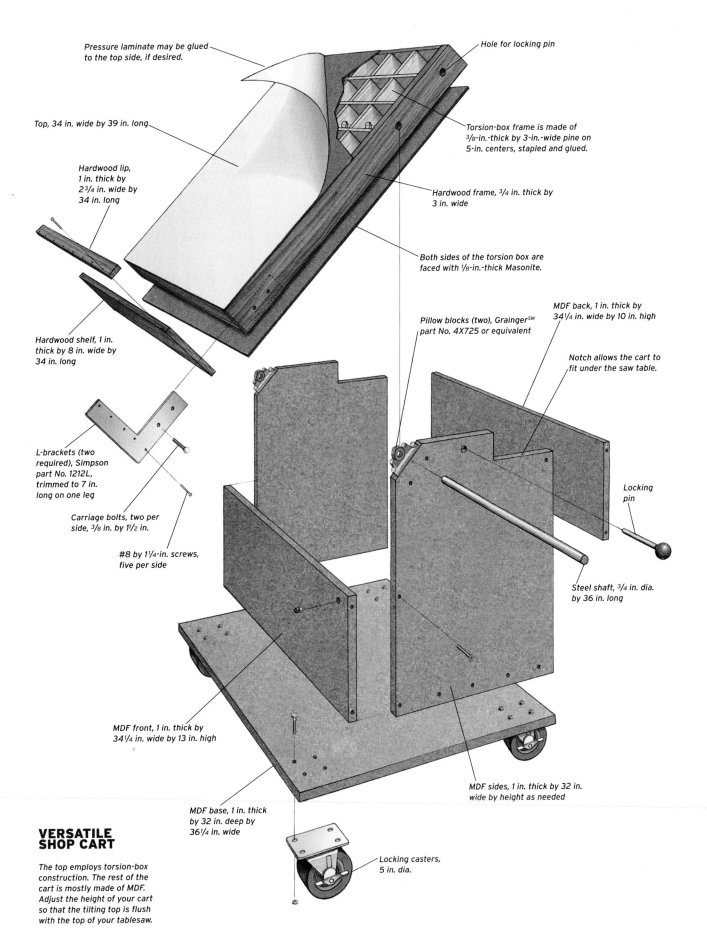

Pressure laminate may be glued to the top side, if desired.

Hole for locking pin

Top, 34 in. wide by 39 in. long.

Torsion-box frame is made of 3/8-in.-thick by 3-in.-wide pine on 5-in. centers, stapled and glued.

Hardwood lip, 1 in. thick by 2 3/4 in. wide by 34 in. long

Hardwood frame, 3/4 in. thick by 3 in. wide

Both sides of the torsion box are faced with 1/8-in.-thick Masonite.

Hardwood shelf, 1 in. thick by 8 in. wide by 34 in. long

MDF back, 1 in. thick by 34 1/4 in. wide by 10 in. high

Pillow blocks (two), Grainger^{SM} part No. 4X725 or equivalent

Notch allows the cart to fit under the saw table.

L-brackets (two required), Simpson part No. 1212L, trimmed to 7 in. long on one leg

Locking pin

Carriage bolts, two per side, 3/8 in. by 1 1/2 in.

#8 by 1 1/4-in. screws, five per side

Steel shaft, 3/4 in. dia. by 36 in. long

MDF front, 1 in. thick by 34 1/4 in. wide by 13 in. high

MDF sides, 1 in. thick by 32 in. wide by height as needed

MDF base, 1 in. thick by 32 in. deep by 36 1/4 in. wide

VERSATILE SHOP CART

The top employs torsion-box construction. The rest of the cart is mostly made of MDF. Adjust the height of your cart so that the tilting top is flush with the top of your tablesaw.

Locking casters, 5 in. dia.

ROLLING COMPOUND-MITER SAW STAND SAVES SPACE

By Charles Jacoby

My shop is pretty crowded, so when I acquire a new tool, I have to create efficient ways to store and use it. Such was the case after I bought a new sliding compound-miter saw. The saw needed a permanent, but mobile, home where I could do accurate cut-off and miter work. I first tried using the saw on planks and horses. This worked fine for single cuts, but I really needed a fence with a stop for cutting multiples. And the extensions that came with the saw limited its cutting to short pieces. Also, I still had to break things down to put the saw away.

About this time, my wife, Rosemary, gave me a benchtop oscillating-spindle sander. Again I wondered where I would store the tool. Building a stand to house both tools was the answer—make that a movable stand with folding extension wings. I designed the stand with crosscutting and mitering in mind but with a place to store the sander. I also left room for a top drawer to hold my shaper cutters and accessories. When I'm not using the saw, I drop the wings and roll the stand into a corner (see the photo). And even with the wings folded down, I can still do short miter-saw work by clamping a stop block to the saw's auxiliary fence.

For the stand's carcase, I made a ³/₄-in. birch-plywood box. To make storing the sander easy, I left the stand's lower compartment open (back and front). I plate joined maple face frames to the front and back of the carcase to make the box rigid. Because my miter saw has its own base with four feet, I recessed the top of the cabinet so that the saw's work surface would be at the same height as the wings (see the drawing).

What make the stand accurate and maneuverable are the folding pair of wings attached to the side of

Workstation with a small footprint. *After a well-executed cutting performance, Jacoby's saw stand (with a sander stowaway) gets its wings lowered and is rolled to a tidy corner in the shop. The stand, with its wings extended, makes a level assistant when mitering the ends of long stock or crosscutting exact-length workpieces.*

the cabinet. Each wing basically consists of a table, a support, and a fence. The tables are ³/₄-in. plywood, and the supports are made from ¹/₂-in.-thick Baltic-birch plywood for strength.

By securing a flip stop to the left fence, I'm able to measure precise lengths. I purposely made my fence higher than what the flip stop requires to permit a full 2×4 to go under the stop. Because of the extra height, I had to make a metal stop extension to get it low enough for thin boards.

The collapsible wings are strong; I can crosscut 14-ft.-long 2×8s in half on the fully extended stand. To achieve this kind of load, I had to first add blocks and stiffeners to reinforce the cabinet where the wing-table and wing-support hinges attach. I secured 1³/₄-in.-thick support blocks to the top of the cabinet sides. Then I fastened ³/₄-in.-thick strips of maple to the plywood sides. For the hinges, I fastened two Corbin® ball-bearing (large door) hinges to the wing tables and mounted a pair of 2-in. by 24-in. piano hinges to the wing supports.

Once the wings were in position, I screwed the table hinges to the support blocks and the piano hinges to the stiffener strips.

To complete the stand, I made a simple drawer for the upper cabinet opening. I sealed the drawer, cabinet, and wings with clear Watco® oil. Once my mobile stand was finished, I put the saw right to work, cutting everything from baseboard to pull-out dish racks for the kitchen.

Charles Jacoby is a retired men's clothing store owner who enjoys making furniture for his family in Helena, Montana.

MOBILE STATION WITH FOLDING WINGS

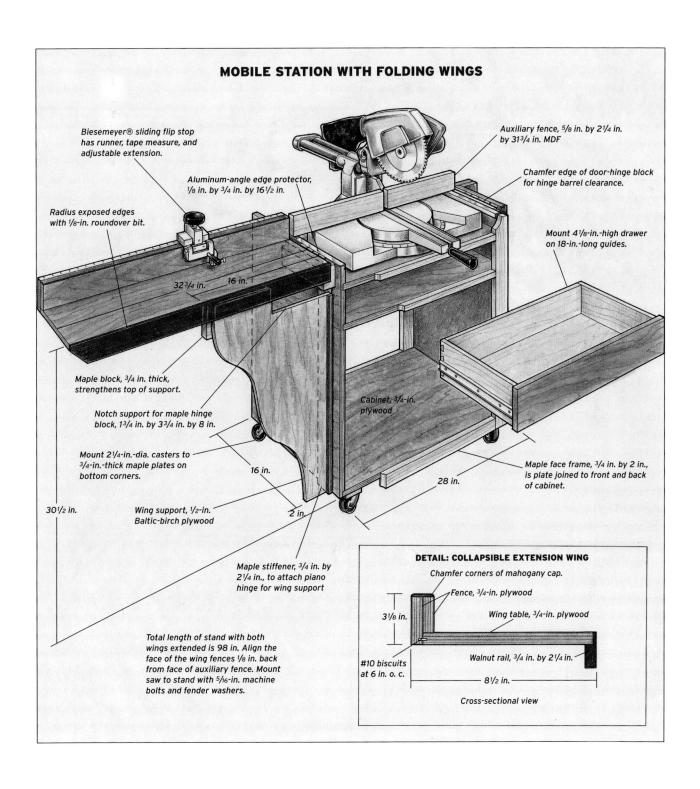

Biesemeyer® sliding flip stop has runner, tape measure, and adjustable extension.

Aluminum-angle edge protector, 1/8 in. by 3/4 in. by 16 1/2 in.

Radius exposed edges with 1/8-in. roundover bit.

Auxiliary fence, 5/8 in. by 2 1/4 in. by 31 3/4 in. MDF

Chamfer edge of door-hinge block for hinge barrel clearance.

Mount 4 1/8-in.-high drawer on 18-in.-long guides.

32 3/4 in.

16 in.

Maple block, 3/4 in. thick, strengthens top of support.

Notch support for maple hinge block, 1 3/4 in. by 3 3/4 in. by 8 in.

Mount 2 1/4-in.-dia. casters to 3/4-in.-thick maple plates on bottom corners.

Cabinet, 3/4-in. plywood

16 in.

30 1/2 in.

Wing support, 1/2-in. Baltic-birch plywood

2 in.

28 in.

Maple face frame, 3/4 in. by 2 in., is plate joined to front and back of cabinet.

Maple stiffener, 3/4 in. by 2 1/4 in., to attach piano hinge for wing support

Total length of stand with both wings extended is 98 in. Align the face of the wing fences 1/8 in. back from face of auxiliary fence. Mount saw to stand with 5/16-in. machine bolts and fender washers.

DETAIL: COLLAPSIBLE EXTENSION WING

Chamfer corners of mahogany cap.

Fence, 3/4-in. plywood

Wing table, 3/4-in. plywood

3 1/8 in.

Walnut rail, 3/4 in. by 2 1/4 in.

#10 biscuits at 6 in. o. c.

8 1/2 in.

Cross-sectional view

SAWHORSES FOR THE SHOP

by Christian Becksvoort

Sawhorses are an indispensable part of my shop equipment. No matter what the process or project, I reach for a horse to saw boards, to stand on, to lay out panels and joints, to hold parts, and to elevate cabinets for sanding or planing. I also use sawhorses for drill-press work supports, assembly, finishing, outdoor power carving and routing, changing lightbulbs, and even photography. I've constructed a pair each of three different heights: 1 ft., 2 ft., and 3 ft. The 3-ft. set includes height extenders for even more versatility.

Sawhorses are not fine furniture. I built these horses quick and dirty, to be useful but sturdy. The material is whatever I happened to have on hand at the time: pine, ash, oak, fir and even the ever-plentiful

cherry scraps. For joinery I relied on butt joints held together with glue and screws. I spent a lot of time and effort on my toolbox and will do the same when I have to replace my aging workbench. But sawhorses are a different story. I give them the roughest treatment without a second thought. While studying and restoring Shaker pieces, I noticed that although most of such work reflects meticulous craftsmanship and graceful design, many Shaker tables, stands, and cases intended for shop use are merely glued and nailed together. They had the same idea.

Christian Becksvoort is a furniture maker and contributing editor to Fine Woodworking.

Wide-topped short horse serves two purposes

Essentially, this horse is a stool, but it can be used as a short bench for sawing, holding tall work in a vise, and holding casework off the floor for finishing.

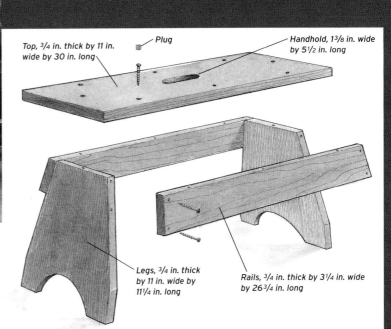

Top, ³/₄ in. thick by 11 in. wide by 30 in. long

Plug

Handhold, 1³/₈ in. wide by 5¹/₂ in. long

Legs, ³/₄ in. thick by 11 in. wide by 11¹/₄ in. long

Rails, ³/₄ in. thick by 3¹/₄ in. wide by 26³/₄ in. long

Stepping up for crosscuts. The 1-ft.-tall horse raises the workpiece so that you can use a crosscut saw comfortably.

7³/₄ in.

30 in.

2¹/₂ in.

10° angle

11 in.

CONSTRUCTION TIP
Use square-drive screws with round heads because they are less likely to strip out and, unlike flat-head screws, won't act as a wedge.

My shortest sawhorse is a larger version of a footstool or a small bench. It's a foot tall and is assembled with screws. Because the top of this horse is relatively large, it has a handhold in the middle to make it easy to pick up the horse and move it with one hand.

Generally, I use the short horse for sawing long planks to rough length. If I'm cutting off just a couple of inches from the end of a long plank, a pair of these horses goes under the long section. If I'm cutting the plank near the middle, the sawcut is made between the horses to support the cutoff.

Most often I'll use the short horses to bring a case piece up to a comfortable working height. For example, I'm over 6 ft. tall, so a 30-in.-tall cabinet that needs to be planed or sanded is in a much better working position for me with this horse placed underneath it.

When edging wide panels or case backs, I set one end into my bench vise and support the other end on the short horse. My ancient Skil® belt sander weighs close to 15 lb., and I prefer to use it in the horizontal position. Consequently, when finish-sanding the top of a 5-ft.-tall cabinet, I stand on the short horse to make sanding easier. When working on a nearly completed piece, I pad the top of the horse with carpet scraps to protect the piece from unwanted dings, dents, and scratches. I'm not the only one who finds my short sawhorses useful. The short horse gives every *Fine Woodworking* photographer who comes into my shop a great view of work in progress on my tall workbench.

The footprint of the base is the same size as the top so that the horse is safe to stand on, and a pair can be

(continued on p. 10)

stacked. The legs are cut at 10 degrees along both sides and are tilted at the same angle when attaching the side rails. A V or half-round cutout on both ends results in four feet. The rails are screwed in place, and the top is attached to the base with screws. I plugged the screw holes to keep chips and oil from accumulating in them, and I beveled all edges with a block plane before putting this horse into service.

When I build a pair of these horses again, I'll make one improvement: The rails will be 4 in. to 6 in. wide for added strength and racking resistance. My set, after 20 years of use, is starting to wobble a bit. Otherwise, I'm pretty happy with them.

Use horses in conjunction with your bench. While a workpiece is secure in the vise, the short horse provides solid support from below.

A pair of medium-size horses makes an impromptu workbench. At 2 ft. tall, these horses are the right height for doing finish work on a large case piece. The carpeting protects the workpiece.

The 2-ft. sawhorse is the workhorse in my shop. This style is easy to make and move around. I make them in pairs, and the design allows the horses to be stacked when not in use. I also stapled carpeting to the top to prevent pieces from being damaged while they are on the horses.

Their primary use is for holding case pieces at working height. When fitting face frames, backs, or doors or when sanding or installing hinges, I find these midheight horses indispensable. Standing on these puppies brings me right up to the ceiling in my shop: I can change lightbulbs or sand the tops of tall cabinets. And because the braces are inboard of the legs, I can clamp onto the ends as well as the middle of the top. I sometimes use these horses to clamp case sides up-right when laying out and transferring dovetails from the top to the sides. This is a real handy feature when working alone.

2-ft. sawhorse is the most useful

This is a standard-size horse for general carpentry, but it also can be handy for holding case pieces. The shelf is optional, though it provides additional stability to the horse.

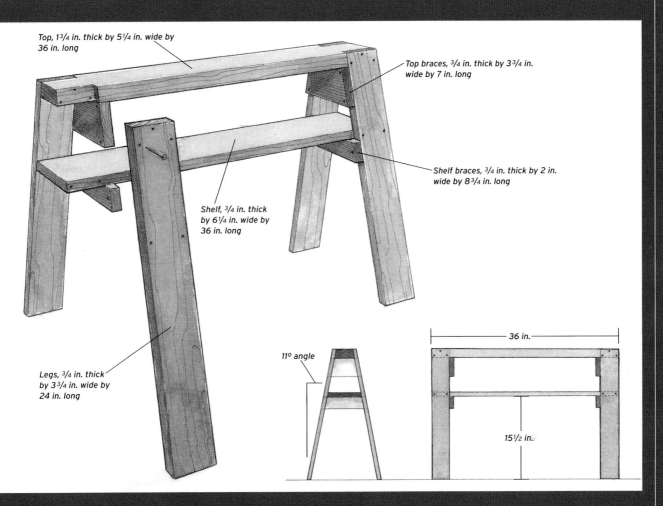

Top, 1³/₄ in. thick by 5¹/₄ in. wide by 36 in. long

Top braces, ³/₄ in. thick by 3³/₄ in. wide by 7 in. long

Shelf braces, ³/₄ in. thick by 2 in. wide by 8³/₄ in. long

Shelf, ³/₄ in. thick by 6¹/₄ in. wide by 36 in. long

Legs, ³/₄ in. thick by 3³/₄ in. wide by 24 in. long

11° angle

36 in.

15¹/₂ in.

There are many ways to construct a 2-ft. sawhorse. On mine, the legs are let into notches in the top piece. Braces provide racking resistance in two locations, and a shelf is handy for storage or as a step. The legs are splayed out 11 degrees to the sides. For the top, you can rip the sides of a 2x4 to 11 degrees and simply attach the legs. Or you can use a 2x6 and let in the legs. The 2x6 gives you a wider top, which provides extra stability should you wish to stand on it. In addition to the two pairs of braces shown in the drawing, one of my 2-ft. horses has additional bracing just above the floor (see the top photo on the facing page).

A shelf on the braces not only adds strength to the horse but also is strong enough to act as a lower step. The braces under the shelf provide enough support that I can stand on the shelf without it flexing. For a while I had side strips along the shelf that kept tools from rolling off. They worked, but they collected all sorts of debris and the shelf was difficult to keep clean, so I took them off.

CONSTRUCTION TIP

Make the shelf braces after the legs have been completed. Place the shelf braces 8¹/₂ in. down from the top and scribe your cut lines.

Legs

Scribe line here.

Shelf brace

Tall horse is adjustable in height

The extenders on this horse raise your work to a comfortable height.
The ends of the horse are made flush so that you can clamp tall
pieces to them.

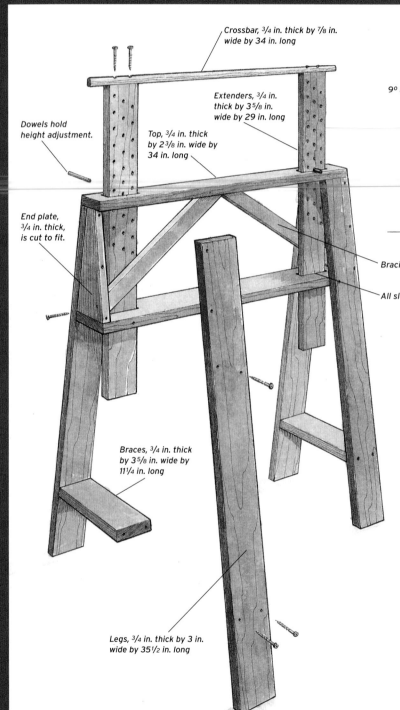

Crossbar, 3/4 in. thick by 7/8 in. wide by 34 in. long

Dowels hold height adjustment.

Extenders, 3/4 in. thick by 3 5/8 in. wide by 29 in. long

Top, 3/4 in. thick by 2 3/8 in. wide by 34 in. long

End plate, 3/4 in. thick, is cut to fit.

Braces, 3/4 in. thick by 3 5/8 in. wide by 11 1/4 in. long

Legs, 3/4 in. thick by 3 in. wide by 35 1/2 in. long

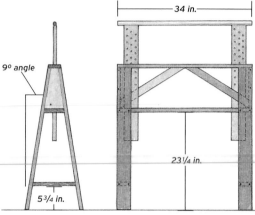

9° angle

34 in.

5 3/4 in.

23 1/4 in.

Bracing, 3/4 in. thick by 1 3/4 in. wide

All slots are 1 1/2 in. from the ends.

CONSTRUCTION TIP

Stack your extenders together and drill the dowel holes in one step to ensure proper alignment.

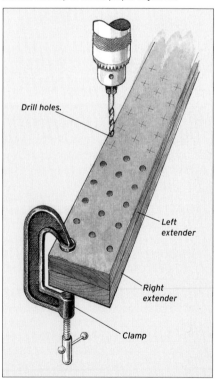

Drill holes.

Left extender

Right extender

Clamp

I recently added a third pair of sawhorses that can be adjusted in height between 36 in. and 55 in.

I use these horses mainly for sanding and finishing. Even though they're 36 in. tall, I still have to bend over slightly, hence the extenders. For my height, 42 in. to 44 in. is ideal for sanding and finishing, especially tabletops. For fine, close-up work like carving or inlaying, I prefer 48 in. to 54 in. That's about midchest height for me, just right for the real fussy stuff. When I have messy work to do, I haul these horses outside, remove the extenders, and use them like a bench for seat carving, grinding, sanding, and routing. At the drill press, the extenders are useful for holding long work at the correct height.

The tall horses are built almost like the two-footers. The major difference is that I have enclosed the ends and added diagonal braces for strength. The extenders consist of two 3⁵⁄₈-in.-wide boards connected to a ³⁄₄-in.-thick crossbar. The boards are drilled at ¹⁄₂-in. intervals and fit into slots in the top and the shelf, much like a centerboard of a sailboat. Two ³⁄₈-in.-dia. dowels through the ²⁵⁄₆₄-in. holes hold the extenders at the desired height. The crossbar is padded with ³⁄₄-in.-dia. foam pipe insulation to protect the workpiece. It also provides grip to prevent panels from sliding around when they're being sanded.

Feel free to customize these horses as needed for specific applications. For example, the crossbar is fine for supporting wide panels, but it won't take the weight of a 4-in.-thick plank. A wider board or even a T-shaped crosspiece would make a good substitute. On occasion, when I use the horses as a single unit, I have scrap V boards fitted between them. Two bar clamps hold the whole unit together so that I can use it as a bench.

Adjustable-height sawhorses are versatile. Avoid back fatigue by raising the work up to a comfortable height.

Height adjustment is made with a dowel. The holes are numbered on both sides for quick alignment.

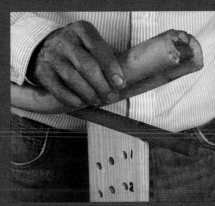

Pad the crossbars to protect your work. Foam pipe insulation works well and easily slips on and off the top.

LOW ASSEMBLY BENCH PUTS WORK AT THE RIGHT HEIGHT

By Bill Nyberg

My father learned woodworking in Sweden, and when he came to this country, he got a job building reproduction early American furniture. The shop had been in operation since the late 1700s; and like those who worked before him, my father was assigned a huge bench with many drawers. He stored his tools and ate his lunch at the bench, but much of his actual work took place nearby on a low table he called "the platform."

When I inherited his big bench, I also found myself doing most of my work at a low platform improvised from sawhorses and planks. I have bad shoulders and the occasional sore back, so using a full-height bench is difficult and unproductive. I needed a bench that suited the way I really work, so I built a low platform that incorporates some features of a traditional full-size bench.

A clamping machine

My low platform bench is made for clamping. The edges overhang enough for clamps to get a good grip anywhere along the length of the bench. A 4-in.-wide space down the middle increases the clamping options.

This platform bench has four tail vises made from Pony® no. 53 double-pipe clamps, which can be used by themselves or in combination with a row of dogs on the centerline between the screws, as the drawing shows. Unlike most bench arrangements, with a single row of dogs along one edge, this one doesn't twist or buckle the piece. I can use each vise singly or with the others because the pipes are pinned into the benchtops at each end with ¼-in. by 2-in. roll pins. Without the pins, the pipes would slide through the bench when tightening one end.

Rather than using traditional square bench dogs, I bored ¾-in. holes for a variety of manufactured dog fixtures or shopmade dowel dogs (see the drawing).

Building the benchtops

The bench is made from eight straight, clear 8-ft. 2×4s that I had kept in the shop for a few months to dry. I jointed the edges and then ran each of the boards through the planer until the radiused corners were square.

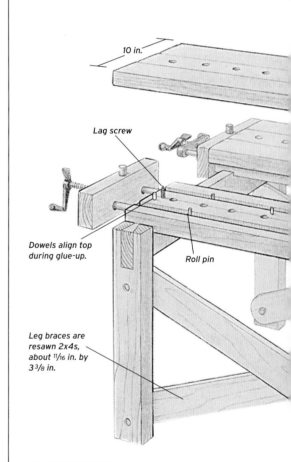

10 in.

Lag screw

Dowels align top during glue-up.

Roll pin

Leg braces are resawn 2x4s, about ¹¹⁄₁₆ in. by 3³⁄₈ in.

A LOW BENCH MADE FOR CLAMPING

This bench is 24 in. high, a convenient height for working on many projects. The benchtops are 42½ in. long, which gives more than 4 ft. between the jaws. At about 70 lb., the bench is light enough to move around yet heavy enough for stability.

Building the legs and base according to the dimensions on the drawing is straightforward. The only point to note is the dovetail connecting the beams to the legs. Because of the orientation of the beams and legs, the dovetail is only 1½ in. at its widest point, but it's 3½ in. from top to bottom. I tilted the tablesaw blade to cut the tails on the beam and cut the pins on the legs in the bandsaw. Almost any method would work to join the beam to the leg; my first version of the bench used a bolted slip joint.

The pipes run through the tops

The tops are made in two sections and glued up with the pipes and vises in place. The upper sections are made of three boards and the lower section from two. I edge-glued them with alternating growth rings to eliminate cupping.

The double-pipe clamps are sold with a tail stop and a screw head. I set aside the tail-stop ends and used only the screw heads. Threading on the vise at one end of the pipe will unscrew the vise at the other end. So I had a plumber cut the threads twice as long on one end of each of the four pipes. I threaded the first vise all the way onto the end with double-long threads so that it was twice as far on the pipe as it needed to go. By the time the second vise was in place, the first one had unscrewed itself to the correct location.

Bill Nyberg is director of ophthalmic photography at the University of Pennsylvania in Philadelphia. He works wood in his spare time.

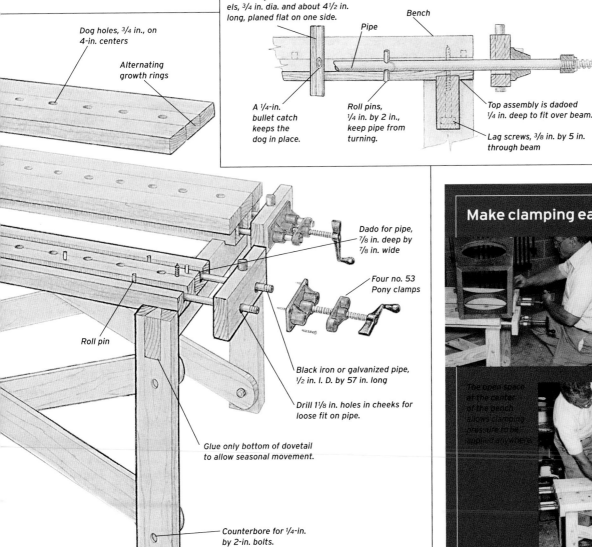

Dog holes, ¾ in., on 4-in. centers

Alternating growth rings

Bench dogs are hardwood dowels, ¾ in. dia. and about 4½ in. long, planed flat on one side.

Pipe

Bench

Cut off one side of handle. When the vise is open, gravity will keep the remaining portion of the handle below the benchtop.

A ¼-in. bullet catch keeps the dog in place.

Roll pins, ¼ in. by 2 in., keep pipe from turning.

Top assembly is dadoed ¼ in. deep to fit over beam.

Lag screws, ⅜ in. by 5 in. through beam

Roll pin

Dado for pipe, ⅞ in. deep by ⅞ in. wide

Four no. 53 Pony clamps

Black iron or galvanized pipe, ½ in. I. D. by 57 in. long

Drill 1⅛ in. holes in cheeks for loose fit on pipe.

Glue only bottom of dovetail to allow seasonal movement.

Counterbore for ¼-in. by 2-in. bolts.

Make clamping easy

Two vises that can be adjusted independently hold even irregular shapes securely.

The open space at the center of the bench allows clamping pressure to be applied anywhere.

DOVETAILER'S BENCH AND CARCASE PRESS

by Charles Durham Jr.

Carcase press Aids Glue-Up. Clamping up a large carcase is much easier with the author's carcase-press clamping system than with ordinary pipe or bar clamps. The press consists of two units, each of which is made of four veneer-press screws; a couple of lengths of heavy metal strapping; a few board feet of hardwood and a handful of nuts, bolts, and washers.

I made my first dovetailed carcase with wide pine boards salvaged from the original kitchen in my first house. Dry, flat, and wide, those boards became a wonderful blanket chest. Since then, much of the lumber I've used on large-carcase projects has been less than ideal. Wide, flat, and dry is more the exception than the rule, whether you use naturally wide boards or glue narrower stock to width. When wide boards are cupped, twisted, or both—even a little—making dovetails that fit well is tough. Yet accurately fitted and squared dovetail corners are crucial to the success of large projects like blanket chests, highboy tops, and slant-front desks.

The other problem with large-carcase projects is the glue-up. Even if you've cut good, accurate dovetails, gluing and clamping big boards can be a real headache or, worse, result in a flawed project—especially if you work alone, as I usually do. Having the pipe clamp I just tightened fall off and dent the carcase as I tighten the next clamp is just one more hassle than I need.

I solved both problems by building two assemblies: a dovetailer's bench to hold the boards flat, secure, and indexed for accurate layout and cutting (see the drawing on the facing page and the photos on p. 18) and a carcase-press clamping system to help me close wide joints with uniform pressure, without having to wrestle an armload of clamps (see the photo at left). Material for both is available at any good lumberyard, and you'll find all the hardware you need either at your local hardware store or through mail order.

Dovetailer's bench

The problem with laying out and cutting dovetails on a typical cabinetmaker's bench is that most benches are about 32 in. off the floor, which constrains you to narrower carcase work. To do bigger jobs on an ordinary bench, you have to jury-rig a support and clamp system to hold things flat and steady at the right height while you mark, saw, and chop. My bench is a large, elevated clamping device that lets me overcome warp on wide boards, allowing me to dovetail the largest boards with ease and precision. The bench's working surface is at elbow height: 42 in. off the floor, which is long enough for the longest pin member I'm likely to encounter.

The deepest carcase I would ever dovetail is about 25 in. So I added space for the clamp heads (see the drawing) to establish the benchtop's width of 28 in. A 72-in.-wide breakfront was the longest project on which I saw myself using the bench, so I decided to make it a bit more than half that length (48 in.) to keep that breakfront's top and bottom from falling off.

I use pipe-clamp heads to hold boards in place (see the photo at left) and cauls extending across the bench's width to take out any warp in either board. An aluminum angle that raises, lowers and locks with a twist of the wooden handles serves as a ledger strip for the pin member (see the drawing).

I cut dovetails in a fairly conventional manner, but with a couple of twists. I lay out the tails first, using a sheet aluminum template I made for the purpose. Then I saw to the line with a Bosch® barrel-grip jigsaw and chop the waste out on my dovetailer's bench. The jigsaw is so much faster than and is at least as accurate (probably more so) as cutting with a backsaw. I mark the pins from the tails, aligning

DOVETAILER'S BENCH

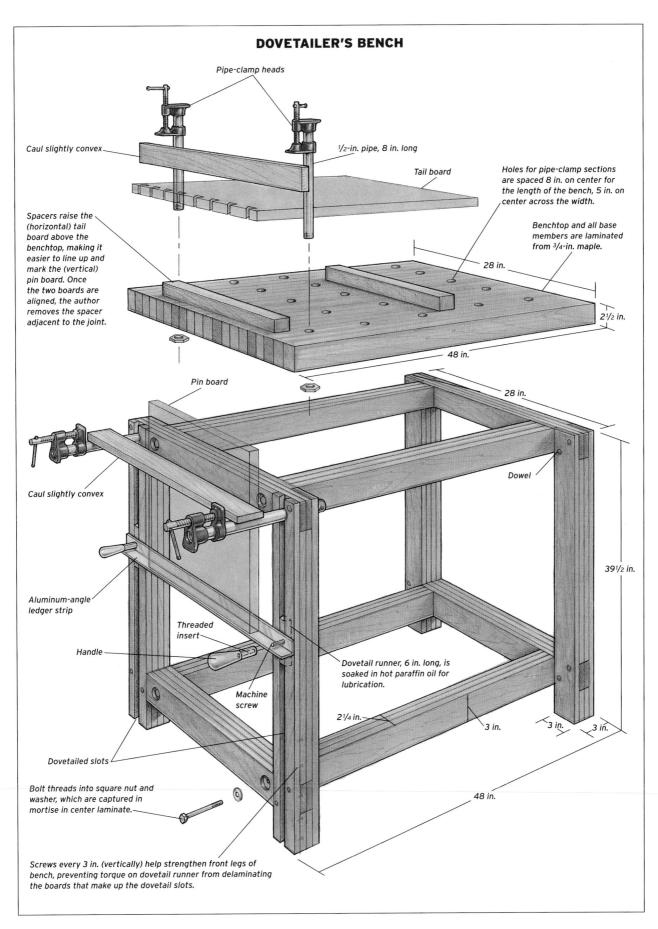

Pipe-clamp heads

Caul slightly convex

½-in. pipe, 8 in. long

Tail board

Holes for pipe-clamp sections are spaced 8 in. on center for the length of the bench, 5 in. on center across the width.

Spacers raise the (horizontal) tail board above the benchtop, making it easier to line up and mark the (vertical) pin board. Once the two boards are aligned, the author removes the spacer adjacent to the joint.

Benchtop and all base members are laminated from ¾-in. maple.

28 in.

2½ in.

48 in.

Pin board

28 in.

Dowel

Caul slightly convex

Aluminum-angle ledger strip

Handle

Threaded insert

Machine screw

Dovetail runner, 6 in. long, is soaked in hot paraffin oil for lubrication.

39½ in.

Dovetailed slots

2¼ in.

3 in.

3 in.

3 in.

Bolt threads into square nut and washer, which are captured in mortise in center laminate.

48 in.

Screws every 3 in. (vertically) help strengthen front legs of bench, preventing torque on dovetail runner from delaminating the boards that make up the dovetail slots.

the tail board on the benchtop with the pin board on the aluminum ledger, using a chisel and mallet to transfer lines (see the top photo below). Again, I use the jigsaw, this time with its base set at approximately 14 degrees (from a bevel-square set on the tail board) to cut to the line and then chop out the waste on the bench. The fit I get with this system is nearly perfect.

Carcase press

My carcase press will close any size project I'll ever build and will do it in much less time than it takes with loose clamps. With the time saved, I can close the

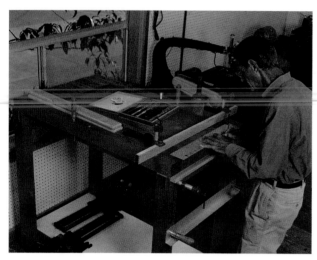

Mark the Tails. *The author uses an aluminum template to mark out the tails on the side board of what will be a mahogany blanket chest. The short sections of pipe, which clamp at the front of the dovetailer's bench, ensure the board remains flat for an accurate layout.*

Transfer the Marks. *Marking pins from tails is more certain with a chisel than with a knife because there's no danger of the chisel following the grain. It's important, though, to make sure the chisel is absolutely perpendicular to the surface of the board you're dovetailing.*

joints correctly before the glue grabs. The only fixed dimension is its internal working height—enough to take those 25-in. boards I produced on the bench. The carcase press consists of a pair of clamping frames made of maple laminations and prepunched, galvanized steel strapping. The head member of each is fixed and has veneer-press screws mounted to it. A foot member moves along the galvanized strapping to accommodate carcases of various widths. The clamping frames can themselves be positioned as near or as far from one another as need be (see the photo on p. 16).

At each end of the maple laminations, I made a sawcut precisely as deep as the strapping is wide and drilled holes for the bolts that connect the wooden end pieces to the metal strapping. The straps I use are 60 in. long, but they're available in virtually any length. Smaller wooden cauls ride on the strapping to transfer the clamping force from the press screws to the carcase. Ideally, the clamping force should bear directly on the corner of the carcase, but I find that placing the force just inside the joint, right on the baseline, works just as well. With the 8-in. press screws and this setup, there's a range of about 4 in., fully opened to fully closed.

The elimination of loose clamps is the major benefit provided by the carcase press. Instead of watching and worrying about clamps falling off, I can monitor the joint. But there's another advantage. Quite often, clamping a project together forces it out of square in one plane or another. With loose clamps, the unending adjustment required to restore squareness can be maddening. None of that has been necessary since I began using the carcase press.

Moreover, when using loose clamps, if a carcase winds (so that the diagonal corners are high), there's nothing you can do with ordinary clamps. With the carcase press, I just wedge shims between press and carcase in the high corners, and it's flat again.

In using the carcase press, I work at table height on a sheet of laminate-covered particleboard. Because the bottoms of both clamping frames that make up the press are square, they stand upright on their own, making it easy to slide the carcase into the press. I get the joints just started outside the press and then place it inside and dry-assemble the carcase. Only after checking to see that everything's going to close up properly do I apply glue and clamp the carcase for good.

Charles Durham is a professional woodworker in San Clemente, California.

ASSEMBLY CART RAISES WORK

By Jerry H. Lyons

A secretary on the move. *This rolling cart allows Lyons to move work around the shop easily. It also keeps a piece at a comfortable working height, with access to all sides.*

This shopmade cart provides a comfortable working height (about 24 in.) and easy access to the back and sides of a large project, like the slant-top secretary pictured here. The cart is made from off-the-shelf lumber and about half a sheet of plywood. Under each leg are 2½-in.-dia. casters, all of which both swivel and lock. To prevent marring projects, the top of the cart is covered with a carpet remnant. Also, the cart makes it easy and safe to roll a piece around my shop to take advantage of natural light. Both shelves are carpeted to protect the edges of the workpiece, and the lower shelf provides storage for components and hardware.

Jerry H. Lyons, who taught furniture making for 21 years, recently built his dream shop near Glasgow, Kentucky.

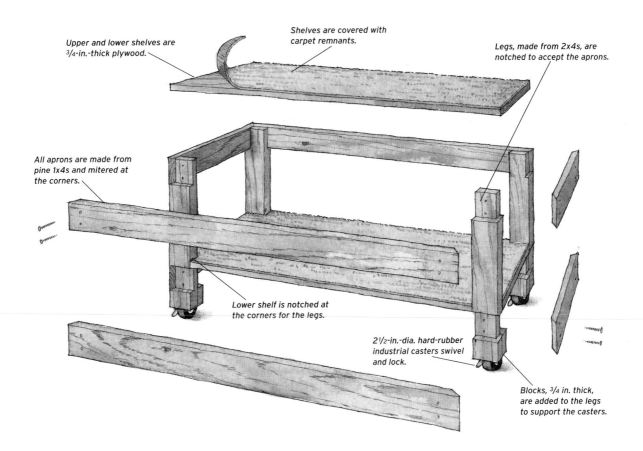

Upper and lower shelves are ¾-in.-thick plywood.

Shelves are covered with carpet remnants.

Legs, made from 2x4s, are notched to accept the aprons.

All aprons are made from pine 1x4s and mitered at the corners.

Lower shelf is notched at the corners for the legs.

2½-in.-dia. hard-rubber industrial casters swivel and lock.

Blocks, ¾ in. thick, are added to the legs to support the casters.

SHOP DRAFTING TABLE FOLDS AWAY

by Dwayne Intveld

Sit or stand. *Intveld's table is designed to be used when either sitting or standing. The table folds flat against a wall, taking up virtually no space while allowing the drawing to be referenced a any time during the construction of a project.*

For a long time, my "drafting table" was a small sink cutout propped at an angle on my workbench. It worked okay, but it was far from ideal. So a couple of years ago, I decided to make a convenient and functional table.

The tabletop is hinged to a lower panel, and both parts fit into a surrounding frame. Two pairs of bearings at the top of the table roll in a groove routed inside the frame, permitting me to adjust the table to eight different working positions, depending on whether I want to sit or stand, or how my back is feeling that day.

For smooth operation, the groove should be about 1/32 in. wider than the diameter of the bearings. I used two light-duty bearings (available from Reid Tool Supply Company®; 800-253-0421) with an inside diameter of 1/4 in. and an outside diameter of 3/4 in. Although I chose maple for the frame, you can use any reasonably dense hardwood, mainly so the bearings that ride in the track have a hard surface to bear against.

Drill 1/4-in.-dia. cross-holes through the routed groove at 6-in. intervals. Drilling these holes before routing helps prevent chipout from breaking into the groove. Two small fillister-head screws slipped into a pair of these holes act as pegs for the bearings to rest on and establish the position of the drawing table. A cupboard-door catch mounted on the crossmember holds the table in its vertical stored position.

For quick assembly, use a biscuit joiner on all of the joints in the frame.

TABLE ADJUSTS TO VARYING HEIGHTS

Intveld wanted the range of table motion to start from a fully horizontal position at a comfortable working height and transition smoothly to a vertical position against the wall at eye level, with stops in between.

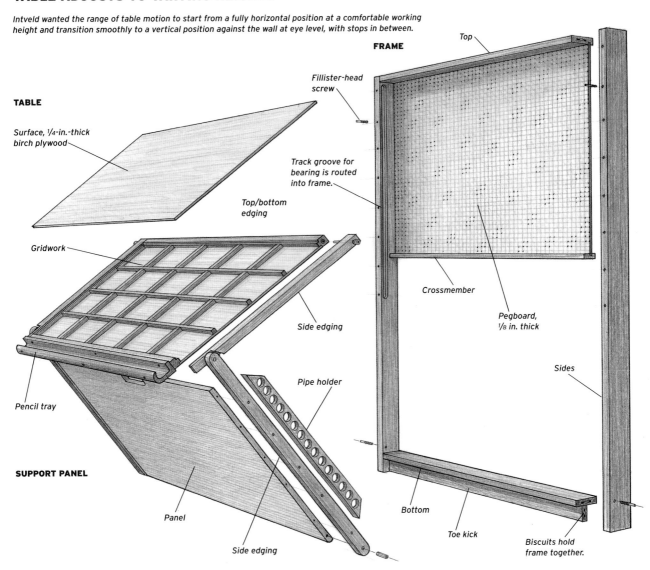

FRAME

TABLE

Surface, 1/4-in.-thick birch plywood

Fillister-head screw

Track groove for bearing is routed into frame.

Top/bottom edging

Gridwork

Side edging

Top

Crossmember

Pegboard, 1/8 in. thick

Pipe holder

Side edging

Pencil tray

Sides

SUPPORT PANEL

Panel

Bottom

Toe kick

Biscuits hold frame together.

Then rout a groove in the back of the frame to accept the 1/8-in.-thick pegboard panel. Finally, apply a water-based polyurethane finish to protect all exposed wood parts.

Table is light but rigid

The table is made using torsion-box construction. Using half-lap joints, glue together a 3/4-in.-thick pine grid and sandwich it between two 1/4-in.-thick birch-plywood panels with the edges trimmed in maple. This construction, though only 1 1/4 in. thick, keeps the table flat and light yet rigid and resistant to twisting. The bearings

are attached to each upper corner of the table with 1/4-in. bolts. The bolts thread first into nuts epoxied into the table and then into blind holes drilled and tapped into the table's maple trim.

Mount a pencil tray to the bottom of the table. I shaped the bottom of this tray to capture pencils, erasers, and rules, whether the table is in a horizontal or vertical position. A vinyl drawing-board cover, clamped along the edge of the top, provides an optimum drawing surface. Although I installed a commercial parallel rule that keeps all horizontally

drawn lines parallel automatically, a T-square would function fine.

The lower panel consists of a 3/4-in.-thick maple-plywood sheet with maple edging screwed on each side. Lengths of 1 1/2-in. dia. plastic pipe store rolled-up drawings behind the lower panel. The PVC pipe sections are held in counter-bored holes in three brackets screwed to the back of the lower panel. There is space behind the panel for mailing tubes that store large batches of drawings.

All four pivot points that hinge the table and support panel are made with threaded-rod connectors and T-nuts. Drill the holes 1/32 in. smaller than the 5/16-in. threaded-rod connector bodies, and press and epoxy the connectors into these holes. After the 5/16-in. T-nuts are recessed and epoxied into the mating piece, drill out the threads to provide a smooth bearing for the pivots. The pivots themselves are 5/16-in. bolts with the hex heads cut off and screwdriver slots hacksawed in the end.

Putting it all together

Position the frame against the wall and secure it in place by driving two screws through the center crossmember into the wall studs. Then, with the table positioned horizontally, slip one of the bearings into its track and tip the other end of the table down slightly to engage the opposite bearing. With the table rotated up to a vertical position and lifted to the top of the track, insert two pegs into the top holes to hold the table in its top position.

Next, put the lower panel in place, inserting two pivot screws through the frame sides into the threaded-rod connectors in the bottom of the lower panel. Swing the lower panel up to mate with the drawing table, and install the last pivot screws.

Dwayne Intveld builds custom furniture and cabinets in Hazel Green, Wisconsin.

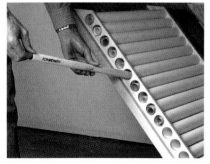

A place to store finished drawings. Completed drawings can be rolled up and stored in PVC tubes mounted behind the support panel.

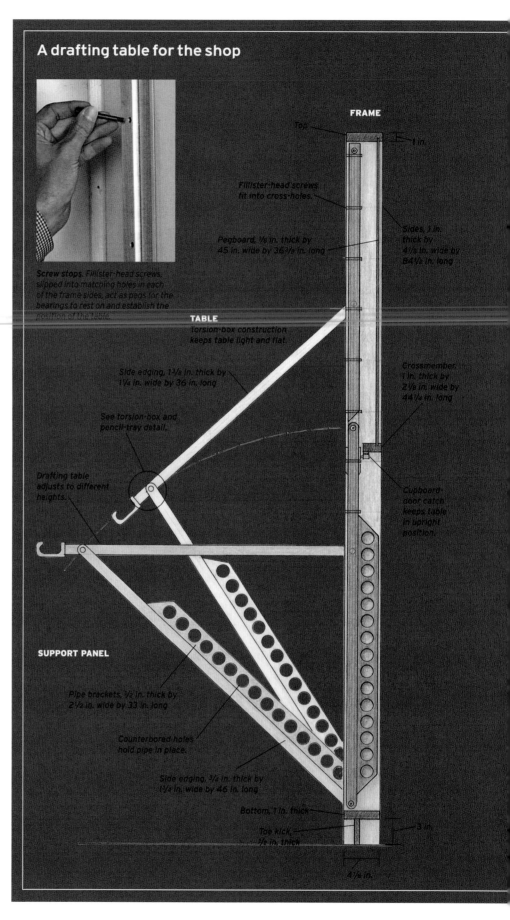

A drafting table for the shop

Screw stops. *Fillister-head screws, slipped into matching holes in each of the frame sides, act as pegs for the bearings to rest on and establish the position of the table.*

FRAME

Top

1 in.

Fillister-head screws fit into cross-holes.

Pegboard, 1/8 in. thick by 45 in. wide by 36-3/8 in. long

Sides, 1 in. thick by 4-1/8 in. wide by 84-1/2 in. long

TABLE
Torsion-box construction keeps table light and flat.

Side edging, 1-3/8 in. thick by 1-1/4 in. wide by 36 in. long

Crossmember, 1 in. thick by 2-1/8 in. wide by 44-1/4 in. long

See torsion-box and pencil-tray detail.

Drafting table adjusts to different heights.

Cupboard-door catch keeps table in upright position.

SUPPORT PANEL

Pipe brackets, 1/2 in. thick by 2-1/2 in. wide by 33 in. long

Counterbored holes hold pipe in place.

Side edging, 3/4 in. thick by 1-1/4 in. wide by 46 in. long

Bottom, 1 in. thick

Toe kick, 3/8 in. thick

3 in.

4-1/8 in.

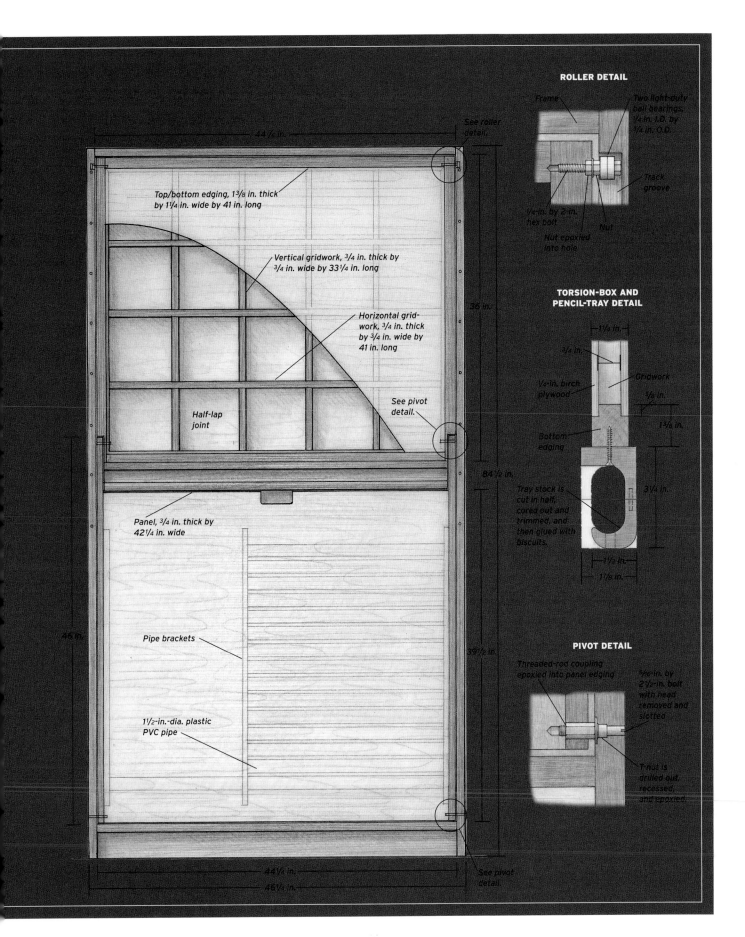

ROLLER DETAIL

Frame

Two light-duty ball bearings, 1/4 in. I.D. by 3/4 in. O.D.

Track groove

1/4-in. by 2-in. hex bolt

Nut

Nut epoxied into hole

Top/bottom edging, 1 3/8 in. thick by 1 1/4 in. wide by 41 in. long

See roller detail.

44 1/4 in.

Vertical gridwork, 3/4 in. thick by 3/4 in. wide by 33 1/4 in. long

36 in.

Horizontal gridwork, 3/4 in. thick by 3/4 in. wide by 41 in. long

TORSION-BOX AND PENCIL-TRAY DETAIL

1 1/4 in.

3/4 in.

Gridwork

1/4-in. birch plywood

5/8 in.

1 3/8 in.

Bottom edging

Half-lap joint

See pivot detail.

Tray stock is cut in half, cored out and trimmed, and then glued with biscuits.

3 1/4 in.

84 1/2 in.

Panel, 3/4 in. thick by 42 1/4 in. wide

1 1/2 in.

1 7/8 in.

46 in.

Pipe brackets

39 1/2 in.

PIVOT DETAIL

Threaded-rod coupling epoxied into panel edging

5/16-in. by 2 1/2-in. bolt with head removed and slotted

1 1/2-in.-dia. plastic PVC pipe

T-nut is drilled out, recessed, and epoxied.

44 1/2 in.

46 1/4 in.

See pivot detail.

VACUUM HOLD-DOWN TABLE

By Mike M. McCallum

When I'm constructing a set of custom cabinets, I frequently need an extra pair of hands, especially when I'm sanding drawer fronts or drilling odd-shaped pieces. Occasionally, I also need a table-mounted router. More often than not, I require that router table or those pair of hands at a job site. After putting up with cobbled scraps, make-shift clamps, and excessive router dust one too many times, I came up with a design for a router table that's also a vacuum hold-down. Using scrap materials, I built the table so that I could easily disassemble it for storage or transport.

I call my knockdown platform a super router/hold-down table for a couple of reasons. First, it's stout, turning my router into a light-capacity shaper. Second, it enables my shop vacuum to serve dual functions by providing suction for the hold-down surface or collecting dust from the router table. And while I don't use the hold-down to freehand-rout large workpieces, I do rely on its substantial holding power for most of my sanding and finishing work (see the left photo below).

The dimensions of the hold-down table are not critical. I made my table out of ⅝-in. high-density particleboard and covered exposed surfaces with scraps of plastic laminate. The top is removable, so I can use the vacuum table on my benchtop. I stiffened the table's top and bottom by gluing on a particleboard framework, as shown in the drawing. The top and bottom frames hold the sides and center divider in place without fasteners, allowing easy knockdown of the unit. After assembling the top and bottom oversize, I trimmed the parts square. I laminated all the pieces, and then I bored two holes in the edge of the table so I can connect my shop vacuum to either the router-table or hold-down side (see the right photo below). To power the table, I ran a heavy-duty extension cord to a 4-in. by 4-in. electrical box and mounted the box's stud bracket to the inside of the platform. The box houses switched receptacles for both the router (or sander) and shop vacuum. I also added a plywood shelf to the table to hold tools, bits, guide bushings, and adapters.

I made a clear window for the router table from Lexan®, which I recycled from a computer-store display. The window is a good safety feature because it lets in enough light to see the collet when I'm adjusting the

Vacuum side has plenty of clamping power. The vacuum surface (left) clamps a drawer front as the author sands its face. An open hole on the edge of the table (right) shows where he connects his shop vacuum when he's routing.

Wire the table. The author fed a 4-in. work box for a pair of switched receptacles: one for the vacuum, one for a router or sander. A shelf at the back of the table holds tools and accessories. He drew outlines of the items and routed recesses to hold each shape, which reminds him when something's missing.

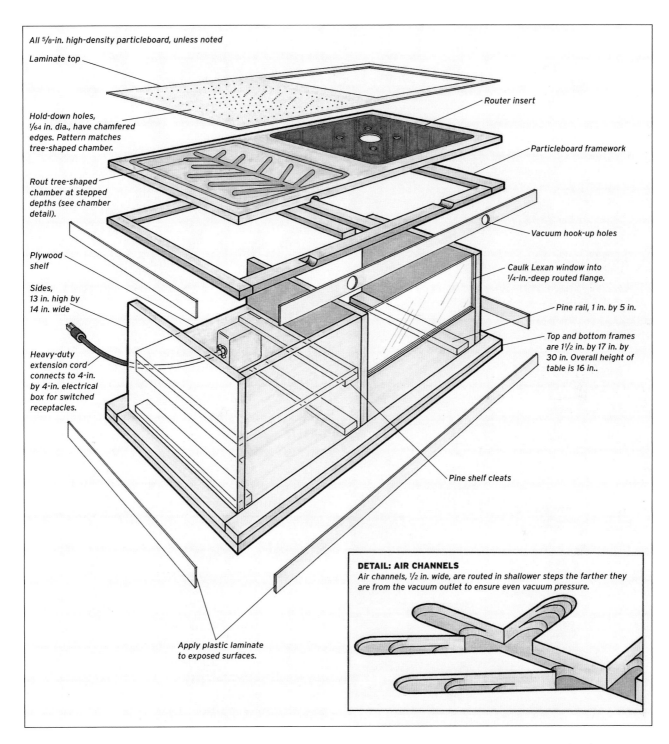

All 5/8-in. high-density particleboard, unless noted

Laminate top

Hold-down holes, 1/64 in. dia., have chamfered edges. Pattern matches tree-shaped chamber.

Rout tree-shaped chamber at stepped depths (see chamber detail).

Plywood shelf

Sides, 13 in. high by 14 in. wide

Heavy-duty extension cord connects to 4-in. by 4-in. electrical box for switched receptacles.

Apply plastic laminate to exposed surfaces.

Router insert

Particleboard framework

Vacuum hook-up holes

Caulk Lexan window into 1/4-in.-deep routed flange.

Pine rail, 1 in. by 5 in.

Top and bottom frames are 1 1/2 in. by 17 in. by 30 in. Overall height of table is 16 in..

Pine shelf cleats

DETAIL: AIR CHANNELS
Air channels, 1/2 in. wide, are routed in shallower steps the farther they are from the vacuum outlet to ensure even vacuum pressure.

bit height or using the router table. The router insert is a standard one—it fits whatever bit I'm using.

As long as my workpiece has a flat surface to put down on the hold-down table, I've found that there's plenty of suction—enough to grip a piece of low-grade plywood. To increase the holding pressure, you could also block off holes that are not covered by the workpiece. On rough surfaces, I take a 1/8-in.-thick piece of closed-cell plastic (shipper's foam) to make a gasket. With a utility knife, I cut out an appropriate shape that still allows the vacuum to suck the workpiece down. I use a couple of pieces of masking tape to hold the gasket to the table. So far, I've been delighted with the possibilities of the hold-down table. In fact, I'm working on a sliding saw table that uses a similar vacuum hold-down system.

Mike M. McCallum is an artist who does custom architectural woodworking in Portland, Oregon.

A DOWNDRAFT SANDING TABLE

by Peter Brown

My shop was originally a 20-ft. by 40-ft. hog barn. In the early years, before it could really be called a shop, I conveniently ignored the dust created from sanding. However, after I added a floor and finished the interior, I became more conscious of the dust and began to take large sanding projects out to another barn, where I could let the dust fly. The solution was clear: I had to find some way to collect sanding dust.

When I first noticed downdraft sanding tables that were for sale, I was intrigued. They were just what I needed, but I could not afford any of them. It was then that I decided to make my own downdraft table using the central dust-collection system in my shop. I use a shopmade system built with the motor and impeller from a portable Dust Boy®—rated to move 1,100 cu. ft. of air per minute (cfm) at a velocity of 5,400 ft. per minute (fpm)—adapted to an Oneida Air Systems® cyclone. I was confident that by locating my 2-hp Dust Boy close to the downdraft table, my system would do the job.

I based the size of the sanding tabletop—24 in. deep by 36 in. wide—on the average dimension of my workpieces.

After making the frame, I made the first mock-up of the table interior. The mock-up had a flat bottom with straight sides and an 8-in.-dia. duct at the bottom of the table. Regardless of what adjustments I made, the airflow wasn't evenly distributed across the table: It was fair near the outlet but poor elsewhere. For the second mock-up, I changed the outlet duct from the round to a standard 4-in. by 12-in. heating duct made of sheet metal, and I moved the outlet to the back of the table. I sloped the interior bottom from front to back and added the side pieces that slope toward the center and the back of the table.

The second mock-up made a significant improvement in the airflow, giving me good dust collection. I replaced the cardboard mock-up with 1/8-in.-thick Masonite. The addition of the 1/2-in.-thick medium-density fiberboard (MDF) back and side apron pieces at the top of the table adds rigidity to the frame and keeps stray dust within the collection area.

Peter Brown works as an engineer developing repairs for jet engines in Lebanon, Ohio.

SHOPMADE DOWNDRAFT TABLE

This downdraft sanding table is connected to a standard shop dust-collection system with a 4-in.-dia. hose. A sheet-metal fixture at the back of the table is a standard 90 degree heating and air-conditioning duct.

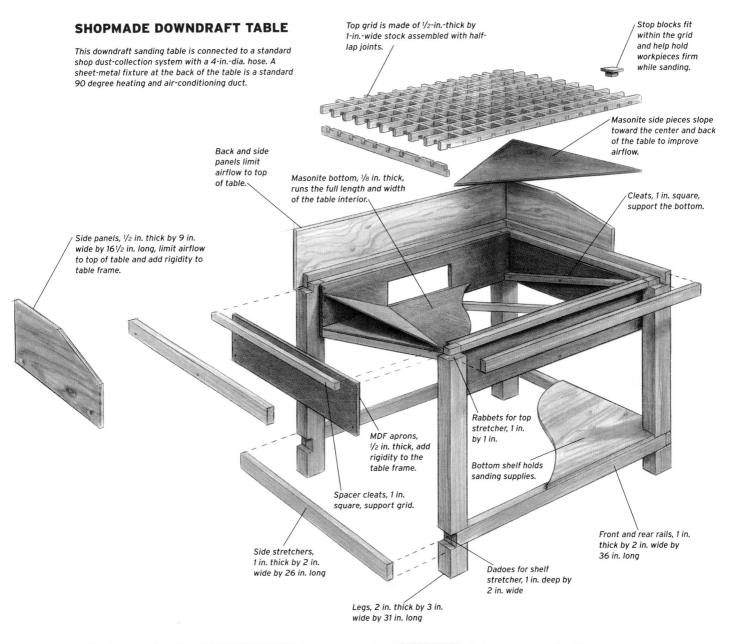

Top grid is made of ½-in.-thick by 1-in.-wide stock assembled with half-lap joints.

Stop blocks fit within the grid and help hold workpieces firm while sanding.

Back and side panels limit airflow to top of table.

Masonite bottom, ⅛ in. thick, runs the full length and width of the table interior.

Masonite side pieces slope toward the center and back of the table to improve airflow.

Side panels, ½ in. thick by 9 in. wide by 16½ in. long, limit airflow to top of table and add rigidity to table frame.

Cleats, 1 in. square, support the bottom.

Rabbets for top stretcher, 1 in. by 1 in.

MDF aprons, ½ in. thick, add rigidity to the table frame.

Bottom shelf holds sanding supplies.

Spacer cleats, 1 in. square, support grid.

Front and rear rails, 1 in. thick by 2 in. wide by 36 in. long

Side stretchers, 1 in. thick by 2 in. wide by 26 in. long

Dadoes for shelf stretcher, 1 in. deep by 2 in. wide

Legs, 2 in. thick by 3 in. wide by 31 in. long

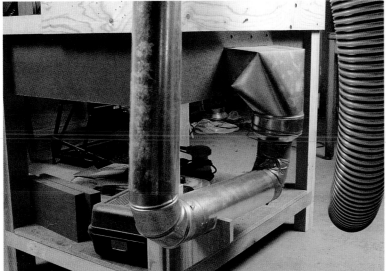

An inexpensive connection. Brown used a standard sheet-metal air-conditioning duct to tie the sanding table to his shop dust system.

FOLD-DOWN SANDING TABLE COLLECTS DUST

by David DiRanna

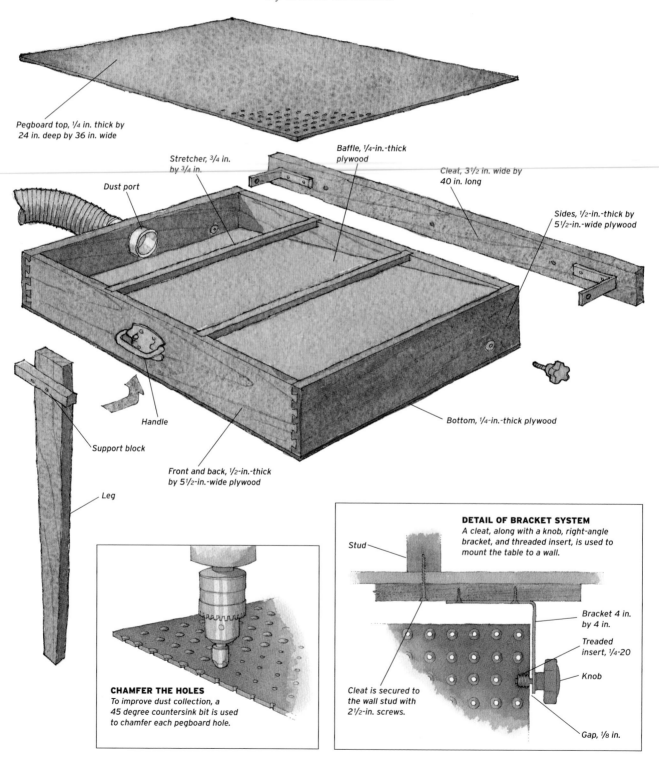

Pegboard top, ¼ in. thick by 24 in. deep by 36 in. wide

Stretcher, ¾ in. by ¾ in.

Dust port

Baffle, ¼-in.-thick plywood

Cleat, 3½ in. wide by 40 in. long

Sides, ½-in.-thick by 5½-in.-wide plywood

Handle

Support block

Leg

Front and back, ½-in.-thick by 5½-in.-wide plywood

Bottom, ¼-in.-thick plywood

CHAMFER THE HOLES
To improve dust collection, a 45 degree countersink bit is used to chamfer each pegboard hole.

DETAIL OF BRACKET SYSTEM
A cleat, along with a knob, right-angle bracket, and threaded insert, is used to mount the table to a wall.

Stud

Cleat is secured to the wall stud with 2½-in. screws.

Bracket 4 in. by 4 in.

Treaded insert, ¼-20

Knob

Gap, ⅛ in.

In December 2002, a U.S. Department of Health and Human Services report officially designated wood dust as a human carcinogen. According to the report, "unprotected workers have a higher risk of cancers to the nasal cavities and sinuses."

Such blunt facts make it clear that it's important to control wood dust in the shop. As part of that effort, I built a fold-down sanding table that allows me to collect dust at the source as I sand.

The design is pretty basic. The table itself essentially is a shallow rectangular box with a pegboard top. A port in the side connects to the hose from my dust-collection system. When fired up, the dust collector draws air from above the table down through the holes in the top, taking along a good deal of the dust generated while I sand. Inside the box, a plywood baffle extending from one corner to the other helps improve the dust-collection effectiveness. The table mounts to the wall via a simple bracket system (see the detail on the facing page).

I own a dovetail jig, so it was easy to join the front, back, and sides of the table with dovetails. But I could have created strong enough joints simply by butting the parts and screwing them together.

Before assembling any of these joints, I used a drill press and a circle cutter to cut a hole in one of the sides, with the hole diameter just big enough to create a snug fit for the dust port. I used a 3-in. PVC pipe coupling here. The 4-in. outside diameter of the coupling was a perfect fit for the dust collector's 4-in. hose.

I wanted the pegboard top to be removable, just in case I needed to open the table for cleaning or repair. So the top is secured using only flat-head wood screws.

David DiRanna builds furniture in his home shop in Fountain Valley, California.

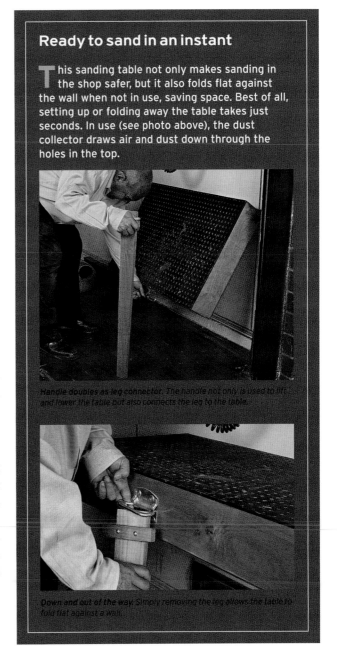

Ready to sand in an instant

This sanding table not only makes sanding in the shop safer, but it also folds flat against the wall when not in use, saving space. Best of all, setting up or folding away the table takes just seconds. In use (see photo above), the dust collector draws air and dust down through the holes in the top.

Handle doubles as leg connector. The handle not only is used to lift and lower the table but also connects the leg to the table.

Down and out of the way. Simply removing the leg allows the table to fold flat against a wall.

SHOOTING BOARD

by Ed Speas

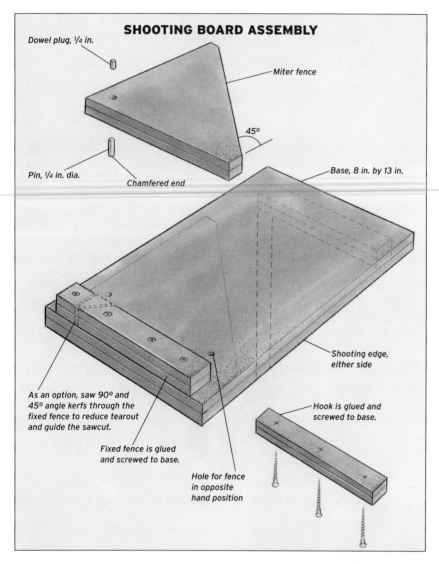

SHOOTING BOARD ASSEMBLY

Dowel plug, 1/4 in.

Miter fence

45°

Pin, 1/4 in. dia.

Chamfered end

Base, 8 in. by 13 in.

Shooting edge, either side

As an option, saw 90° and 45° angle kerfs through the fixed fence to reduce tearout and guide the sawcut.

Hook is glued and screwed to base.

Fixed fence is glued and screwed to base.

Hole for fence in opposite hand position

Fitting miters has been every woodworker's problem at one time or another. If your angle of cut or your piece lengths are not perfect, you have to repeatedly shave a smidgen to get a tight joint. A compound-miter or a tablesaw may not be the best choice for extremely clean and accurate cuts. If you use a handsaw, it tends to wander if not precisely guided. And even then, I don't know too many folks who can really get consistent 45s with a hand miter box alone.

You can eliminate these difficulties by using a simple fixture called a shooting board. When guided by a shooting board, a plane with a razor-sharp edge, can accurately slice off wispy thin shavings. And the end grain will be left with the smoothest surface possible. To use one of these fixtures, first place a workpiece against the fence, and lay a handplane on its side with the sole against the edge of the base. Butt the work up to the plane sole, and then push the plane by the work in several passes.

The shooting board I use is an adaptation of an old bench hook, or sawing board. I made this combination bench hook/shooting board so it would either hold stock while sawing or precisely plane the ends of stock. The entire jig is made out of medium density fiberboard (MDF). It also features a removable 45-degree fence, which makes it both a miter and a right-angle shooting board. The fence is reversible as well, so I can pare miters from the left or the right side.

Ed Speas is a woodworker in Ballground, Georgia.

Perfect miters. Guided by Ed Speas's shooting board, a Lie-Nielsen® #9 miter plane easily shaves a 45-degree miter on molding. The fence is reversible, so the fixture can handle left- and right-hand cuts.

Fixture doubles as a bench hook. To convert the shooting board to a bench hook for 90-degree sawing, the author simply removed the miter fence (here resting in the bench trough).

ROLLING TOOL CABINETS SAVE SPACE

By Bill Endress

After many years living in central Florida, I received an invitation to relocate to Tucson, Ariz. Having been an active woodworker for 18 years, I placed adequate shop space high on my list when it came time to buy a home. While it would have been nice to find a house with a separate workshop, my wife and I settled on one with a spacious 23-ft. by 23-ft. two-car garage.

This presented me with a challenge: create an efficient and comfortable workshop that could accommodate big projects but still make room for the family cars. The primary requirement was to keep at least one car in the garage at night, even if a half-finished project occupied floor space. The flexibility to park two vehicles in the garage on occasion also was essential. The challenge was balancing these requirements with the elements of a good shop: one that is attractive to work in, easy to clean, and has plenty of organized storage. My philosophy throughout was "a place for everything, and everything in its place."

Room for rough cutting. Endress starts his work flow by milling boards at the thickness planer. Rolling cabinets support the stock on its way in and out of the planer and can be moved to support boards of various lengths.

Making do with limited space

To have plenty of workspace and be able to cut long boards with my radial-arm saw, I knew I would build a long workbench along one of the garage walls.

While paging through magazines, I came upon an article for a roll-around tool-storage cabinet designed to be tucked under one wing of a tablesaw. It dawned on me that I could use a similar concept to save space in my garage. Beneath the workbench I could house roll-around cabinets to store tools.

The more I thought about it, the more advantages I could see of this system. With the rolling cabinets built to well-planned heights, they could serve as infeed and outfeed supports for stationary tools. Work areas also could be adapted to accommodate different projects just by rearranging the rolling cabinets.

Once I knew the workbench measurements, it was easy to back out the dimensions for the rolling cabinets. The cabinets follow the same basic design but are configured differently, according to their functions.

All of the cabinets roll on swivel casters. Handles are attached to the cabinet faces so that they can be maneuvered around the garage. The handles, drawer pulls, and cabinet-door handles are all matching brushed chrome, giving the final profile of the workbench a handsome look.

Storage cabinets double as work surfaces

The cabinet used for storing power tools has six sliding shelves that pull out to the left for storing sanders, a jigsaw, and other tools. A second cabinet is built in a mirror image. By butting these two cabinets together, a continuous work surface is created while leaving the shelves accessible.

BASIC CONSTRUCTION OF ROLLING CABINETS

Each rolling cabinet has the same overall dimensions: 26 in. deep by 22 in. wide by 32½ in. high (the compound-miter saw, planer, and scrollsaw cabinets are shorter but follow a similar construction method). Locking swivel casters account for 3 in. of the height. The basic construction allows for variations in the placement of drawers and shelves. Each cabinet is constructed from ¾-in.-thick plywood and finished with two coats of water-based varnish.

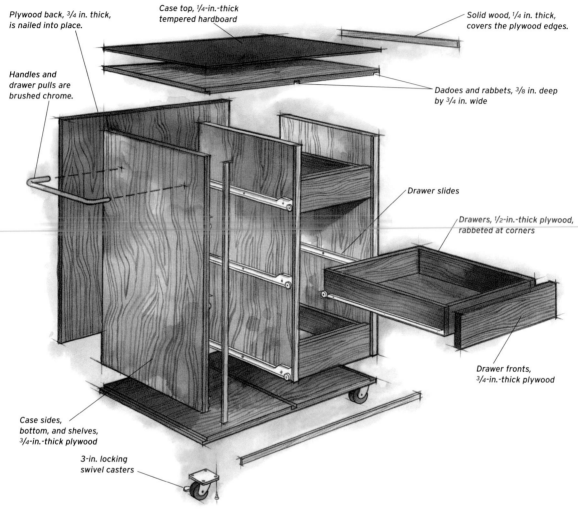

Plywood back, ¾ in. thick, is nailed into place.

Case top, ¼-in.-thick tempered hardboard

Solid wood, ¼ in. thick, covers the plywood edges.

Handles and drawer pulls are brushed chrome.

Dadoes and rabbets, ⅜ in. deep by ¾ in. wide

Drawer slides

Drawers, ½-in.-thick plywood, rabbeted at corners

Drawer fronts, ¾-in.-thick plywood

Case sides, bottom, and shelves, ¾-in.-thick plywood

3-in. locking swivel casters

Configure the cabinet for various uses

While confined to set dimensions, Endress designed the rolling cabinets with various arrangements of shelves and drawers so that each one serves a unique purpose.

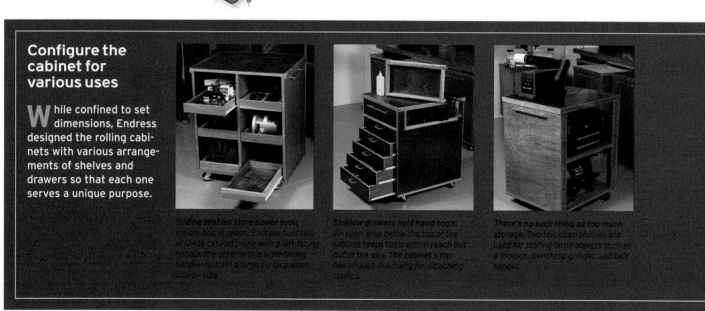

Sliding shelves store power tools visibly and in reach. Endress built two of these cabinets—one with a left-facing handle, the other with a right-facing handle—to form a large surface when side by side.

Shallow drawers hold hand tools. An open area below the top of the cabinet keeps tools within reach but out of the way. The cabinet's top has enough overhang for attaching clamps.

There's no such thing as too much storage. Two tall open shelves are used for storing large objects such as a toolbox, benchtop grinder, and belt sander.

A third rolling cabinet has five drawers to hold hand tools. A shelf underneath the top of the cabinet is open on three sides, providing a place to set tools and keep them out of the way. The opening also is useful for clamping workpieces to the tabletop.

The fourth rolling cabinet simply has two shelves that are accessible from three sides. One shelf holds two toolboxes, and the other holds my bench grinder and a small belt sander.

The height of the cabinets is consistent and makes them ideal to serve as infeed and outfeed tables for my miter saw, planer, and tablesaw.

Stationary tools get wheels too

The first four cabinets provide adequate storage for my hand tools. But I also needed storage for my assortment of power tools.

The scrollsaw fits below the workbench, sitting on a low, rolling cabinet. While it seems quite short at first glance, the cabinet is just the right height to use the saw while sitting comfortably in a chair. The router-table cabinet also is on wheels. The table is equipped with a router lift. The lift is offset from the center of the work surface, leaving room for drawers on one side of the cabinet.

Following the same design, I built rolling cabinets to hold my planer, miter saw, and tablesaw. Rather than getting stored out of sight, these cabinets fit along the walls of my shop and can be moved easily. The cabinets for these tools also have plenty of storage for any accessories.

Bill Endress is an aerospace engineer in Tucson, Arizona. In his spare time, he works wood in his two-car garage.

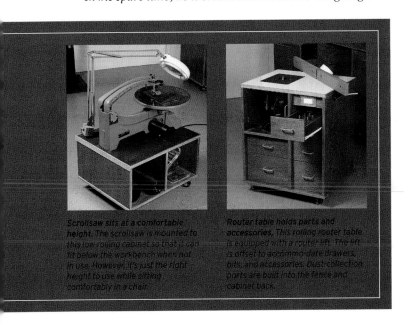

Scrollsaw sits at a comfortable height. The scrollsaw is mounted to this low rolling cabinet so that it can fit below the workbench when not in use. However, it's just the right height to use while sitting comfortably in a chair.

Router table holds parts and accessories. This rolling router table is equipped with a router lift. The lift is offset to accommodate drawers, bits, and accessories. Dust-collection ports are built into the fence and cabinet back.

Mobile tools and cabinets improve work flow

With the cabinets and tool stands built to corresponding heights, they can be arranged for use in a variety of combinations. The four-station arrangement shown here will accommodate a work flow that includes benchtop planing, ripping on the tablesaw, crosscutting on the miter saw, and routing at the router table. After an operation has been completed at one station, the outfeed table is rolled to the next station, where it becomes the infeed table.

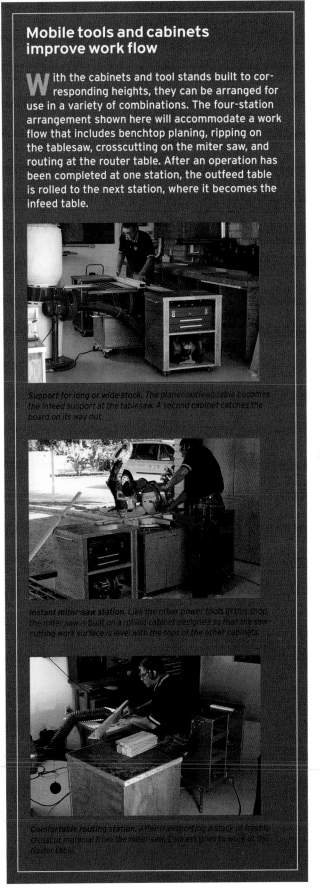

Support for long or wide stock. The planer outfeed table becomes the infeed support at the tablesaw. A second cabinet catches the board on its way out.

Instant miter-saw station. Like the other power tools in this shop, the miter saw is built on a rolling cabinet designed so that the saw-cutting work surface is level with the tops of the other cabinets.

Comfortable routing station. After transporting a stack of freshly crosscut material from the miter saw, Endress goes to work at the router table.

VERTICAL PRESS SIMPLIFIES PANEL GLUE-UPS

By Jim Tolpin

Large panels can be clamped easily in a vertical press. Wedges along the joint keep the boards aligned. Other wedges at the top, as well as pipe or bar clamps, provide the edge-clamping pressure.

When I need to glue up small panels, I just gather up a few pipe or bar clamps and work right on my bench. When I have everything clamped, I take the assembly and set it against a wall, taking care not to rack it when I set it down.

Large panels, like tabletops, and large glue-ups, like full-size entry or interior doors, aren't so easy. Moving heavy pieces like these can be more than a little unwieldy, making racking much more likely. And leaving the whole assembly on my bench until it dries isn't a good solution either. That's why I built a vertical press (see the photo at left).

Awhile back, I saw a professionally made vertical press in an industrial cabinet shop and realized that the press was the solution to my problem. But the press cost a lot more than I was willing or able to spend. So I designed my own and made it from 2x4s and 2x6s and common hardware (see the drawing on the facing page).

Besides keeping my bench free when I'm doing large glue-ups, the vertical press virtually ensures that the panels will be flat and correctly aligned. And because the press is made from 2x stock, it's light, easily movable and priced right.

There are other advantages to my vertical press. Both sides of the assembly are readily accessible, making it easy to inspect the joints front and back and to remove any excess glue. Because the press is inexpensive, I can afford to build a number of them. And plastic laminate on the inside face of the back 2x4 of each upright keeps the boards I'm edge-gluing from becoming part of the press.

Using the press

To clamp up a panel or a flat assembly, such as a door, I start by measuring the overall width of the panel or assembly. Then I add a little space for a wedge at the top, maybe 2 in. or so. I bolt the lower stop block in place at this distance from the fixed top block.

Then I run the first board of the panel between the uprights and spread out the individual presses, spacing them from 12 in. to 16 in. apart. I tap a wedge or wedges (also faced with laminate to prevent them from adhering to the panel) between the face of the board and the front upright to hold the board in place. I apply glue to the edge of this first board as well as to the mating edge of the next board, which I then slide into the press.

Once the second board is in the press, I reposition the first set of wedges, so they're right on the joint between the first two boards. The wedges keep the boards flush. I add more near the top of the second board to hold it against the back upright.

I continue in this way to the last board and then drive wedges under the top blocks to press the lamination together. These wedges get the panel or assembly together quickly and also provide a good amount of clamping pressure.

To ensure that clamping pressure is uniform over the full length of the boards, I insert pipe or bar clamps across the boards, as shown in the photo on the facing page. I use wood scraps or clamp pads to protect the outer edges. I make sure the joints are flush across their faces and drive additional wedges wherever necessary to get the whole panel flat.

Jim Tolpin is a writer and woodworker in Port Townsend, Washington.

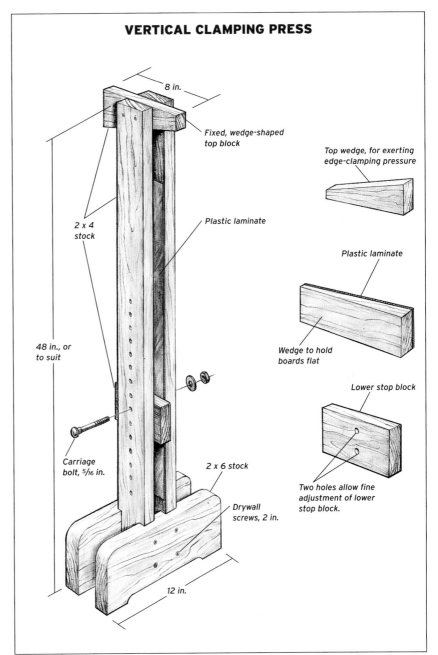

VERTICAL CLAMPING PRESS

8 in.

Fixed, wedge-shaped top block

Top wedge, for exerting edge-clamping pressure

2 x 4 stock

Plastic laminate

Plastic laminate

Wedge to hold boards flat

48 in., or to suit

Lower stop block

Carriage bolt, 5/16 in.

2 x 6 stock

Drywall screws, 2 in.

Two holes allow fine adjustment of lower stop block.

12 in.

CONVERTIBLE CLAMPING WORKSTATION

By Gary B. Foster

Widthwise panels,
3/4 in. thick by
15 1/2 in. high by
35 in. long

After working for months on my knees building a large bookcase, I decided I needed a low table in my shop for assembling large projects. I didn't want to take up room with a low table that would find only part-time use. It needed to do more. So I designed a workstation that also fulfilled a number of other shop needs, including a place to store my clamps and to glue up furniture parts. The workstation is built in two sections and can be reconfigured to accommodate its various uses.

The lower portion of the workstation is constructed as a tall torsion box. A plywood grid makes up its interior, consisting of five panels running widthwise and three longer panels running lengthwise. The panels, which stand on end, cross one another with cross-lap joints, and they are sandwiched between two 3/4-in.-thick plywood skins. Built into the lower torsion box is a web of PVC pipes, that hold clamps up to 6 ft. long.

The upper section of the table stacks on top of the lower section and is designed to support clamps when assembling furniture parts. It also is constructed as a tall torsion box with panels that lock together with cross-lap joints. However, this torsion box is not glued, so it can be reconfigured to hold clamps in different arrangements.

The upper section also can be used as a work surface by laying a sheet of 3/4-in.-thick Melamine® on top of the plywood grid. With the top on, the table is level with my workbench and tablesaw, so it is useful as an infeed or outfeed support.

Gary B. Foster is a longtime woodworker and manages the tools department at the Lowe's® in his hometown of Folsom, California.

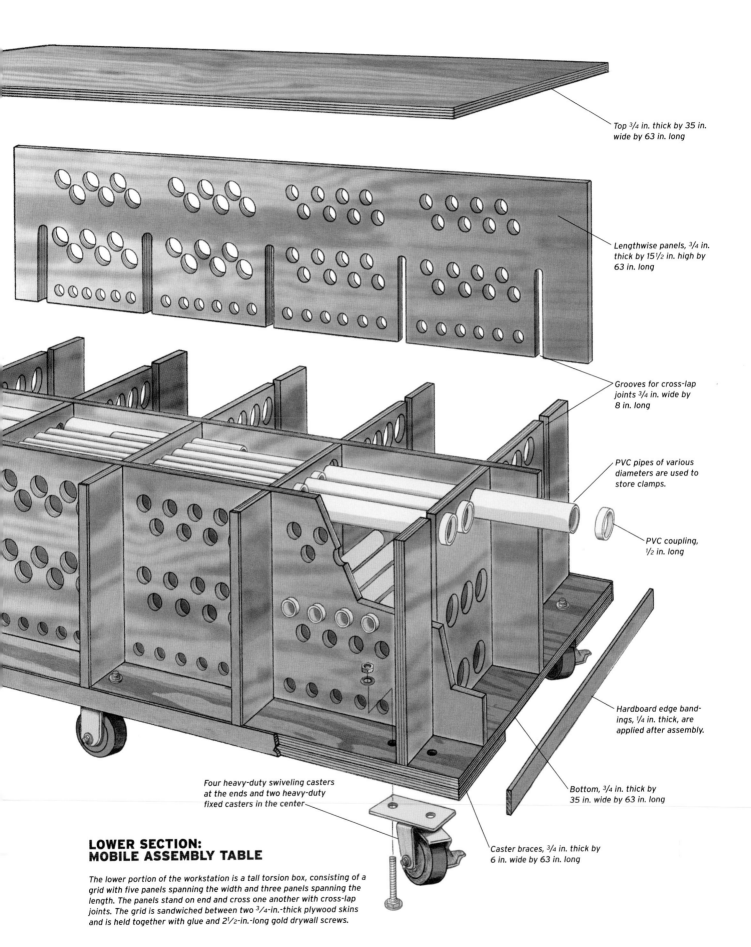

Top ³/₄ in. thick by 35 in. wide by 63 in. long

Lengthwise panels, ³/₄ in. thick by 15¹/₂ in. high by 63 in. long

Grooves for cross-lap joints ³/₄ in. wide by 8 in. long

PVC pipes of various diameters are used to store clamps.

PVC coupling, ¹/₂ in. long

Hardboard edge bandings, ¹/₄ in. thick, are applied after assembly.

Bottom, ³/₄ in. thick by 35 in. wide by 63 in. long

Four heavy-duty swiveling casters at the ends and two heavy-duty fixed casters in the center

Caster braces, ³/₄ in. thick by 6 in. wide by 63 in. long

LOWER SECTION: MOBILE ASSEMBLY TABLE

The lower portion of the workstation is a tall torsion box, consisting of a grid with five panels spanning the width and three panels spanning the length. The panels stand on end and cross one another with cross-lap joints. The grid is sandwiched between two ³/₄-in.-thick plywood skins and is held together with glue and 2¹/₂-in.-long gold drywall screws.

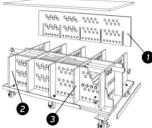

HOLE LAYOUT FOR PLYWOOD PANELS

PVC pipes, with diameters based on the size of the clamps they will hold, are fed through holes drilled in the plywood panels. Lay out the pipes so that those spanning the width of the table don't interfere with those running lengthwise. Prepare templates to cut matching hole patterns on each plywood panel. The end panels are mirror images of each other and are laid out with the same template. The center panels combine the layouts of the two end panels.

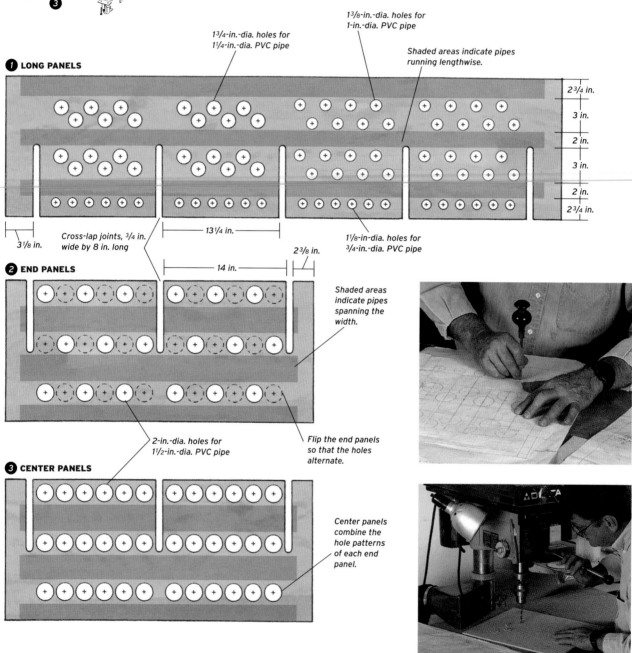

1³/₈-in.-dia. holes for
1-in.-dia. PVC pipe

1³/₄-in.-dia. holes for
1¹/₄-in.-dia. PVC pipe

Shaded areas indicate pipes
running lengthwise.

1 LONG PANELS

2³/₄ in.

3 in.

2 in.

3 in.

2 in.

2³/₄ in.

3¹/₈ in.

Cross-lap joints, ³/₄ in.
wide by 8 in. long

13¹/₄ in.

1¹/₈-in-dia. holes for
³/₄-in.-dia. PVC pipe

14 in.

2³/₈ in.

2 END PANELS

Shaded areas
indicate pipes
spanning the
width.

Flip the end panels
so that the holes
alternate.

2-in.-dia. holes for
1¹/₂-in.-dia. PVC pipe

3 CENTER PANELS

Center panels
combine the
hole patterns
of each end
panel.

Templates guarantee matching holes. Center points
are transferred from a paper template to a ¹/₄-in.-thick
plywood template. The template is then used to lay out
each section of the final panels.

UPPER SECTION:
KNOCKDOWN TABLE DOUBLES AS CLAMPING GRID

The upper section of the workstation is a torsion box consisting of tall plywood panels connected by cross-lap joints. The panels are not glued together, so they can be reconfigured for different clamping arrangements. Grooves in the top edges of the panels support clamps during glue-up. In one configuration, grooves in the lengthwise panels are twice as deep as those in the widthwise panels. This allows clamps to be arranged front to back and side to side without interference. With the top panel in place, the workstation can be used as a large work surface.

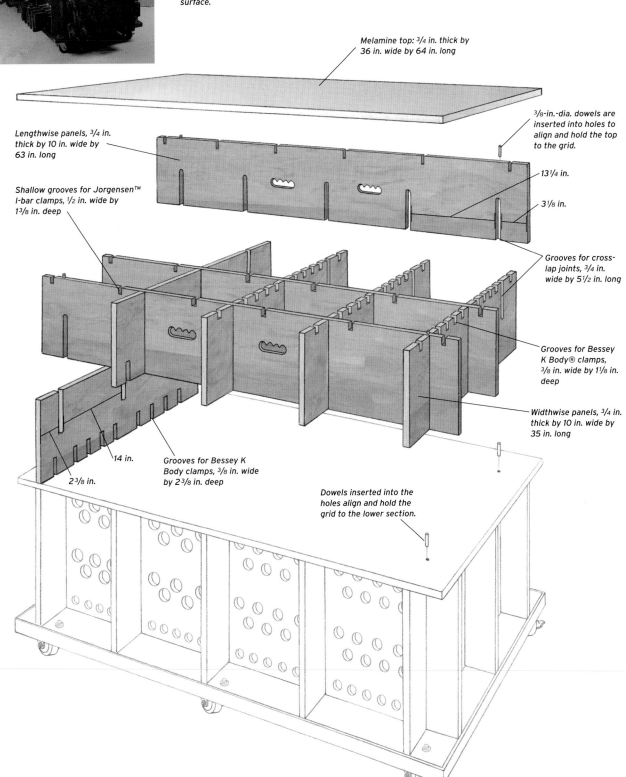

Melamine top: ³/₄ in. thick by 36 in. wide by 64 in. long

³/₈-in.-dia. dowels are inserted into holes to align and hold the top to the grid.

Lengthwise panels, ³/₄ in. thick by 10 in. wide by 63 in. long

13¹/₄ in.

3¹/₈ in.

Shallow grooves for Jorgensen™ I-bar clamps, ¹/₂ in. wide by 1³/₈ in. deep

Grooves for cross-lap joints, ³/₄ in. wide by 5¹/₂ in. long

Grooves for Bessey K Body® clamps, ³/₈ in. wide by 1¹/₈ in. deep

Widthwise panels, ³/₄ in. thick by 10 in. wide by 35 in. long

14 in.

Grooves for Bessey K Body clamps, ³/₈ in. wide by 2³/₈ in. deep

2³/₈ in.

Dowels inserted into the holes align and hold the grid to the lower section.

A BENCH BUILT TO LAST

By Dick McDonough

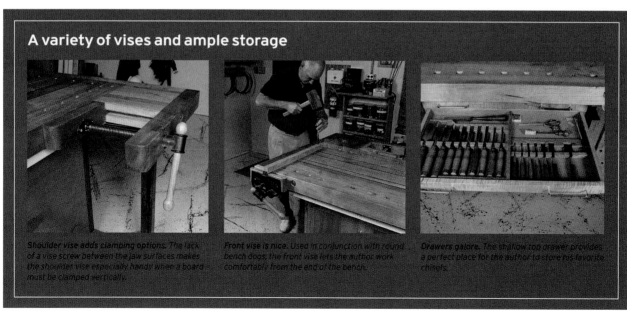

A variety of vises and ample storage

Shoulder vise adds clamping options. The lack of a vise screw between the jaw surfaces makes the shoulder vise especially handy when a board must be clamped vertically.

Front vise is nice. Used in conjunction with round bench dogs, the front vise lets the author work comfortably from the end of the bench.

Drawers galore. The shallow top drawer provides a perfect place for the author to store his favorite chisels.

SHOULDER VISE AND END CAP

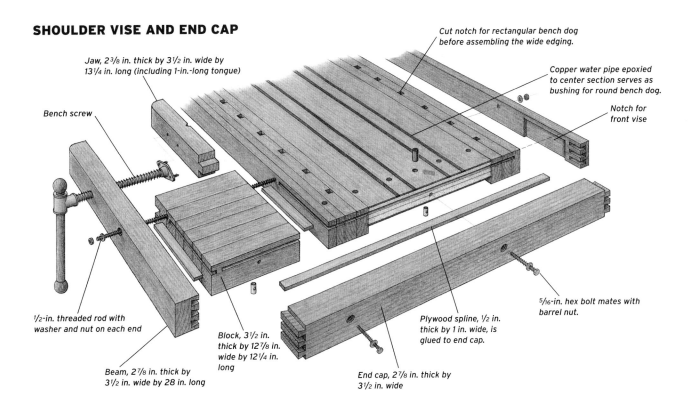

Jaw, 2³/₈ in. thick by 3¹/₂ in. wide by 13¹/₄ in. long (including 1-in.-long tongue)

Bench screw

Cut notch for rectangular bench dog before assembling the wide edging.

Copper water pipe epoxied to center section serves as bushing for round bench dog.

Notch for front vise

¹/₂-in. threaded rod with washer and nut on each end

Beam, 2⁷/₈ in. thick by 3¹/₂ in. wide by 28 in. long

Block, 3¹/₂ in. thick by 12⁷/₈ in. wide by 12¹/₄ in. long

Plywood spline, ¹/₂ in. thick by 1 in. wide, is glued to end cap.

End cap, 2⁷/₈ in. thick by 3¹/₂ in. wide

⁵/₁₆-in. hex bolt mates with barrel nut.

I f this workbench played football, I'm certain it would be a lineman. Because, like the guards and tackles found on the gridiron, my bench is big and solid. And I wouldn't have it any other way.

Most of my work involves the fabrication of large case goods—entertainment centers, bookcases, and other types of storage furniture. And although much of the machine work gets done using a tablesaw and router, I still do a good deal of work at the bench. So when it was time to replace my older, smallish, and somewhat rickety workbench, I opted to make a new one with all the bells and whistles. The bench would provide plenty of size and sturdiness. *Sturdiness* is the operative word here. Indeed, no matter how aggressive I get with a saw, a handplane, or a mallet and chisel, the bench doesn't wobble. The result is a workbench that has just about everything I need.

The supersize top is another important feature. With about 22 sq. ft. of surface area, the top is great for supporting long boards and wide sheet goods. Two end vises, a front vise, and a shoulder vise, along with a small army of bench-dog holes, make it easy to secure almost any size stock to the bench.

My bench is considered left-handed, based on the location of the shoulder vise. If you prefer a right-handed bench, just build the shoulder vise on the right side.

The base creates a sturdy foundation

The bench owes much of its sturdiness to the design of the base. Yet its construction is pretty straightforward. It has just five main parts: three support frames and a pair of boxes. Screwing the frames and boxes together creates a single, rock-solid unit that can accept almost any kind of top. And the two boxes provide a ton of space for adding cabinets or drawers.

The center and right-side support frames are identical. But to provide additional support for the shoulder vise, the left-side support frame is longer and has an extra leg. I added seven heavy-duty levelers—one under each leg of the support frame. I leveled the top surface using winding sticks and the seven levelers. Then I was ready to build the top right on the base.

Once the support frames and boxes were put together, I was able to assemble the base without much fuss.

The top has three main parts. There's a center section made from veneered particleboard. Attached to the center section are two 6-in.-wide edgings—one in front, the other in back—and both made from glued-up solid maple. To help keep costs under control, I face-glued three pieces of particleboard together—a ⁵/₈-in.-thick piece sandwiched between two ³/₄-in.-thick pieces.

A workbench top gets a lot of wear and tear, so I used a ³/₁₆-in.-thick veneer on top. And to make sure any movement stresses would be equal, I also veneered the bottom.

The wide edgings that run along the front and back of the bench are made of solid maple. That way the bench dogs have plenty of support when in use.

Those big boxes in the base provide plenty of storage space. I placed eight drawers in the right-hand box, a shallow through-drawer that extends from front to back, and a left-hand box to hold project parts.

The board jacks (one in front and one in back) are handy additions to the bench. When a board is clamped in the front, or shoulder, vise, the jack holds up the unsupported end. To accommodate boards of different lengths, the jack is able to slide along the full length of the bench.

Because my bench is several feet from a wall, I added power strips along the front and back edges, making it easy to use power tools at the bench.

The bench has been serving me well for several years now. During that time, it has picked up plenty of scratches and dents, but it's as solid as ever. And I expect it's going to stay that way for many years to come.

Dick McDonough lives in Flint, Michigan, where he's a full-time finish carpenter and part-time woodworking teacher.

A MASSIVE TOP ON A STURDY MODULAR BASE

To help keep costs under control, the top is a hybrid, a mix of solid maple, thick veneer, and particleboard. The base construction is surprisingly simple—a pair of plywood boxes sandwiched between three frames—yet the single unit that results is as solid as a '72 Buick®.

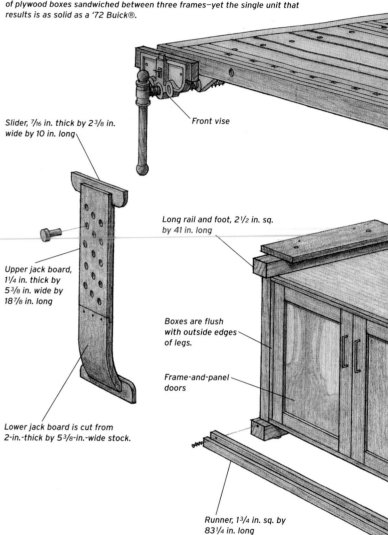

Slider, ⁷/₁₆ in. thick by 2³/₈ in. wide by 10 in. long

Front vise

Long rail and foot, 2¹/₂ in. sq. by 41 in. long

Upper jack board, 1¹/₄ in. thick by 5³/₈ in. wide by 18⁷/₈ in. long

Boxes are flush with outside edges of legs.

Frame-and-panel doors

Lower jack board is cut from 2-in.-thick by 5³/₈-in.-wide stock.

Runner, 1³/₄ in. sq. by 83¹/₄ in. long

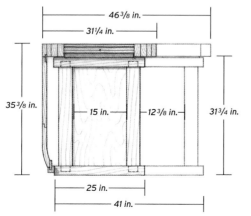

46³/₈ in.

31¹/₄ in.

35³/₈ in.

15 in.

12³/₈ in.

31³/₄ in.

25 in.

41 in.

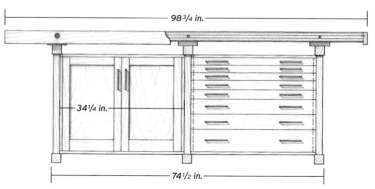

98³/₄ in.

34¹/₄ in.

74¹/₂ in.

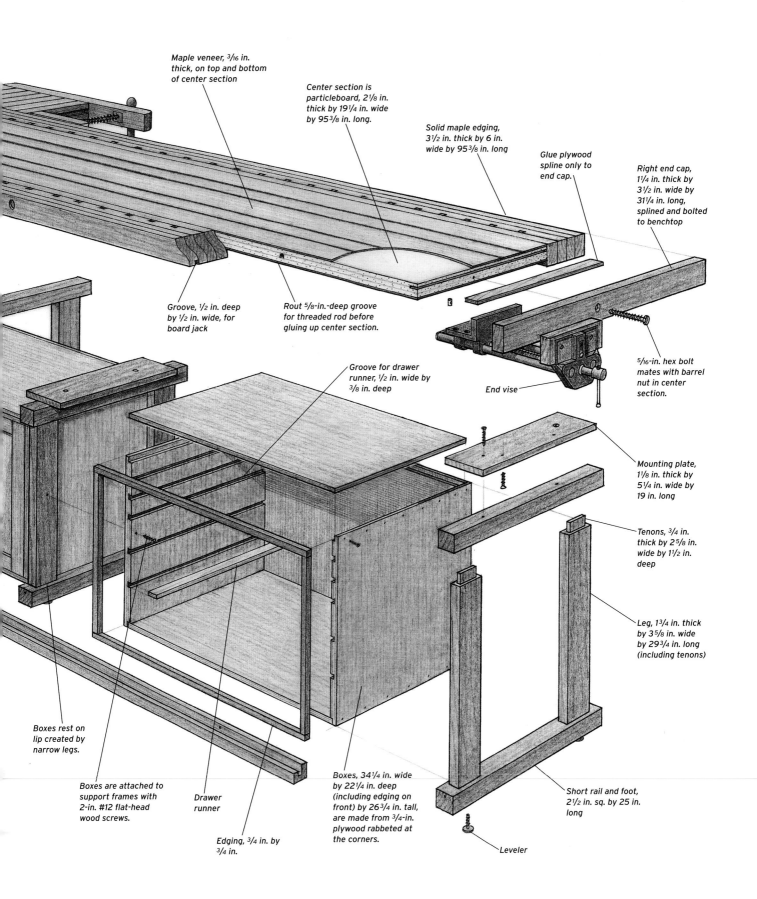

Maple veneer, 3/16 in. thick, on top and bottom of center section

Center section is particleboard, 2 1/8 in. thick by 19 1/4 in. wide by 95 3/8 in. long.

Solid maple edging, 3 1/2 in. thick by 6 in. wide by 95 3/8 in. long

Glue plywood spline only to end cap.

Right end cap, 1 1/4 in. thick by 3 1/2 in. wide by 31 1/4 in. long, splined and bolted to benchtop

Groove, 1/2 in. deep by 1/2 in. wide, for board jack

Rout 5/8-in.-deep groove for threaded rod before gluing up center section.

5/16-in. hex bolt mates with barrel nut in center section.

End vise

Groove for drawer runner, 1/2 in. wide by 3/8 in. deep

Mounting plate, 1 1/8 in. thick by 5 1/4 in. wide by 19 in. long

Tenons, 3/4 in. thick by 2 5/8 in. wide by 1 1/2 in. deep

Leg, 1 3/4 in. thick by 3 5/8 in. wide by 29 3/4 in. long (including tenons)

Boxes rest on lip created by narrow legs.

Boxes are attached to support frames with 2-in. #12 flat-head wood screws.

Drawer runner

Edging, 3/4 in. by 3/4 in.

Boxes, 34 1/4 in. wide by 22 1/4 in. deep (including edging on front) by 26 3/4 in. tall, are made from 3/4-in. plywood rabbeted at the corners.

Leveler

Short rail and foot, 2 1/2 in. sq. by 25 in. long

ROCK-SOLID
PLYWOOD BENCH

By Cecil Braeden

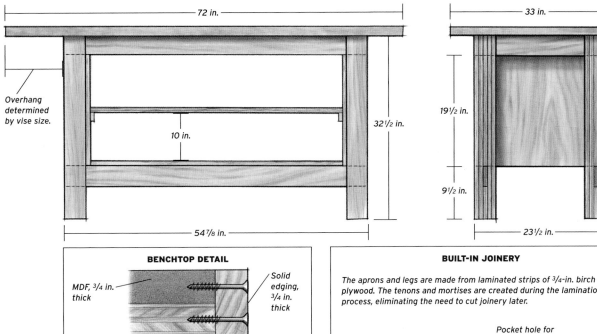

72 in.

33 in.

Overhang determined by vise size.

32½ in.

10 in.

19½ in.

9½ in.

54⅞ in.

23½ in.

BENCHTOP DETAIL

MDF, ¾ in. thick

Solid edging, ¾ in. thick

Plywood, ¾ in. thick

BUILT-IN JOINERY

The aprons and legs are made from laminated strips of ¾-in. birch plywood. The tenons and mortises are created during the lamination process, eliminating the need to cut joinery later.

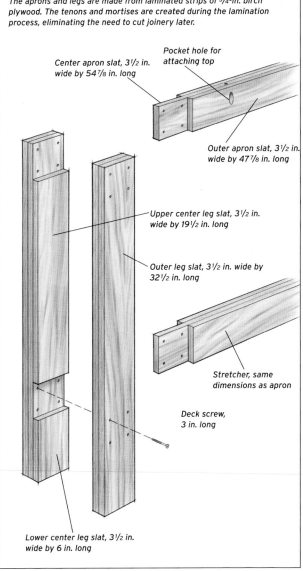

Center apron slat, 3½ in. wide by 54⅞ in. long

Pocket hole for attaching top

Outer apron slat, 3½ in. wide by 47⅞ in. long

Upper center leg slat, 3½ in. wide by 19½ in. long

Outer leg slat, 3½ in. wide by 32½ in. long

Stretcher, same dimensions as apron

Deck screw, 3 in. long

Lower center leg slat, 3½ in. wide by 6 in. long

I had wanted to build a sturdy workbench for some time but was put off by the cost and complexity of a traditional hardwood bench. I knew that such benches derive much of their strength and rigidity from the mortises and tenons that join the framework, and I wondered if there was a way to combine this joinery with the inherent strength, rigidity, and dimensional accuracy of plywood. The design I created has a base of laminated sections of plywood and a top of plywood and medium-density fiberboard (MDF).

An advantage of this design is that the piece can be built without a planer or jointer, perfect for someone just getting started in woodworking. Including a vise, I have a bench with the rigidity I desired without breaking the bank.

This method of construction can be adapted to almost any size and type of bench: You could even construct just the base and purchase a ready-made hardwood top. My bench is 33 in. wide by 72 in. long by 34 in. tall, a comfortable height for me to work at. It is also ⅛ in. lower than my tablesaw, allowing me to use the bench as an auxiliary outfeed table. The cut plan I used (see drawings on p. 46) allows you to create a bench with legs up to 36 in. long, giving a bench height of 37½ in. All base components—legs, aprons, and stretchers—are laminations made from 3⁹⁄₁₆-in.-wide slats of ¾-in.-thick plywood.

Cecil Braeden is a woodworker near Anacortes, Washington.

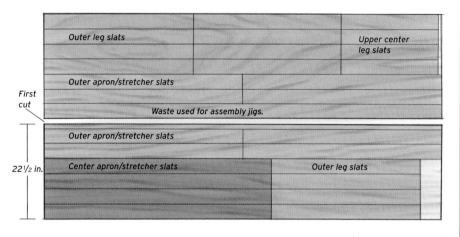

Outer leg slats

Upper center leg slats

Outer apron/stretcher slats

Waste used for assembly jigs.

First cut

Outer apron/stretcher slats

Center apron/stretcher slats

Outer leg slats

22½ in.

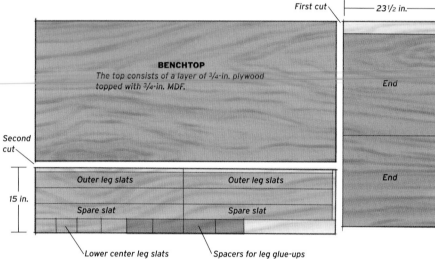

First cut

23½ in.

BENCHTOP
The top consists of a layer of ¾-in. plywood topped with ¾-in. MDF.

End

End

Second cut

15 in.

Outer leg slats

Outer leg slats

Spare slat

Spare slat

Lower center leg slats

Spacers for leg glue-ups

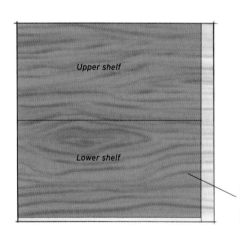

Upper shelf

Lower shelf

The two optional shelves come out of a half sheet of ¾-in.-thick plywood.

Make the most of your plywood

If you decide to build a bench that is the same size as mine, or one that is slightly taller, use these cut plans. I used 2½ sheets of 4x8 birch plywood and a sheet of MDF from my local home center. Have your plywood seller make the first and second cuts as shown to ease handling the material.

Other materials needed are 2-, 2½-, and 3-in.-long deck screws, and a quart of fresh PVA woodworking glue. I've used both Titebond® II and III; but particularly in hot, dry conditions, glues with extended open times make alignment of the laminations easier.

MULTIPURPOSE SUPPORT STAND

By John White

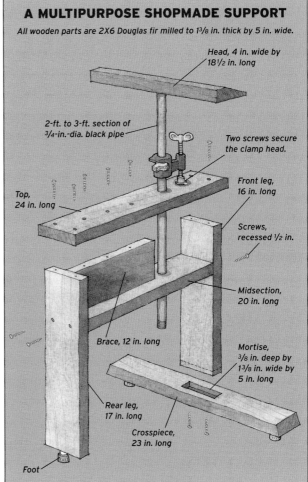

A MULTIPURPOSE SHOPMADE SUPPORT

All wooden parts are 2X6 Douglas fir milled to 1⅜ in. thick by 5 in. wide.

Head, 4 in. wide by 18½ in. long

2-ft. to 3-ft. section of ¾-in.-dia. black pipe

Two screws secure the clamp head.

Front leg, 16 in. long

Top, 24 in. long

Screws, recessed ½ in.

Midsection, 20 in. long

Brace, 12 in. long

Mortise, ⅜ in. deep by 1⅜ in. wide by 5 in. long

Rear leg, 17 in. long

Crosspiece, 23 in. long

Foot

After studying the roller stands on the market, I decided that it should be possible to create one that is quick and easy to build, economical, and combines the best features of various commercial stands. My design appears unorthodox; however, it is stable, fine-tuning the height is a breeze, and I can use a variety of support surfaces.

The stand is assembled with simple butt joints held by drywall screws. For added strength, the front leg is set into a ⅜-in.-deep mortise in the crosspiece.

The stand uses a #56 Pony brand pipe clamp sold in hardware stores. Depending on the bed height of your tools, you'll also need a length of ¾-in.-dia. black pipe between 2 ft. and 3 ft. long.

The base sits on three rubber crutch tips to prevent it from sliding. The tips are slipped over 1¼-in. O.D. plastic plumbing pipe caps, which are screwed to the bottom of the stand.

John White is Fine Woodworking's *shop manager.*

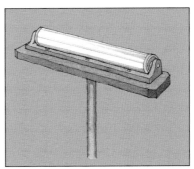

THREE HEADS ARE BETTER THAN ONE

The beauty of this shopmade stand is its interchangeable head design. All three heads illustrated here mount to the threaded pipe via pipe flanges screwed to the bottom of each head. Use your own head to determine which one is best for the task at hand.

HEFTY WORKBENCH WITH ALL THE FRILLS

By Jon Leppo

Vises, bench dogs, and a board jack help anchor workpieces

The front and end vises, along with bench dogs and a board jack, offer plenty of clamping options.

In the front of the bench I had planned to use a typical cast-iron vise with wood jaws until I ran across an Internet ad for a used patternmaker's vise, and I couldn't resist the temptation to buy. The vise, built in the 1930s by the Emmert® Manufacturing Co., allows me to clamp a workpiece in almost any position. Patternmakers favor this type of vise because it adjusts in several planes, making it possible to hold work of almost any shape. Like me, you'll occasionally see a used Emmert vise offered for sale on the Internet. Also, you can sometimes find them at vintage tool dealers or, more rarely, at flea markets. Expect to pay upwards of $500* for one in good condition. My vise is one of the larger ones Emmert produced. Modern reproductions of the vise are available in mostly smaller sizes, generally about 15 in. long. Some of these are fairly inexpensive, about $300*, and the quality is decent. Higher-quality ones can cost more than $1,000*.

A sliding board jack helps support long, wide stock, with the front end of the stock held in the Emmert vise. The board jack is adapted directly from one I found in *The Workbench Book* by Scott Landis (The Taunton Press, 1987), modified only slightly to fit my bench. The bottom track screws to the bottom frame, capturing the board jack. An occasional application of paste wax to the tracks keeps the jack sliding smoothly.

End vise adds versatility

I originally considered a commercially made twin-screw end vise, but in the end the extra versatility

I knew that when I eventually got around to building my dream workbench, it would have to meet a few basic requirements. It would have to be sturdy enough to last a few lifetimes. It would have to have storage underneath. And it would have to have good front and end vises so that I wouldn't have to do a lot to get a workpiece held securely.

In 1998, I finally built my bench. It's rock solid and has plenty of useful storage, thanks to 15 drawers and an area of open space between the base and the top.

Building such a large workbench can be an intimidating task, but it's actually basic woodworking. The only parts of the bench that call for anything other than straightforward biscuit and mortise-and-tenon joinery is the end vise. Whether you decide to build this bench using the drawings or add the end vise to a bench you already have, this chapter walks you through the process.

that a traditional vise offers has made the effort worthwhile. Whether you build my bench from the ground up or not, adding an end vise to a workbench will make it much more user-friendly. Building the end vise is also the trickiest part of the process.

The end-vise hardware consists of four parts (the vise hardware is available from Woodcraft®, 800-225-1153): a main plate, which includes a cylindrical nut; a long screw with a flanged bracket and handle collar; a top guide plate with a lengthwise groove and a pair of threaded bolt holes; and a bottom guide plate with a corresponding groove and a pair of countersunk through holes. A pair of bolts is also included. By the way, it's important to have the hardware on hand before making the vise. Some of the dimensions are taken directly off the steel parts.

The main plate is screwed to the edge of the benchtop. All of the other parts, effectively working as one component, simply slide along the main plate. One end of the long screw is attached to the outside end of the vise, while the other end is threaded into the nut on the main plate. As the screw is turned, it threads in or out of the fixed nut; and in the process the vise is carried along for the ride. The top and bottom guide plates connect the vise and the main plate while allowing the vise to slide. The secret here is the single lengthwise groove near one edge of each guide plate. The grooves in the guide plates simply slide over the main plate, held apart by the wooden core.

* Price estimates from 2003.

Jon Leppo is an amateur woodworker in Denver, Colorado.

VICE CONSTRUCTION

The core connects the vise to the hardware

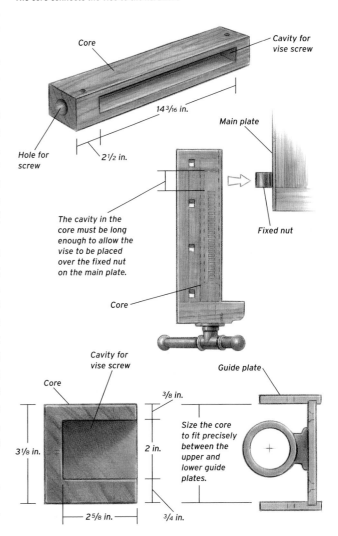

Core

Cavity for vise screw

14 3/16 in.

Main plate

Hole for screw

2 1/2 in.

The cavity in the core must be long enough to allow the vise to be placed over the fixed nut on the main plate.

Fixed nut

Core

Cavity for vise screw

Core

3/8 in.

Guide plate

3 1/8 in.

2 in.

Size the core to fit precisely between the upper and lower guide plates.

2 5/8 in.

3/4 in.

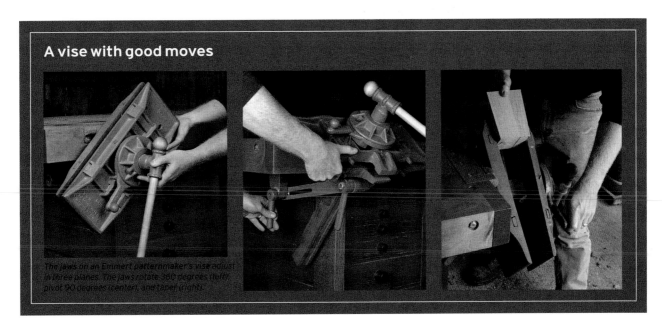

A vise with good moves

The jaws on an Emmert patternmaker's vise adjust in three planes. The jaws rotate 360 degrees (left), pivot 90 degrees (center), and taper (right).

Anatomy of a sturdy bench

The base of this bench, modeled after the one master woodworker Robert Whitley built for his bench, consists of five frame-and-panel assemblies—two end frames, a back frame, and two horizontal frames—bolted together with carriage bolts. And while I wouldn't exactly call this a knockdown bench, it can be disassembled.

I joined the panel frames with a double row of #20 biscuits, mostly because of speed and convenience. The base carcase sees mostly compression loads on vertical grain members rather than racking forces, which would stress the biscuit joints. A purist would have used mortises and tenons here. But I've had no trouble using biscuits in this kind of application.

The top is made from hard-maple laminations face-glued together. Each end of the bench has a long tenon. Later, when a pair of caps is made, each tenon fits into a mortise in the corresponding cap pieces.

I used a circular saw to cut the tenons. With a straightedge clamped to the benchtop to guide the saw, I made several crosscut kerfs and chiseled away the waste.

Both the long and short end caps are mortised to accept the tenons on each end of the bench.

To allow the top to move, the end caps aren't glued in place. Instead, each one is held in place with a pair of bolts. One of the bolt holes on each end cap is slotted so that it can move with the top. Once I had the end caps mounted, I flattened the entire benchtop using handplanes and winding sticks. Mounting an Emmert vise is relatively simple, although they are often heavy (mine is about 85 lb.). The vise itself mounts on a large hinge that's mortised into the top face of the benchtop and also the front face of the front apron. To allow clearance for the vise screw, a channel is cut into the underside of the apron and the benchtop.

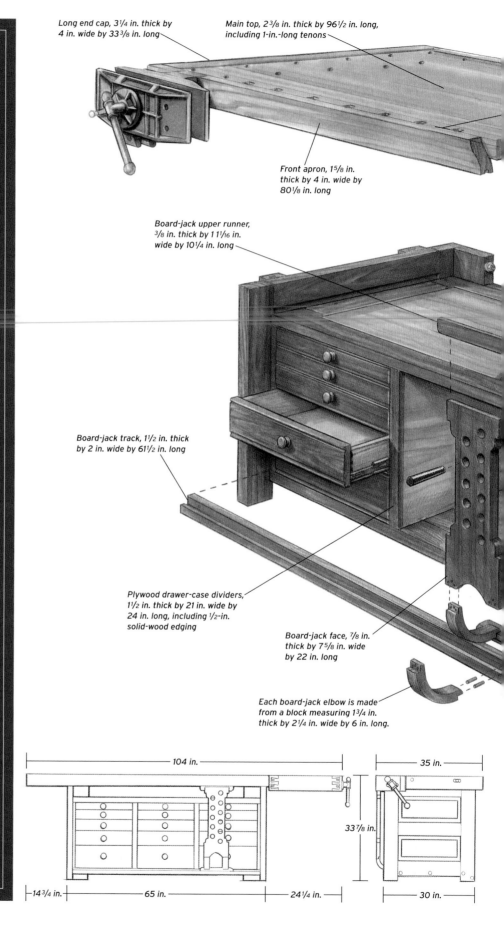

Long end cap, 3¼ in. thick by 4 in. wide by 33⅜ in. long

Main top, 2⅜ in. thick by 96½ in. long, including 1-in.-long tenons

Front apron, 1⅝ in. thick by 4 in. wide by 80⅛ in. long

Board-jack upper runner, ⅜ in. thick by 1 11/16 in. wide by 10¼ in. long

Board-jack track, 1½ in. thick by 2 in. wide by 61½ in. long

Plywood drawer-case dividers, 1½ in. thick by 21 in. wide by 24 in. long, including ½-in. solid-wood edging

Board-jack face, ⅞ in. thick by 7⅝ in. wide by 22 in. long

Each board-jack elbow is made from a block measuring 1¾ in. thick by 2¼ in. wide by 6 in. long.

104 in.

35 in.

33⅞ in.

14¾ in.

65 in.

24¼ in.

30 in.

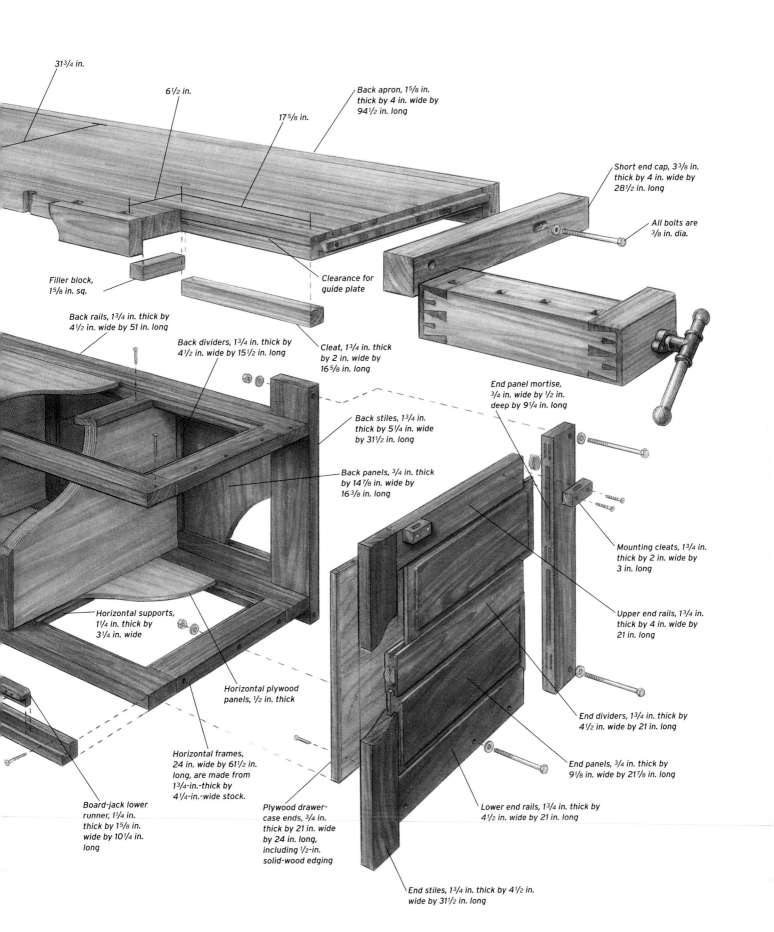

31³⁄₄ in.

6¹⁄₂ in.

17⁵⁄₈ in.

Back apron, 1⁵⁄₈ in.
thick by 4 in. wide by
94¹⁄₂ in. long

Short end cap, 3³⁄₈ in.
thick by 4 in. wide by
28¹⁄₂ in. long

All bolts are
³⁄₈ in. dia.

Filler block,
1⁵⁄₈ in. sq.

Clearance for
guide plate

Back rails, 1³⁄₄ in. thick by
4¹⁄₂ in. wide by 51 in. long

Back dividers, 1³⁄₄ in. thick by
4¹⁄₂ in. wide by 15¹⁄₂ in. long

Cleat, 1³⁄₄ in. thick
by 2 in. wide by
16⁵⁄₈ in. long

End panel mortise,
³⁄₄ in. wide by ¹⁄₂ in.
deep by 9¹⁄₄ in. long

Back stiles, 1³⁄₄ in.
thick by 5¹⁄₄ in. wide
by 31¹⁄₂ in. long

Back panels, ³⁄₄ in. thick
by 14⁷⁄₈ in. wide by
16³⁄₈ in. long

Mounting cleats, 1³⁄₄ in.
thick by 2 in. wide by
3 in. long

Horizontal supports,
1¹⁄₄ in. thick by
3¹⁄₄ in. wide

Upper end rails, 1³⁄₄ in.
thick by 4 in. wide by
21 in. long

Horizontal plywood
panels, ¹⁄₂ in. thick

Horizontal frames,
24 in. wide by 61¹⁄₂ in.
long, are made from
1³⁄₄-in.-thick by
4¹⁄₄-in.-wide stock.

End dividers, 1³⁄₄ in. thick by
4¹⁄₂ in. wide by 21 in. long

Board-jack lower
runner, 1¹⁄₄ in.
thick by 1⁵⁄₈ in.
wide by 10¹⁄₄ in.
long

Plywood drawer-
case ends, ³⁄₄ in.
thick by 21 in. wide
by 24 in. long,
including ¹⁄₂-in.
solid-wood edging

Lower end rails, 1³⁄₄ in. thick by
4¹⁄₂ in. wide by 21 in. long

End panels, ³⁄₄ in. thick by
9¹⁄₈ in. wide by 21⁷⁄₈ in. long

End stiles, 1³⁄₄ in. thick by 4¹⁄₂ in.
wide by 31¹⁄₂ in. long

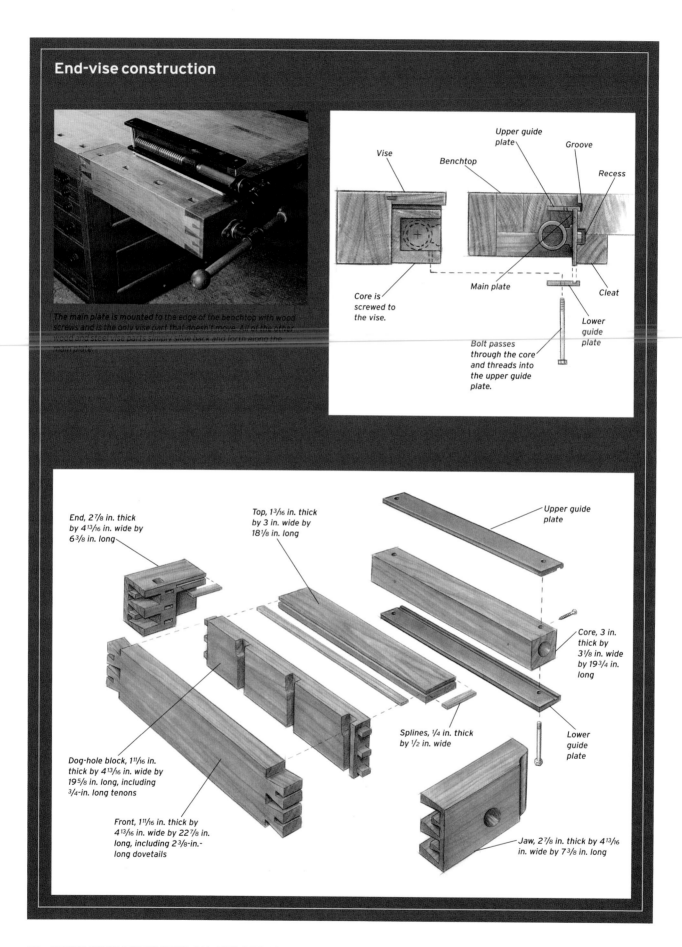

End-vise construction

The main plate is mounted to the edge of the benchtop with wood screws and is the only vise part that doesn't move. All of the other wood and steel vise parts simply slide back and forth along the main plate.

Vise

Upper guide plate

Benchtop

Groove

Recess

Core is screwed to the vise.

Main plate

Cleat

Bolt passes through the core and threads into the upper guide plate.

Lower guide plate

End, 2 7/8 in. thick by 4 13/16 in. wide by 6 3/8 in. long

Top, 1 3/16 in. thick by 3 in. wide by 18 1/8 in. long

Upper guide plate

Core, 3 in. thick by 3 1/8 in. wide by 19 3/4 in. long

Dog-hole block, 1 11/16 in. thick by 4 13/16 in. wide by 19 5/8 in. long, including 3/4-in. long tenons

Splines, 1/4 in. thick by 1/2 in. wide

Lower guide plate

Front, 1 11/16 in. thick by 4 13/16 in. wide by 22 7/8 in. long, including 2 3/8-in.-long dovetails

Jaw, 2 7/8 in. thick by 4 13/16 in. wide by 7 3/8 in. long

MOBILE TABLE SERVES MANY NEEDS

By Jerry H. Lyons

This table is my heavyweight shop assistant: With a 1,000-lb. capacity, it never complains of backache; four wheels means it can move anywhere on the heavy-machinery floor; and because its wheels lock, the table never backs out when I need it most. The table is ⅛ in. below the height of the tablesaw to eliminate boards getting caught on it when being ripped. It can be positioned either lengthwise or widthwise, depending on the shape of the board being cut. It also makes a nice outfeed surface when planing long parts. In addition, it is a handy table for layout work as well as a good place to store clamps and other accessories. The dimensions of your table will depend on your tools and the work you do.

Jerry H. Lyons, who taught furniture making for 21 years, recently built his dream shop near Glasgow, Kentucky.

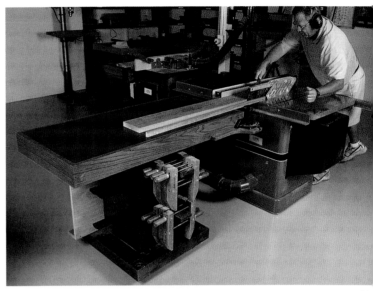

A multipurpose support table. This table can be wheeled to support operations at the tablesaw or the jointer, while the base stores clamps and jigs.

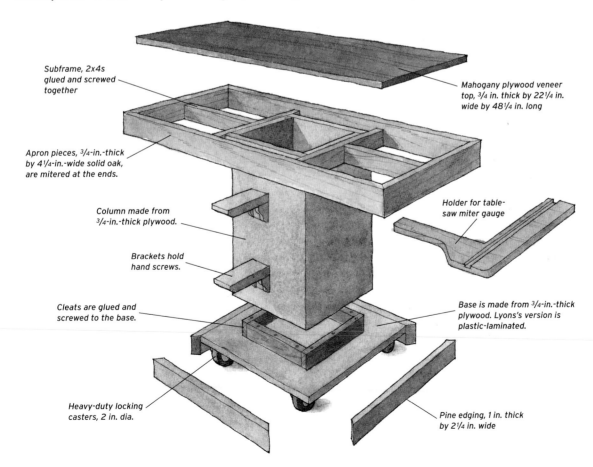

Subframe, 2x4s glued and screwed together

Mahogany plywood veneer top, ¾ in. thick by 22¼ in. wide by 48¼ in. long

Apron pieces, ¾-in.-thick by 4¼-in.-wide solid oak, are mitered at the ends.

Column made from ¾-in.-thick plywood.

Brackets hold hand screws.

Holder for table-saw miter gauge

Cleats are glued and screwed to the base.

Base is made from ¾-in.-thick plywood. Lyons's version is plastic-laminated.

Heavy-duty locking casters, 2 in. dia.

Pine edging, 1 in. thick by 2¼ in. wide

POWER-TOOL WORKBENCH

by Lars Mikkelsen

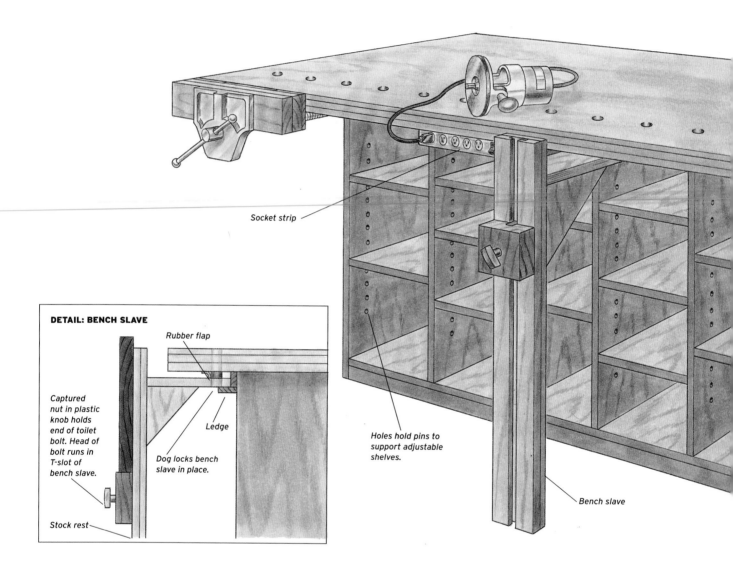

Socket strip

DETAIL: BENCH SLAVE

Rubber flap

Captured nut in plastic knob holds end of toilet bolt. Head of bolt runs in T-slot of bench slave.

Ledge

Dog locks bench slave in place.

Stock rest

Holes hold pins to support adjustable shelves.

Bench slave

Space is at a premium in my small shop, so the more functions any one thing can serve the better. I had two things that needed improvement—my hand power tools were cramped in a small cabinet, their cords always entwined, and my bench needed a good base. So I decided to kill two birds with one stone and build a base cabinet for the bench with cubbies for my tools.

These cubbies have worked out very well for me. Each tool has its place, where I also keep the miscellaneous wrenches and screwdrivers needed for that particular tool. The small size of the cubbies makes the tools much easier to find than if they were stored on long shelves. The cords never get tangled, and it's so easy to get and put away a tool that I avoid the usual clutter on the benchtop. The power strip that I attached to the bench makes it possible for a tool to be in its cubby while still plugged in ready to go.

I made the base cabinet from ³⁄₄-in. birch plywood edged with ¹⁄₄-in. strips of solid birch and biscuited together, as shown in the drawing. The biscuits could be replaced with tongue-and-groove joints or dadoes and rabbets, but biscuits are the simplest. I measured my biggest tool to determine the maximum width and depth of the sections.

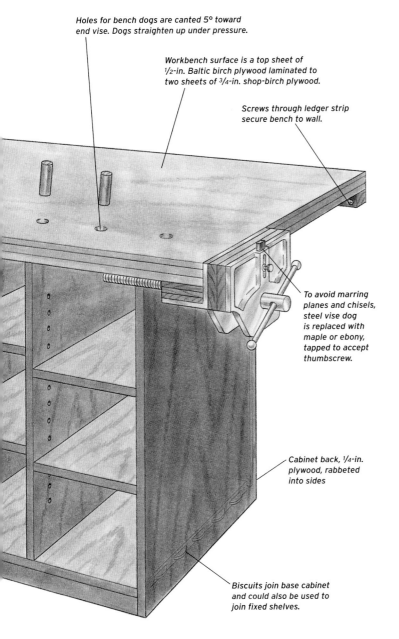

Holes for bench dogs are canted 5° toward end vise. Dogs straighten up under pressure.

Workbench surface is a top sheet of ½-in. Baltic birch plywood laminated to two sheets of ¾-in. shop-birch plywood.

Screws through ledger strip secure bench to wall.

To avoid marring planes and chisels, steel vise dog is replaced with maple or ebony, tapped to accept thumbscrew.

Cabinet back, ¼-in. plywood, rabbeted into sides

Biscuits join base cabinet and could also be used to join fixed shelves.

Both have wooden jaw faces. I drilled a series of 1-in. holes for the dogs in line with the end vise dog. The holes angle toward the vise at 5 degrees so the bench dogs straighten up under pressure. To keep the dogs from sliding down when in use, I tacked small strips of rubber to the underside of the bench, partially overlapping the dog holes. But I was afraid vigorous pounding on the bench might make the dogs fall out, so I screwed and glued a ledge to the base that supports the inside half of the dogs. I can easily reach under the bench to push the dogs up, and when not in use, they are firm against the ledge.

For the times when I have a long piece of stock clamped in the front vise, I made a bench slave to support the free end (see the photo below). The outer face of the slave leg is in the same plane as the inner jaw of the shoulder vise. I use the bench dogs and the ledge beneath them as a way of locking the slave to the table.

The stock rest, a block of solid wood, is attached to the leg with a toilet bolt that slides in a T-slot (as shown in the drawing detail on the facing page) and can be locked at any height on the slave.

My bench was relatively inexpensive to build and serves my purpose well. I like the big top, and the vises can hold everything I work on, from big doors to the occasional miniature. Doors on a base like this might look good, but the ease of access would be lost, and in a shop, efficiency comes before aesthetics.

Lars Mikkelsen is a professional woodworker in Santa Margarita, California.

Bench slave holds long stock. *The author made a bench slave with a brace at the top that locks into the 1-in. dowel bench dogs he uses. Round dogs are easier to make and install than traditional square dogs.*

The top of my bench is made from two layers of ¾-in. shop-birch plywood and one layer of ½-in. Baltic birch plywood. Unlike shop-birch plywood, which has a core of thick softwood veneers between thin outer layers of birch, Baltic birch is all birch with a core of thin, high-quality veneers, free of voids. This sandwich of shop birch and Baltic birch makes the benchtop amply stiff, and the Baltic birch has a surface hard enough and thick enough to withstand some abuse.

I mounted two Record® #52½ ED vises to the top, one as an end vise, the other as a front vise.

THE ESSENTIAL WORKBENCH

By Lon Schleining

Square dog holes, made to fit metal dogs, tilting 3° toward end vise and 6 in. o.c., are aligned with dogs in end vise.

Round dog holes, 3/4 in. dia., are aligned with dog holes in front vise jaw.

Front apron, 1³/4 in. thick by 6 in. wide by 75 in. long

Front vise jaw, 3 in. thick by 6 in. wide by 18 in. long; inside face beveled 1/8 in. top to bottom

Roundover on trestle members and vise jaws, 2 1/8-in. radius

Dowels, 7/16 in. dia., chamfered on tip

Stretchers, 1³/4 in. thick by 4 in. wide by 50 5/8 in. long overall (includes an extra 1/16 in. on each tenon for trimming after wedging)

Tenons, 1 in. thick by 3¹/4 in. wide by 3¹/16 in. long

Several *Fine Woodworking* editors and I recently collaborated on designing an essential workbench for today's woodworker, one that is straightforward to build without compromising performance. We did not include traditional components simply for history's sake, and we took advantage of modern innovations.

We decided on an overall size of 28 in. wide by 6 ft. long. Add a few inches for vise jaws, and it's a nice, big top.

Many benches I've seen look like top-heavy slabs on spindly legs. It was important that the bench not rack or skid across the floor under heavy handplaning. A thick trestle base, joined with pinned or wedged mortise-and-tenons, guarantees stability.

Splitting the stretchers, two high and two low, leaves a perfect opening for a future cabinet with drawers.

The Veritas® Twin-Screw Vise incorporates some of the capabilities of both tail and shoulder vises, allowing long boards or large panels to be clamped with bench dogs as well as clamping and upright board up to 15 in. wide for operations such as dovetailing.

I was tempted to install a cast-iron, quick-action Record-style vise, until I found a German-made quick-action vise screw and guide bars at Woodcraft. That allowed me to design a wooden front jaw to match the one I made for the Veritas end vise and still have quick action.

Lon Schleining is a contributing editor to Fine Woodworking.

ANATOMY OF A WORKBENCH

This bench consists of (and construction proceeds in this order): a trestle base joined with mortise-and-tenons; a thick top laminated from boards set on edge; and front and end vises, both with wood jaws.

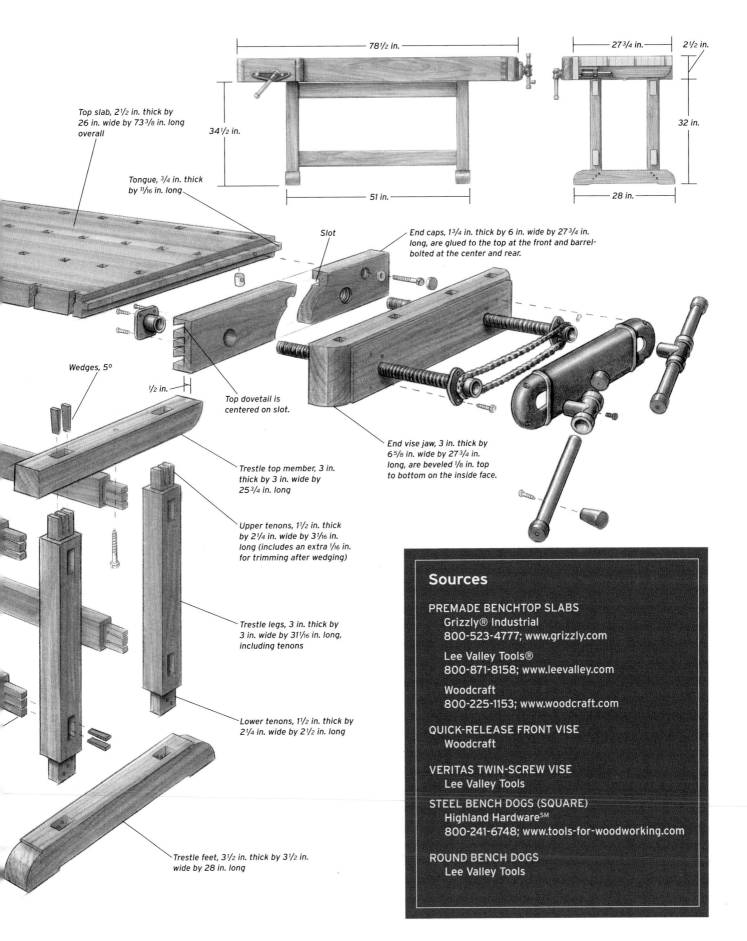

Top slab, 2½ in. thick by 26 in. wide by 73⅜ in. long overall

Tongue, ¾ in. thick by 11/16 in. long

78½ in.

34½ in.

51 in.

27¾ in.

2½ in.

32 in.

28 in.

Slot

End caps, 1¾ in. thick by 6 in. wide by 27¾ in. long, are glued to the top at the front and barrel-bolted at the center and rear.

Wedges, 5°

½ in.

Top dovetail is centered on slot.

End vise jaw, 3 in. thick by 6⅝ in. wide by 27¾ in. long, are beveled ⅛ in. top to bottom on the inside face.

Trestle top member, 3 in. thick by 3 in. wide by 25¾ in. long

Upper tenons, 1½ in. thick by 2¼ in. wide by 3 1/16 in. long (includes an extra 1/16 in. for trimming after wedging)

Trestle legs, 3 in. thick by 3 in. wide by 31 1/16 in. long, including tenons

Lower tenons, 1½ in. thick by 2¼ in. wide by 2½ in. long

Trestle feet, 3½ in. thick by 3½ in. wide by 28 in. long

Sources

PREMADE BENCHTOP SLABS
Grizzly® Industrial
800-523-4777; www.grizzly.com

Lee Valley Tools®
800-871-8158; www.leevalley.com

Woodcraft
800-225-1153; www.woodcraft.com

QUICK-RELEASE FRONT VISE
Woodcraft

VERITAS TWIN-SCREW VISE
Lee Valley Tools

STEEL BENCH DOGS (SQUARE)
Highland Hardware℠
800-241-6748; www.tools-for-woodworking.com

ROUND BENCH DOGS
Lee Valley Tools

HEAVY-DUTY BENCH WITH A KNOCKDOWN BASE

By Mike Dunbar

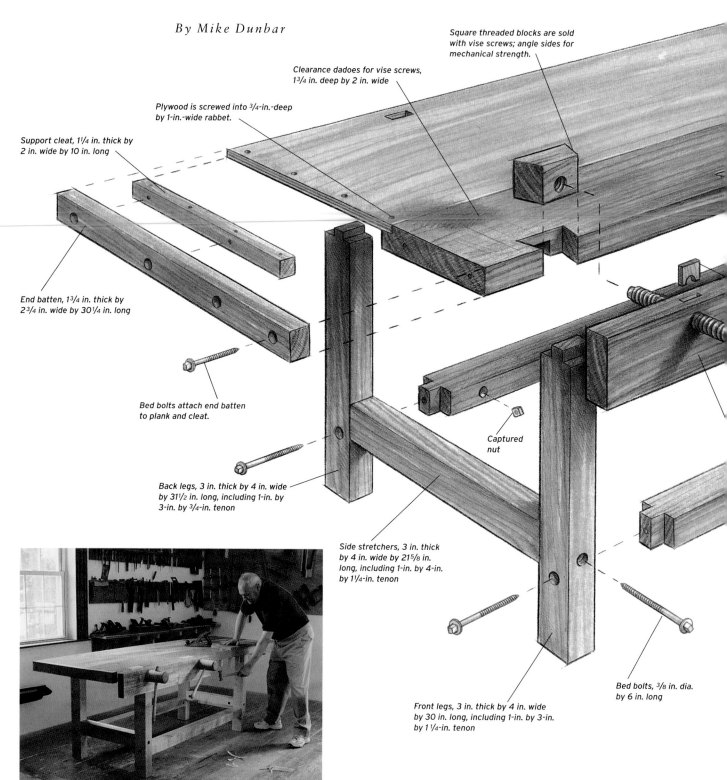

Square threaded blocks are sold with vise screws; angle sides for mechanical strength.

Clearance dadoes for vise screws, 1¾ in. deep by 2 in. wide

Plywood is screwed into ¾-in.-deep by 1-in.-wide rabbet.

Support cleat, 1¼ in. thick by 2 in. wide by 10 in. long

End batten, 1¾ in. thick by 2¾ in. wide by 30¼ in. long

Bed bolts attach end batten to plank and cleat.

Back legs, 3 in. thick by 4 in. wide by 31½ in. long, including 1-in. by 3-in. by ¾-in. tenon

Captured nut

Side stretchers, 3 in. thick by 4 in. wide by 21⅝ in. long, including 1-in. by 4-in. by 1¼-in. tenon

Front legs, 3 in. thick by 4 in. wide by 30 in. long, including 1-in. by 3-in. by 1¼-in. tenon

Bed bolts, ⅜ in. dia. by 6 in. long

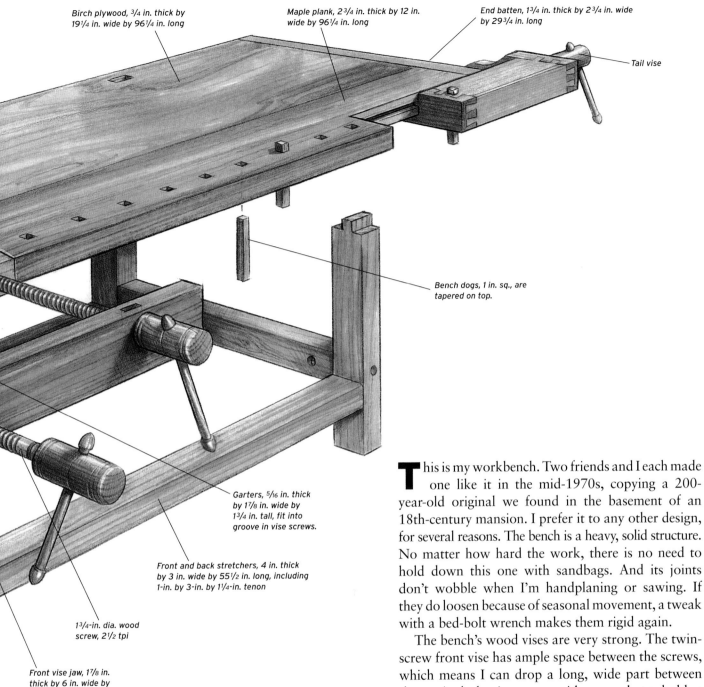

Birch plywood, 3/4 in. thick by 19 1/4 in. wide by 96 1/4 in. long

Maple plank, 2 3/4 in. thick by 12 in. wide by 96 1/4 in. long

End batten, 1 3/4 in. thick by 2 3/4 in. wide by 29 3/4 in. long

Tail vise

Bench dogs, 1 in. sq., are tapered on top.

Garters, 5/16 in. thick by 1 7/8 in. wide by 1 3/4 in. tall, fit into groove in vise screws.

Front and back stretchers, 4 in. thick by 3 in. wide by 55 1/2 in. long, including 1-in. by 3-in. by 1 1/4-in. tenon

1 3/4-in. dia. wood screw, 2 1/2 tpi

Front vise jaw, 1 7/8 in. thick by 6 in. wide by 55 in. long

This is my workbench. Two friends and I each made one like it in the mid-1970s, copying a 200-year-old original we found in the basement of an 18th-century mansion. I prefer it to any other design, for several reasons. The bench is a heavy, solid structure. No matter how hard the work, there is no need to hold down this one with sandbags. And its joints don't wobble when I'm handplaning or sawing. If they do loosen because of seasonal movement, a tweak with a bed-bolt wrench makes them rigid again.

The bench's wood vises are very strong. The twin-screw front vise has ample space between the screws, which means I can drop a long, wide part between them. And the jaws are wide enough to hold a 6-ft.-long board for edge-jointing without additional support.

The bench does not have a tool tray, leaving its entire wide top available not just for woodworking but also for assembly. When I worked by myself as a professional furniture maker, this bench was all I needed. Finally, I am a woodworker, and a bench made entirely of wood has a deep appeal for me.

Mike Dunbar and his wife, Sue, run a Windsor chair-making school in Hampton, New Hampshire.

TAIL VISE

This complex-looking unit is basically a three-sided box that slides back and forth on the tip of the bench's end batten. One wrinkle: The threaded nut included with the screw set must be joined to the end batten.

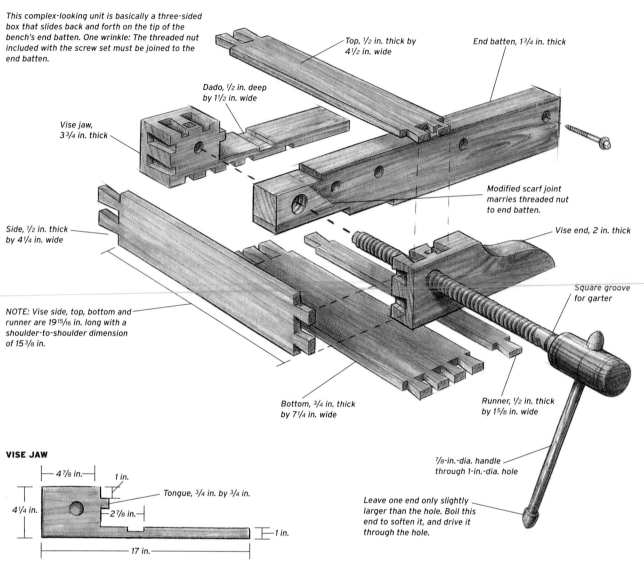

Top, 1/2 in. thick by 4 1/2 in. wide

End batten, 1 3/4 in. thick

Dado, 1/2 in. deep by 1 1/2 in. wide

Vise jaw, 3 3/4 in. thick

Modified scarf joint marries threaded nut to end batten.

Side, 1/2 in. thick by 4 1/4 in. wide

Vise end, 2 in. thick

NOTE: Vise side, top, bottom and runner are 19 15/16 in. long with a shoulder-to-shoulder dimension of 15 3/8 in.

Square groove for garter

Bottom, 3/4 in. thick by 7 1/4 in. wide

Runner, 1/2 in. thick by 1 5/8 in. wide

7/8-in.-dia. handle through 1-in.-dia. hole

Leave one end only slightly larger than the hole. Boil this end to soften it, and drive it through the hole.

VISE JAW

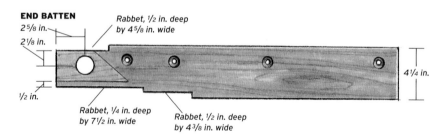

4 7/8 in.

1 in.

Tongue, 3/4 in. by 3/4 in.

4 1/4 in.

2 7/8 in.

1 in.

17 in.

END BATTEN

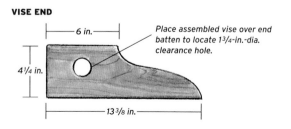

2 5/8 in.

2 1/8 in.

Rabbet, 1/2 in. deep by 4 5/8 in. wide

1/2 in.

4 1/4 in.

Rabbet, 1/4 in. deep by 7 1/2 in. wide

Rabbet, 1/2 in. deep by 4 3/8 in. wide

VISE END

6 in.

Place assembled vise over end batten to locate 1 3/4-in.-dia. clearance hole.

4 1/4 in.

13 3/8 in.

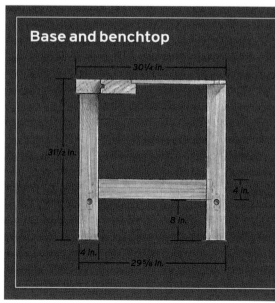

Base and benchtop

30 1/4 in.

31 1/2 in.

4 in.

8 in.

4 in.

29 5/8 in.

Think of the vise as a three-sided box with closed ends. *Build up the jaw end (foreground) from thinner stock. An ogee contour decorates the opposite end piece. The top, side, and bottom are joined to the ends with large dovetails.*

Attaching the Vise. *Slide the assembled tail vise into place to locate the holes for the vise screw. This measurement determines where the vise screw will pass through the end of the tail vise and where it will enter the jaw end.*

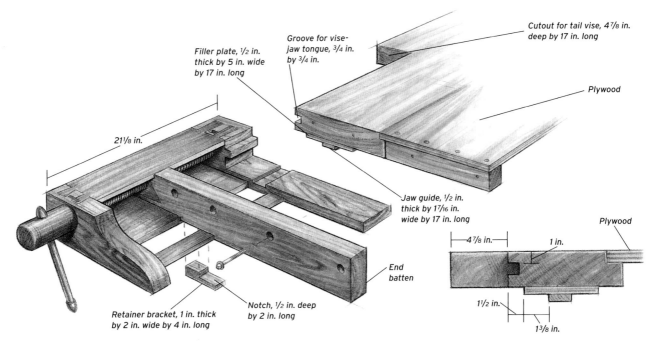

Filler plate, ½ in. thick by 5 in. wide by 17 in. long

Groove for vise-jaw tongue, ¾ in. by ¾ in.

Cutout for tail vise, 4⅞ in. deep by 17 in. long

Plywood

21⅛ in.

Jaw guide, ½ in. thick by 1⁷⁄₁₆ in. wide by 17 in. long

End batten

Retainer bracket, 1 in. thick by 2 in. wide by 4 in. long

Notch, ½ in. deep by 2 in. long

Plywood

4⅞ in.   1 in.

1½ in.

1⅜ in.

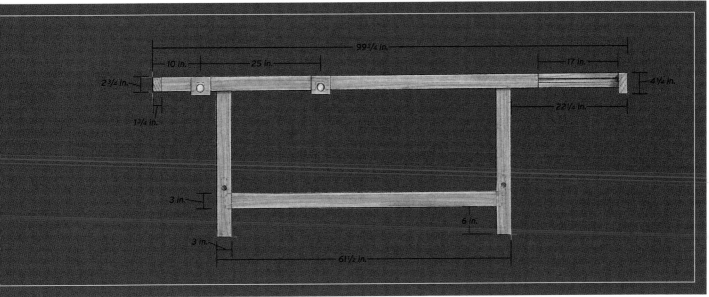

99¾ in.

10 in.   25 in.   17 in.

2¾ in.   4¼ in.

1¾ in.   22¼ in.

3 in.

6 in.

3 in.

61½ in.

A BENCHTOP BENCH

by Jeff Miller

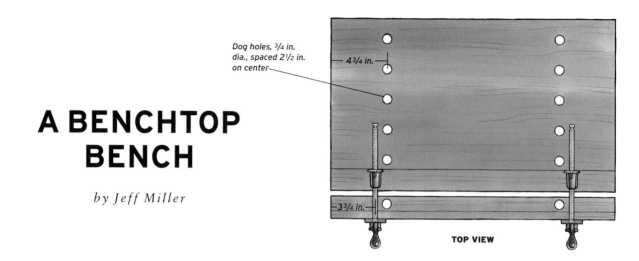

Dog holes, ³/₄ in. dia., spaced 2¹/₂ in. on center

4³/₄ in.

3³/₄ in.

TOP VIEW

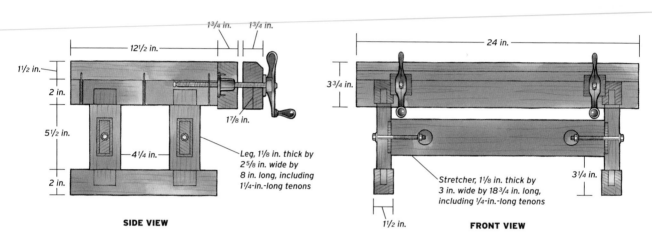

1³/₄ in. 1³/₄ in.

12¹/₂ in.

1¹/₂ in.

2 in.

5¹/₂ in.

4¹/₄ in.

2 in.

1⁷/₈ in.

Leg, 1¹/₈ in. thick by 2⁵/₈ in. wide by 8 in. long, including 1¹/₄-in.-long tenons

SIDE VIEW

24 in.

3³/₄ in.

Stretcher, 1¹/₈ in. thick by 3 in. wide by 18³/₄ in. long, including ¹/₄-in.-long tenons

3¹/₄ in.

1¹/₂ in.

FRONT VIEW

Elevated bench saves your back

This benchtop bench elevates a workpiece several inches above a regular workbench, so it is more comfortable to do such tasks as cutting, carving, and routing.

Woodworking benches are designed to place a workpiece at a height that's ideal for handplaning. But the perfect height for planing often is too low for other common bench tasks. For example, when routing, carving, cutting dovetails, or doing layout, I frequently have found myself bent over at an uncomfortable angle so that I could see clearly and work effectively. When performing these tasks, I like to have a workpiece positioned 6 in. to 10 in. above my waist level.

To bring a workpiece to my ideal height range, I made a small workbench that mounts quickly to my regular bench. When extra height is needed, the minibench effectively raises the work surface to my comfort zone. The bench is easy to move, stores nicely under my bigger bench, and includes a vise that provides plenty of holding force. I made the bench out of maple, but any hard, dense wood will work.

Trestle design is simple yet strong

I wanted the benchtop bench to be as sturdy as my regular bench. I settled on a trestle-table design, which ensured a solid bench and simplified construction.

I chose a mortise-and-tenon joint to connect the legs to the aprons and feet, but half-lap joints would work well, too. The trestle base is screwed to the top through three countersunk holes in the bottom of each apron.

Vise adds versatility

The front vise makes it easy to clamp a workpiece either to the front of the bench or on top of it. While I wanted the vise to be simple and easy to make, I also needed it to accept wide boards for dovetailing carcases. As it turned out, a couple of veneer-press screws satisfied both requirements.

The addition of Veritas Bench Pups® allows me to hold a workpiece on top of the bench.

Jeff Miller runs a custom furniture shop in Chicago, where he also offers woodworking classes (www. furnituremaking.com).

TRESTLE DESIGN MAKES A STURDY BENCH

BASE ASSEMBLY

The trestles and stretchers are assembled using mortise-and-tenon construction, giving the benchtop bench solid footing.

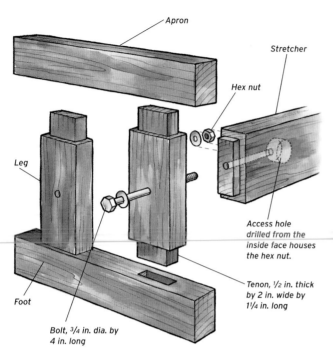

Apron

Stretcher

Hex nut

Leg

Access hole drilled from the inside face houses the hex nut.

Foot

Tenon, 1/2 in. thick by 2 in. wide by 1 1/4 in. long

Bolt, 3/4 in. dia. by 4 in. long

Glue up the trestles, then attach the stretchers. A long bolt connects the end of each stretcher to the trestles. Note the access hole in the stretcher.

VISE ASSEMBLY

Before attaching the bench face to the benchtop, drill the holes for the veneer-press screws and install the hardware. The screws will close the vise jaw, but you'll have to pull it open manually.

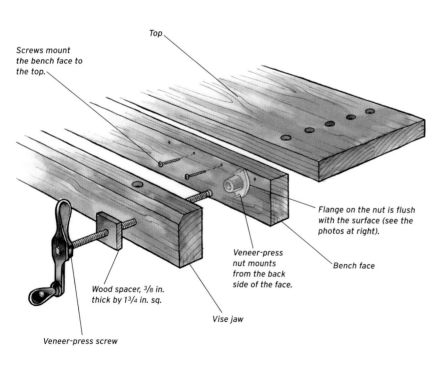

Top

Screws mount the bench face to the top.

Flange on the nut is flush with the surface (see the photos at right).

Veneer-press nut mounts from the back side of the face.

Bench face

Wood spacer, 3/8 in. thick by 1 3/4 in. sq.

Vise jaw

Veneer-press screw

Inset the veneer. Press nuts into the back of the bench face. Trace the flange profile (above) and rout a recess to set the nut flush with the stock. Secure with screws.

CLAMPING TABLE

By Jerry H. Lyons

Less stress and less mess. *The slotted table frame holds clamps in position while gluing up boards. Any glue squeeze-out drips into the newspaper-lined tray.*

Gluing boards into panels often calls for at least three pairs of hands: one to keep the boards aligned, one to stop the clamps from falling over, and one to clean up the surplus glue. I solved this problem by making a dedicated clamping table.

The front and back edgings of the table are slotted to position I-beam bar clamps in an upright position. The tray below is covered with newspapers to catch glue squeeze-out. When done, I simply fold up the newspapers and discard them. This table also has a lower shelf to hold newspapers, jigs, and other used items.

I used a variety of scraps of plywood and solid stock to build the table, then I painted the whole piece with leftover floor paint. This has the bonus of making glue cleanup easier. Size the table based on what scraps are available and the kind of work you do. My table is 30½ in. deep by 65 in. wide by 32 in. tall.

Jerry H. Lyons, who taught furniture making for 21 years, recently built his dream shop near Glasgow, Kentucky.

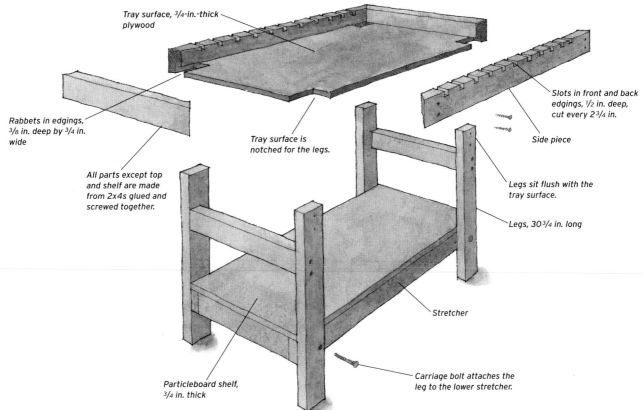

Tray surface, ³/₄-in.-thick plywood

Slots in front and back edgings, ¹/₂ in. deep, cut every 2³/₄ in.

Side piece

Rabbets in edgings, ³/₈ in. deep by ³/₄ in. wide

Tray surface is notched for the legs.

Legs sit flush with the tray surface.

Legs, 30³/₄ in. long

All parts except top and shelf are made from 2x4s glued and screwed together.

Stretcher

Carriage bolt attaches the leg to the lower stretcher.

Particleboard shelf, ³/₄ in. thick

VERSATILE AND AFFORDABLE WORKBENCH

By John White

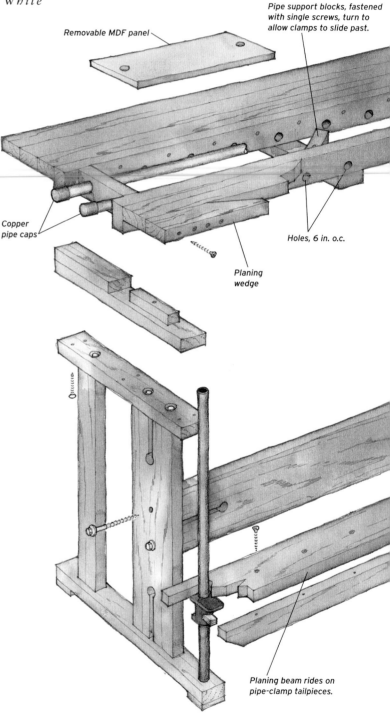

Removable MDF panel

Pipe support blocks, fastened with single screws, turn to allow clamps to slide past.

Copper pipe caps

Holes, 6 in. o.c.

Planing wedge

Planing beam rides on pipe-clamp tailpieces.

For five years I worked as a cabinetmaker in a shop that used only hand tools for the simple reason that electricity wasn't available that far back in the woods. One lesson that I came away with was the importance of a good workbench—and lots of windows. I now work in a shop that is, if anything, overelectrified, but a functional workbench is still important. Just because you're driving a car instead of a buggy doesn't mean you don't need a good road to get where you're going.

On a perfect bench, the various vises and stops would hold any size workpiece in the most convenient position for the job at hand. Traditional workbenches are adequate for clamping smaller pieces, a table leg or frame rail for instance, but most benches can't handle wide boards for edge- and face-planing or frame-and-panel assemblies.

Recently, I moved my shop and needed to build a new bench. I began by researching traditional American and European designs. I found that

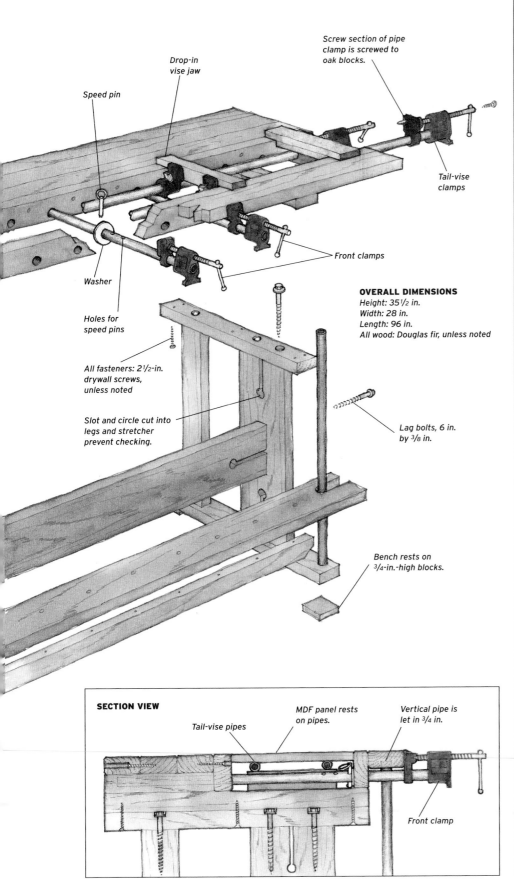

Speed pin

Drop-in vise jaw

Screw section of pipe clamp is screwed to oak blocks.

Tail-vise clamps

Washer

Holes for speed pins

Front clamps

All fasteners: 2 1/2-in. drywall screws, unless noted

Slot and circle cut into legs and stretcher prevent checking.

OVERALL DIMENSIONS
Height: 35 1/2 in.
Width: 28 in.
Length: 96 in.
All wood: Douglas fir, unless noted

Lag bolts, 6 in. by 3/8 in.

Bench rests on 3/4-in.-high blocks.

SECTION VIEW

Tail-vise pipes

MDF panel rests on pipes.

Vertical pipe is let in 3/4 in.

Front clamp

Douglas fir workbench

To minimize costs, the author milled workbench stock from Douglas fir framing lumber, sawing clear sections from the center of 2x10s and 2x12s. The bench is fastened with drywall screws and lag bolts. Six pipe clamps in different configurations are used as vises.

Oak blocks span tail-vise clamps. The screw ends of the pipe clamps are screwed to the end of the bench through holes drilled in the clamp faces.

Pipes rest on blocks that turn. Tail-vise pipe clamps are supported by blocks fastened with one screw. To slide a clamp past, turn the block.

Front clamps are easy to adjust. The clamps fit in holes in the bench front and are secured with large washers and speed pins.

Planing wedge. *When used with the planing beam, long work is held against a wedge-shaped stop at the end of the bench. The harder you push against the work, the tighter it is held in place.*

no one bench solved all or even most of the problems I had encountered in 25 years of woodworking. Frustrated, I finally decided to design a bench from the ground up.

At first I had no success. A design would address one problem but not another, or it would be far too complex. I was about to give up and build a traditional German bench when I came up with a design that incorporates pipe clamps into the bench's top, the front apron, and even the legs.

On the front of the bench is an adjustable, T-shaped planing beam that runs the full length of the bench. It is supported on both ends by the sliding tailpieces of Pony pipe clamps. The ½-in. cast-iron pipes on which the clamps slide are incorporated into the bench's legs.

On the bench's top, two pipe-clamp bars are recessed into a 10-in.-wide well, replacing a conventional tail vise and bench dogs. Both the fixed and movable jaws have oak faces. This clamp setup makes it easy to hold down boards for surface-planing because nothing projects above the board's surface to foul the tool. The top clamp bars have a clamping capacity of just over 7 ft.

The bench, as I built it, is 8 ft. long and was designed to accommodate fairly large work, such as doors and other architectural millwork. The design can be shortened or lengthened, and it could be reversed end for end if you are left-handed.

John White keeps the Fine Woodworking *shop running smoothly.*

Sliding height adjustment. *Pipe-clamp tailpieces slide on cast-iron pipes held captive in the top and bottom of the bench. A T-shaped Douglas fir planing beam rides on the clamps.*

Lift-out MDF panels. *The panels, cut in different lengths from MDF scraps, make a durable yet disposable center surface for the bench. The panels get removed when the tail-vise pipe clamps are in use.*

Horizontal clamps run full length. *A pair of pipe clamps, running under the benchtop, hold work in the same way as a traditional tail vise.*

SLIDING DRILL PRESS TABLE FOR MORTISING

By Gary Rogowski

Before I owned a plunge router, I used my drill press for mortising. A brad-point bit will do a pretty good job of establishing a neat row of holes that can be cleaned up with a chisel. But a sliding table for the drill press makes the mortising process much more efficient. A quality sliding table is also easy to make.

The table has two parts: a movable sled, which is fitted with a pair of runners, and a base, which has grooves for the runners and is bolted to the drill-press table. The sled is made up of a double layer of glued-up material, thick enough to plow grooves for the runners, which are glued in place, without weakening it.

The sliding table has a fence and requires a stop block to locate the start of the mortise. I also clamp a stop block to the underside of the sled to control the length of the mortise. To use the jig, hold or clamp stock in place and use an end mill, a metalworking bit, to bore the mortise. Take light passes. If it chatters, switch to a brad-point bit, smaller in diameter than the end mill; predrill a series of holes; and clean up the walls of the mortise using the end mill.

Gary Rogowski is a contributing editor to Fine Wood-working *and an author and teacher in Portland, Oregon.*

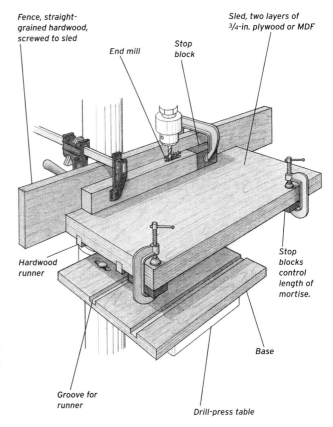

Fence, straight-grained hardwood, screwed to sled

End mill

Stop block

Sled, two layers of 3/4-in. plywood or MDF

Hardwood runner

Stop blocks control length of mortise.

Base

Groove for runner

Drill-press table

Mortising jig

The jig slides back and forth on runners. Using an end mill (a metalworking bit), the author takes light passes to cut a mortise.

AUXILIARY DRILL PRESS TABLE

By Roland Johnson

Originally designed as a tool for machinists, the drill press has become a standard fixture in woodworking shops. It is capable of drilling both small and large holes more accurately and safely than a handheld drill, and it has a built-in depth stop. The rack-and-pinion pressing action of the machine gives easy leverage for boring large holes in hard material. Throw on a simple, shop-built table and fence, and you add the ability to support and stabilize large and small workpieces in precise, repeatable positions. An auxiliary table is a must.

Even though many drill presses are used exclusively for woodworking, they still are equipped with a machinist-oriented table that tends to be too small for many woodworking operations. An auxiliary table that bolts to the drill-press table greatly enhances versatility and safety. A wood or Melamine surface is also kinder to workpieces. My version consists of a ³⁄₄-in. piece of veneer-core plywood, with aluminum T-tracks inset to accommodate a fence and various hold-downs.

Through-holes will tear out without a fresh backer board below the hole. I inset a small, sacrificial piece of plywood into the auxiliary table. For critical holes, flip or rotate the board to find a clean area, and replace it when it is riddled with holes. The replaceable insert also allows the bottom end of a sanding drum to be set below the table surface.

Roland Johnson is a contributing editor to Fine Woodworking.

Using the table

A pin is the simplest stop. It offers a quick way to keep a workpiece from spinning (above). The fence works well for holes in a row (middle). The T-tracks and clamp handles make for quick adjustment and a secure grip.

T-tracks add versatility. Tracks in the table and fence make it easy to secure the fence, end stop, and various hold-downs.

AUXILIARY TABLE IS A MUST

This simple, shopmade table supports long workpieces and offers a number of ways to locate and secure them. It includes a sacrificial backer board to eliminate blowout on the backs of workpieces.

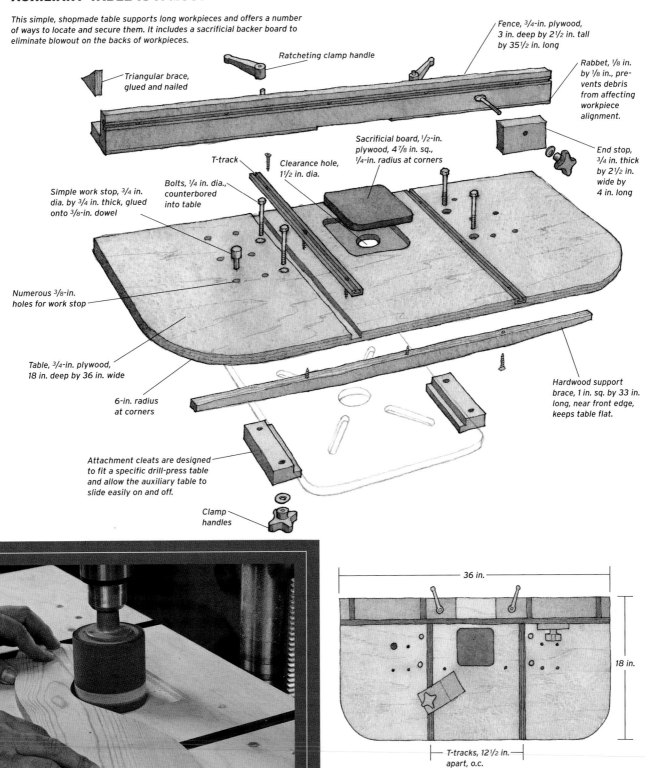

Ratcheting clamp handle

Triangular brace, glued and nailed

Fence, 3/4-in. plywood, 3 in. deep by 2 1/2 in. tall by 35 1/2 in. long

Rabbet, 1/8 in. by 1/8 in., prevents debris from affecting workpiece alignment.

End stop, 3/4 in. thick by 2 1/2 in. wide by 4 in. long

Sacrificial board, 1/2-in. plywood, 4 7/8 in. sq., 1/4-in. radius at corners

T-track

Clearance hole, 1 1/2 in. dia.

Simple work stop, 3/4 in. dia. by 3/4 in. thick, glued onto 3/8-in. dowel

Bolts, 1/4 in. dia., counterbored into table

Numerous 3/8-in. holes for work stop

Table, 3/4-in. plywood, 18 in. deep by 36 in. wide

6-in. radius at corners

Hardwood support brace, 1 in. sq. by 33 in. long, near front edge, keeps table flat.

Attachment cleats are designed to fit a specific drill-press table and allow the auxiliary table to slide easily on and off.

Clamp handles

Sanding drums are good for curved work. The cutout in this table allows the drum to contact the workpiece properly.

36 in.

18 in.

T-tracks, 12 1/2 in. apart, o.c.

ADJUSTABLE END-BORING JIG FOR THE DRILL PRESS

by Jeff Greef

I have built a fair number of custom doors and windows in which I've joined the stiles to rails with dowels. Until recently, I relied on doweling fixtures to position holes. Although fixtures are quick to use, I found them lacking accuracy, particularly for large dowels. The problem is not in locating the fixture's bit guide precisely, but rather it is guaranteeing that the bit drills straight and true.

A horizontal boring machine could solve the problem. But while one of these machines is neither hard to use nor difficult to build, it would eat up precious space in my already cramped shop. Besides, it seemed redundant to buy a motor, bearings, and a thrust mechanism when I had all those things standing in the corner in my drill press.

Boring holes with a drill press is very accurate, but how do you bore holes in the ends of long workpieces? If you turn the press table vertically, clamp a fence to it, and secure the work, the setup is still quite limited in terms of making fine adjustments. So with adjusting (and readjusting) in mind, I made an end-boring jig that mounts to my drill press, as shown in the photo.

Drill-press mounting logistics

Before you build the jig, you need to figure out how you will mount it. Although each type of drill press may require a slightly different setup, you should be able to adapt the principles I used to mount a jig to your press. First, my jig is designed for floor-model

Working on end. *Boring the ends of long workpieces used to present problems for the author, until he devised this end-boring jig for his drill press. A pair of platens mounted to the press's table allows adjustments in and out and left and right.*

presses. If you have a bench press, you'll have to bolt its base to a workbench with the spindle overhanging the edge. You can extend the jig to the floor as I did (see the drawing). Second, the jig is made for presses with at least 14 in. of swing to get the depth to the column needed for mounting. Third, the jig is built for presses with tables that both tilt and swivel. By swivelling the table's arm 90 degrees and tilting the table vertically, you can bolt or clamp the jig to it. If your table doesn't tilt and swivel, remove it. Then make a wooden outrigger with a yoke to clasp the press's column. Mount the jig to the outrigger in line with the spindle.

Designing and building the jig

The boring jig has two main parts: a fixed platen and a movable platen. The fixed platen bolts onto the drill-press table. The movable platen attaches to the fixed one with hinges on one side and adjustment bolts on the other. The hinges allow the movable platen to be positioned in and out from the press's column. The adjustment bolts fine-tune the alignment to the bit. The bolts work in a push-me-pull-you fashion (see the drawing detail on the facing page): One bolt pushes the movable platen away, the other bolt pulls it toward the fixed platen and a spring takes up slack. The movable platen also slides to move work left or right, and an adjustable stop plate sets the height of the work. A toggle clamp secures the workpiece alongside a fixed, vertical fence.

END-BORING JIG ASSEMBLY

Jig consists of a fixed platen that bolts to the drill-press table and a movable platen, which is made up of three layers.

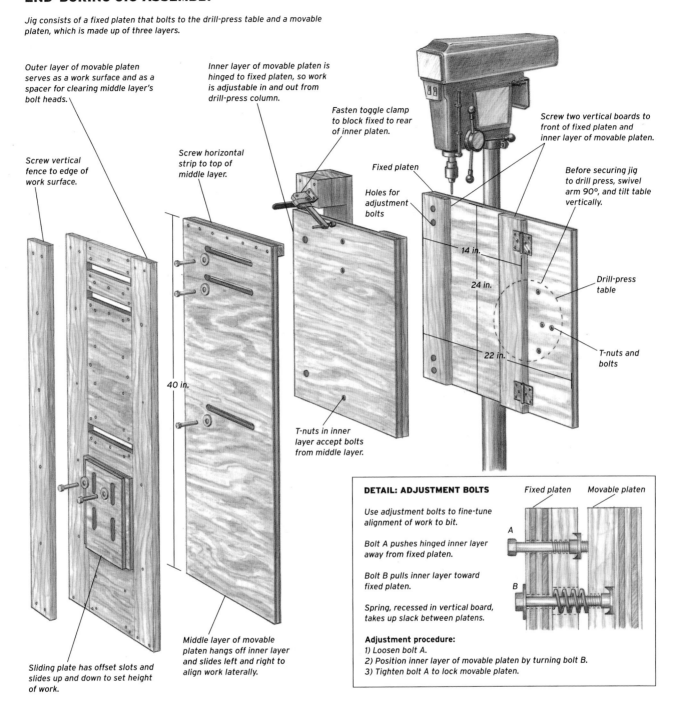

Outer layer of movable platen serves as a work surface and as a spacer for clearing middle layer's bolt heads.

Inner layer of movable platen is hinged to fixed platen, so work is adjustable in and out from drill-press column.

Fasten toggle clamp to block fixed to rear of inner platen.

Screw two vertical boards to front of fixed platen and inner layer of movable platen.

Screw vertical fence to edge of work surface.

Screw horizontal strip to top of middle layer.

Fixed platen

Holes for adjustment bolts

Before securing jig to drill press, swivel arm 90°, and tilt table vertically.

14 in.

24 in.

22 in.

Drill-press table

T-nuts and bolts

40 in.

T-nuts in inner layer accept bolts from middle layer.

Sliding plate has offset slots and slides up and down to set height of work.

Middle layer of movable platen hangs off inner layer and slides left and right to align work laterally.

DETAIL: ADJUSTMENT BOLTS

Fixed platen   Movable platen

Use adjustment bolts to fine-tune alignment of work to bit.

Bolt A pushes hinged inner layer away from fixed platen.

Bolt B pulls inner layer toward fixed platen.

Spring, recessed in vertical board, takes up slack between platens.

A

B

Adjustment procedure:
1) Loosen bolt A.
2) Position inner layer of movable platen by turning bolt B.
3) Tighten bolt A to lock movable platen.

Using the jig

Once I've set up the jig and positioned the work, I wedge in a pair of shims between the bottom of the movable platen and the top of the press's base to stabilize the jig (see the photo on the facing page). Even with the platen wedged in place, I can make up to 1/32-in. corrections using the adjustment bolts.

To break in the jig, I bored holes in the ends of rails on 12 interior doors. The end-boring jig proved a real improvement over my conventional doweling fixtures. Once the work was roughly aligned, it was easy to make fine adjustments on test scraps before boring the actual run of holes. I still keep the old doweling fixtures on hand—but only for those rare situations that the end-boring jig won't handle.

Jeff Greef is a woodworker and journalist in Soquel, California.

VERTICAL BORING JIG FOR THE DRILL PRESS

By Gary Rogowski

Drilling into long boards requires one of two things: great patience or an indispensable jig. You can simply tilt your drill-press table to 90 degrees and maneuver the stock into position and clamp it. That usually entails a lot of fiddling.

Here's a better way. Make up a vertical two-part drilling jig (see the photo and drawing). The jig is similar to the mortising jig seen on p. 69 in that it consists of a base and a movable sled with a fence. Stock clamped to the fence and the workpiece can be moved fore or aft while remaining plumb (or at whatever angle the jig was set to).

Gary Rogowski is a contributing editor to Fine Woodworking *and an author and teacher in Portland, Oregon.*

VERTICAL BORING JIG

For boring into end grain, an adjustable table and fence provide a solid clamping surface. Wedges may be placed between the stock and the base of the drill press for additional stability.

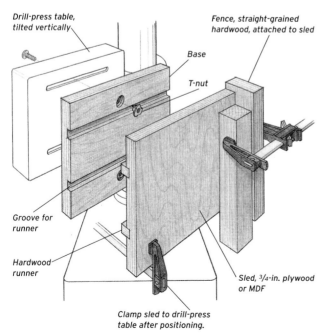

Drill-press table, tilted vertically

Base

T-nut

Fence, straight-grained hardwood, attached to sled

Groove for runner

Hardwood runner

Sled, 3/4-in. plywood or MDF

Clamp sled to drill-press table after positioning.

FOLDING EXTENSION TABLES SAVE SPACE

by Dwayne J. Intveld

When using a tablesaw to cut a large workpiece or a full sheet of plywood, it's important to provide extra support surfaces for the stock. But like many woodworkers, I don't have enough room in my shop to have extension tables permanently fixed in place. So I built a side table that readily folds down out of the way when not needed.

And while I was at it, I replaced my somewhat flimsy portable outfeed roller with a sturdy outfeed table that folds down behind the saw. I have the option of opening it in two stages, depending on my needs at the time. The first stage provides a 36-in. main outfeed table; the next stage produces a secondary outfeed table that adds about another 30 in. to the main table, handy for extralong stock.

With both tables open, a 4×8 sheet of plywood remains supported throughout the entire cut. Yet, when folded, the tables add little to the footprint of the saw.

Remember that the drawing dimensions on pp. 76–77 are based on building the tables to fit my 10-in. Powermatic® 66 tablesaw, which sits on a 2-in.-tall wood frame. The extra couple of inches raises the top of the table to 36 in., a height better suited to my 6-ft. 4-in. frame.

Also, the rip-fence system on my tablesaw is made by Biesemeyer. If you use a different type, unless it's a Biesemeyer clone, you'll likely need to modify the way the tables connect to the saw, especially at the outfeed end.

Finally, because the outfeed table sits just behind the saw when folded up, the table won't work with a saw that has a motor or any other obstruction sticking out the back. The side table, however, should be adaptable to any saw.

Dwayne J. Intveld is an engineering manager living in Hazel Green, Wisconsin.

Foldable outfeed table. *Intveld used torsion-box construction to build the outfeed tables, a technique that makes them both light and strong.*

The tables almost disappear. *Shop space grows considerably when the extension tables fold down.*

SIDE TABLE

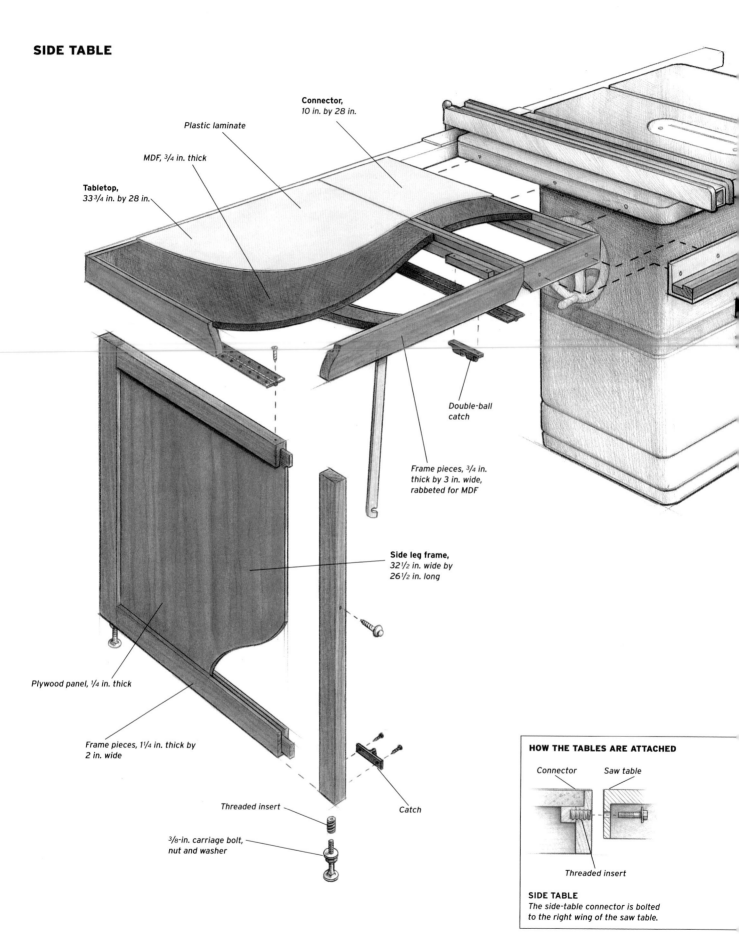

Connector,
10 in. by 28 in.

Plastic laminate

MDF, 3/4 in. thick

Tabletop,
33 3/4 in. by 28 in.

Double-ball catch

Frame pieces, 3/4 in. thick by 3 in. wide, rabbeted for MDF

Side leg frame,
32 1/2 in. wide by 26 1/2 in. long

Plywood panel, 1/4 in. thick

Frame pieces, 1 1/4 in. thick by 2 in. wide

Threaded insert

Catch

3/8-in. carriage bolt, nut and washer

HOW THE TABLES ARE ATTACHED

Connector   *Saw table*

Threaded insert

SIDE TABLE
The side-table connector is bolted to the right wing of the saw table.

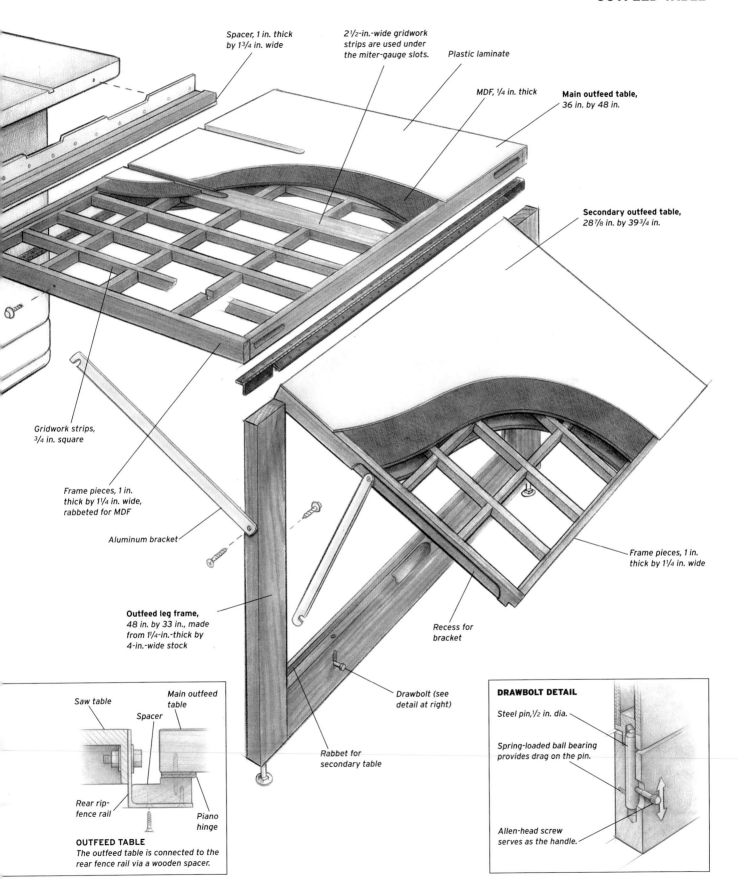

Spacer, 1 in. thick by 1 3/4 in. wide

2 1/2-in.-wide gridwork strips are used under the miter-gauge slots.

Plastic laminate

MDF, 1/4 in. thick

Main outfeed table, 36 in. by 48 in.

Secondary outfeed table, 28 7/8 in. by 39 3/4 in.

Gridwork strips, 3/4 in. square

Frame pieces, 1 in. thick by 1 1/4 in. wide, rabbeted for MDF

Aluminum bracket

Outfeed leg frame, 48 in. by 33 in., made from 1 1/4-in.-thick by 4-in.-wide stock

Frame pieces, 1 in. thick by 1 1/4 in. wide

Recess for bracket

Drawbolt (see detail at right)

Rabbet for secondary table

Saw table

Main outfeed table

Spacer

Rear rip-fence rail

Piano hinge

OUTFEED TABLE
The outfeed table is connected to the rear fence rail via a wooden spacer.

DRAWBOLT DETAIL

Steel pin, 1/2 in. dia.

Spring-loaded ball bearing provides drag on the pin.

Allen-head screw serves as the handle.

PICTURE FRAMER'S MITER JIG

By Robert Hamon

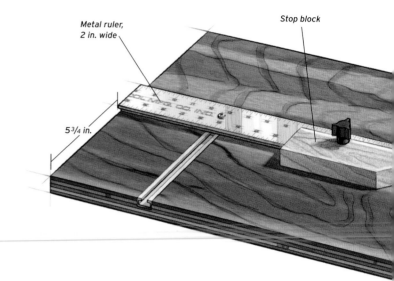

Metal ruler, 2 in. wide

Stop block

5 3/4 in.

Cutting picture-frame miters on a tablesaw using a standard miter gauge is a real challenge. Problems include small amounts of play in the miter gauge and lack of support for the molding near the blade. The traditional solution has been to build a miter sled or a sliding miter jig that eliminates any movement and supports the full length of the workpiece up to the blade. Clamps or hold-downs add to the jig's accuracy. You may have a jig already, but to cut picture-frame molding, you need a jig with two further attributes: It must provide an accurate way to measure and cut the lengths of molding so that the opposing sides are exactly the same, and it must be designed to cut the outside edge of the molding first to eliminate splintering on the most visible edge of the frame.

My jig is designed to miter picture frames. Rather than the typical square board, it is a rectangle, aligned to the miter-gauge slots at a 45-degree angle. Instead of two fences of equal length, one is short for making the first cut on each section of molding, while the fence for the second cut is 36 in. long—the practical limit for cutting frames on a tablesaw. Each fence consists of a base with a ruler attached to it. The ruler on the long fence allows you to measure each piece accurately before it is cut. An adjustable stop helps make accurate duplicate pieces.

When cutting frame molding, always cut the longer sides first. If you should err, you still will be able to cut the longer piece into a shorter side. With your rough-cut section of molding secured to the short fence, miter the right-hand end. Move the molding to the long fence, using the ruler to establish the desired length. Clamp the molding and set the adjustable stop at the end of the molding. Cut the left-hand miter. The parallel section of molding is cut in the same way, but now you have a stop, making the two sections identical in length.

Robert Hamon is a professional picture framer in Mission, Kansas.

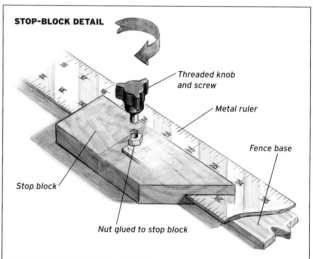

STOP-BLOCK DETAIL

Threaded knob and screw

Metal ruler

Fence base

Stop block

Nut glued to stop block

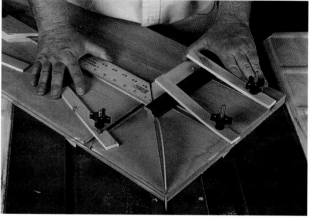

The first miter cut. *Clamp the piece of molding, rough-cut to length, to the short fence of the jig to cut the right-hand miter.*

CUT PERFECT MITERS ON THE TABLESAW

Unlike most tablesaw sleds, this one has two fences of different lengths. A short fence is used to make the first cut on the right-hand side of the molding; a long fence is used to cut the left-hand miter. The longer fence incorporates a ruler and a stop block that allow moldings to be cut to precise and repeatable lengths. Hold-downs support stock over its entire length.

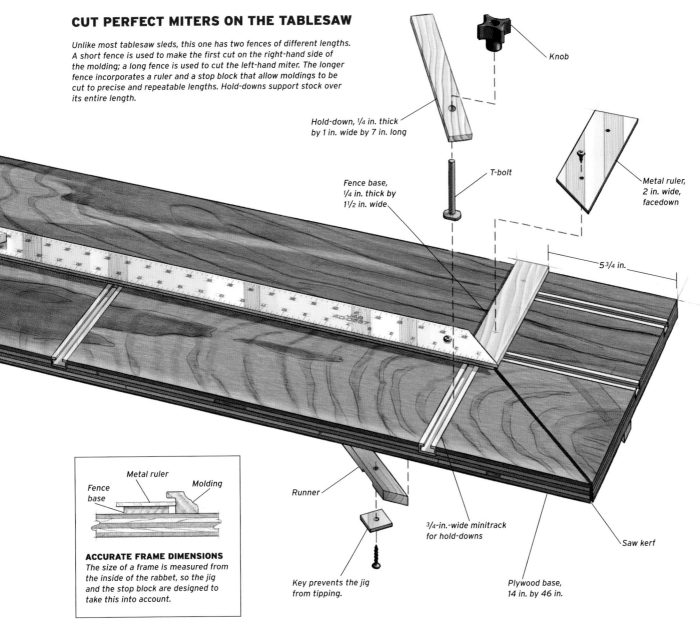

Knob

Hold-down, ¼ in. thick by 1 in. wide by 7 in. long

T-bolt

Fence base, ¼ in. thick by 1½ in. wide

Metal ruler, 2 in. wide, facedown

5¾ in.

Runner

Key prevents the jig from tipping.

¾-in.-wide minitrack for hold-downs

Saw kerf

Plywood base, 14 in. by 46 in.

ACCURATE FRAME DIMENSIONS
The size of a frame is measured from the inside of the rabbet, so the jig and the stop block are designed to take this into account.

Fence base

Metal ruler

Molding

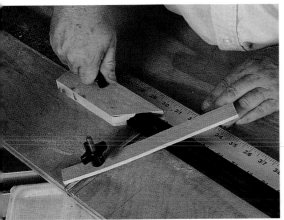

The second cut. Clamp the molding to the long fence and set the stop block at the correct distance from the blade (above). Then cut the left-hand miter (right).

SLIDING MITER GAUGE FENCE LENDS ACCURACY

By Tim Hanson

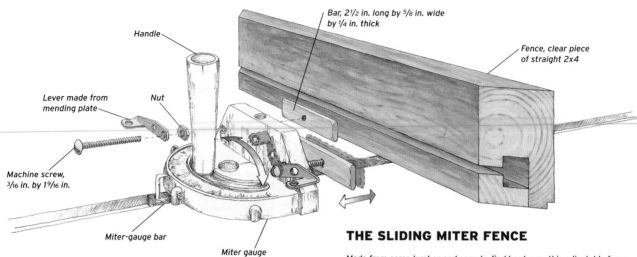

Handle

Bar, 2½ in. long by ⅝ in. wide by ¼ in. thick

Fence, clear piece of straight 2x4

Lever made from mending plate

Nut

Machine screw, ³/₁₆ in. by 1⁹/₁₆ in.

Miter-gauge bar

Miter gauge

THE SLIDING MITER FENCE

Made from scrap lumber and easy-to-find hardware, this adjustable fence supports the work right up to the blade, no matter what the angle. It makes cross-cutting and miter-cutting safer and more efficient.

The piece of scrap I kept bolted to my tablesaw miter gauge was a great improvement over the gauge alone, especially when making crosscuts. This extra fence made the gauge easier to grip, and it supported the workpiece right up to the blade. The problem came when making angled cuts. Each new angle made a new divot in the fence, and pretty soon, it looked like an old comb with missing teeth. I would try to save time by using one of the gaps as a point of reference when cutting, but sooner or later, I'd use the wrong one. Then I'd get ticked off and have to stop work to make a new fence, and the whole cycle would start again.

I finally took the time to make a fence that could be moved right or left and locked in place by simply flipping two little levers. Now I can make minute adjustments in the position of a workpiece by releasing the levers and sliding the fence rather than unclamping and reclamping. The fence makes using the tablesaw faster, safer, and more accurate.

How it works

The wooden fence is held to the miter gauge by a pair of machine screws. The screws go through the miter gauge and are tapped into 2½-in.-long metal bars that ride in T-slots in the back of the fence. When the machine screws are loosened, the fence can be adjusted right or left—exactly where you want it. Flip the levers up, and the fence slides right up to the blade. Flip them down, and the fence is locked in place.

The fence is made from a clear, straight piece of 2x4 construction lumber. I made it 20 in. long thinking

Quick and accurate The lever-action adjustment on this shop-built fence lets you position the fence quickly.

SLIDING FENCE

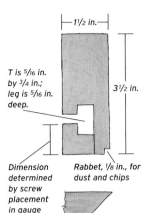

⊢— 1½ in. —⊣

T is 5/16 in. by 3/4 in.; leg is 5/16 in. deep.

3½ in.

Dimension determined by screw placement in gauge

Rabbet, 1/8 in., for dust and chips

Make a T-shaped slot in the fence. Cut the pieces to the dimensions shown at right, and glue together. Make sure the bar stock moves freely in the slot. Miter the ends of the fence at 45°.

LEVERS

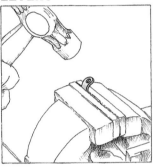

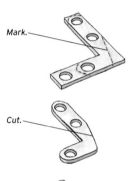

Mark.

Cut.

Bend.

Make two levers. Using 2-in. by 2-in. mending plates, cut one leg about 1/2 in. long, and round all the corners. Make the left lever by bending the short leg toward the back of the vise, as shown. For the right lever, bend the short leg toward the front.

BARS

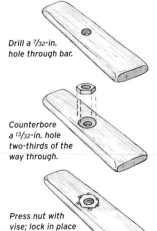

Drill a 7/32-in. hole through bar.

Counterbore a 13/32-in. hole two-thirds of the way through.

Press nut with vise; lock in place by dimpling bar with punch.

Attaching screw to bar. A machine screw threads into the bar to lock the fence in position. If you don't have metal taps to make this connection, you can use a standard nut, as shown at right.

Smooth action, strong support. This sliding fence is easy to grip with hands or clamps, and it supports the work right up to the blade.

I'd shorten it later, but I found the length useful when crosscutting long pieces.

I fashioned the levers from right-angle mending plates, which I purchased at the hardware store. The drawings at right show the parts and how they go together, but the system does need some fine-tuning. Secure the levers under the heads of the machine screws with a wrench-tight nut. Slide the machine-screw assemblies through the miter gauge, and turn the bars onto the screws so the ends of the screws are flush with the bars.

Now turn one lever all the way to the left (at the 9 o'clock position), and slide the bar into the T-slot. Flip the lever to the right. The fence should tighten up against the miter gauge at about the 2 o'clock position without much effort. If it rotates past that point and the fence still isn't tight, the lever has to be repositioned.

Tim Hanson builds furniture and toys in Indianapolis, Indiana.

ONE-STOP CUTTING STATION

by Ken Picou

Tablesaws are excellent for ripping stock, but the standard miter gauge that comes with most tablesaws makes them mediocre at best for crosscutting material or cutting joinery. But by making a simple sliding-crosscut box and a few accessory jigs, you can greatly increase the accuracy and flexibility of your saw and turn it into a one-stop cutting station, capable of crosscutting, tenoning, and slotting.

The system I've developed consists of a basic sliding-crosscut box with a 90-degree back rail, a removable pivoting fence, a tenoning attachment, and a corner slotting jig for cutting the slots for keyed miter joints. This system is inherently safer and more accurate than even the most expensive miter gauge for several reasons. First, it uses both miter slots, so there is less side play than with a miter gauge. Second, the work slides on a moving base, so there's no chance of the work slipping or catching from friction with the saw table. Third, the long back fence provides better support than a miter gauge, which is usually only 4 in. or 5 in. across. Fourth, the sliding-crosscut box is big, so angles can be measured and divided much more accurately than with a miter gauge (the farther from its point of origin an angle is measured, the greater the precision). Finally, the sliding crosscut box is a stable base on which to mount various attachments, such as a tenoning jig or a corner slotting jig, which can greatly expand the versatility of the tablesaw.

I cut the base of my sliding-crosscut box from a nice flat sheet of ½-in.-thick Baltic birch plywood, and then I made it a little bit wider and deeper than my saw's tabletop. A cheaper grade of plywood also would be fine for this jig, but I decided to use a premium material because I wanted the jig to be a permanent addition to my shop.

The runners that slide in the tablesaw's miter-gauge slots can be made from any stable material that wears well.

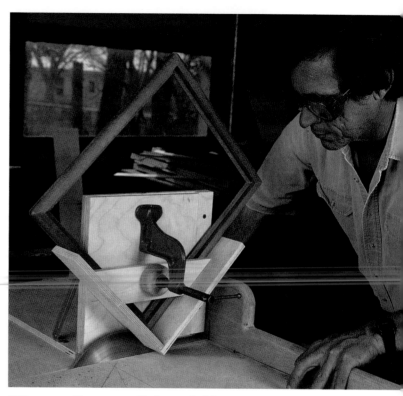

Making a crosscut box more versatile. *An accurate sliding-crosscut box makes a good base for cutting accessories, including this corner-slotting jig. This jig mounts or dismounts in seconds and makes for strong miter joints in picture or mirror frames and in small boxes or drawers.*

A pivoting fence

I wanted a pivoting fence for making angled cuts, but I also wanted to be able to remove the fence quickly when I need to cut wide boards. I accomplished this first by setting a T-nut for the pivot point into the underside of the jig's base about 6 in. forward of the fixed fence. Then I routed an arc-shaped track for a carriage bolt at the end of the fence (see the drawing). The arc runs from 0 degrees to a bit more than 45 degrees, and there's a plunge-routed hole just below the 0-degree point through which the carriage-bolt assembly can be lifted out to remove the fence.

Adding a simple hinged jig that uses the rear fence as a reference surface allows you to cut both regular and angled tenons, rabbets, and angled edges accurately and without too much fuss. I built this jig from Baltic birch plywood as well. I crosscut it in the basic jig and routed the slots in it on my router table.

In use, I slide the workpiece into place and then the brace; finally, I tighten the clamp. The jig feels solid and works well.

Ken Picou is a designer and woodworker in Austin, Texas.

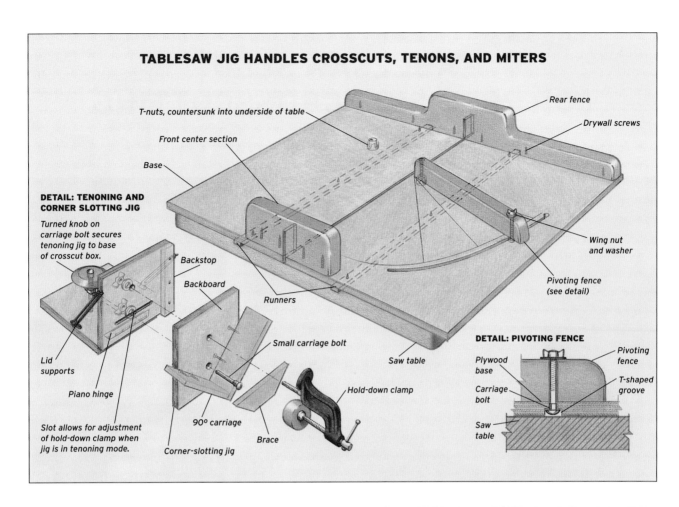

TABLESAW JIG HANDLES CROSSCUTS, TENONS, AND MITERS

T-nuts, countersunk into underside of table

Front center section

Base

Rear fence

Drywall screws

DETAIL: TENONING AND CORNER SLOTTING JIG

Turned knob on carriage bolt secures tenoning jig to base of crosscut box.

Backstop

Backboard

Runners

Lid supports

Piano hinge

Slot allows for adjustment of hold-down clamp when jig is in tenoning mode.

90° carriage

Corner-slotting jig

Small carriage bolt

Brace

Hold-down clamp

Saw table

Wing nut and washer

Pivoting fence (see detail)

DETAIL: PIVOTING FENCE

Plywood base

Carriage bolt

Saw table

Pivoting fence

T-shaped groove

Making adjustments. Setting angles accurately can be done quickly with a miter square or a bevel square. By setting the angle both fore and aft in the tenoning jig, you can be sure the angle will be true across the face of the jig.

Cutting tenons. Quick, accurate tenons, even in large boards, are easy with the author's hinged tenoning jig. A hold-down clamp grabs the workpiece securely and accommodates almost any size workpiece. The big footprint of the tenoning jig's base anchors it securely to the base of the crosscut jig below. The jig is also useful for cutting long miters and angled tenons.

TABLESAW SLED
FOR PRECISION CROSSCUTTING

by Lon Schleining

Miters

Crosscuts

Tenons

Crosscutting with a standard tablesaw miter gauge can be frustrating, inaccurate, even hazardous. Adding an extended fence helps, but the miter gauge still will be limited and imprecise.

A crosscut sled is a sliding table with runners that guide it over the saw in the miter-gauge slots. It has a rear fence set perpendicular to the line of cut to hold the workpiece. Because it uses both miter slots, the sled is remarkably and reliably accurate. It also easily accepts any number of stop blocks, auxiliary fences, and templates, allowing miters, tenons, and many other specialty cuts.

Your sled should fit your work. There's no sense in making a huge, unwieldy sled if you'll use it mostly to cut 3-in. tenons. The one I use is 30 in. wide and 21 in. deep. It's capable of crosscutting a board up to 2 in. thick and 18 in. wide. With a miter template (see the sidebar on the facing page), the sled can cut a 45-degree miter on the end of a 3-in.-wide board. The rear fence is 5 in. high in the middle, 2½ in. high on the ends. Though I rarely crosscut a board thicker than 2 in., the fence needs to be at least 4 in. high to accommodate the height of the sawblade. The extra fence height also supports workpieces on end when I cut tenons.

I used void-free ½-in. Baltic birch plywood for the platform. I prefer to make runners from oak, instead of buying steel ones, because I can control their fit in the miter slots.

Building the Jig

The front brace's only job is to keep the platform in one piece.

It doesn't much matter what size or shape it is as long as it is a few inches higher than the sawblade's maximum cut—about 2 in. above the platform. I made this brace from 1¼-in.-thick red oak, 3¾ in. high, and about as long as the width between the miter slots.

The rear fence should be pretty stout to hold the sled table together. If you don't have 8/4 lumber, laminate two 4/4 pieces together. Make sure the board is perfectly straight on the inside face and square with the edge that will be attached to the platform.

Keeping things square becomes critical when you attach the rear fence. The most important thing to remember is that, for the cut to be square, the rear fence must be square to the line of cut.

Before you attach the rear fence, put the sled on the saw, raise the blade slightly above the thickness of the platform, and cut through the platform about two-thirds of the way from back to front, being very careful not to cut all the way through the platform. Now drill two center pilot holes (of four

A BASIC CROSSCUT SLED

Tailor the size of the sled to fit the work you do. The crucial features are a rear fence perpendicular to the line of cut and runners that slide easily without stop.

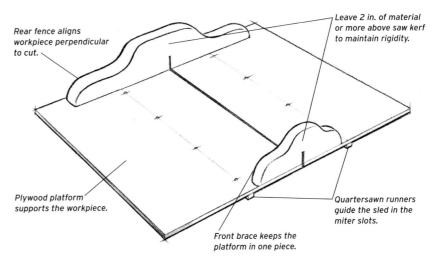

Rear fence aligns workpiece perpendicular to cut.

Leave 2 in. of material or more above saw kerf to maintain rigidity.

Plywood platform supports the workpiece.

Quartersawn runners guide the sled in the miter slots.

Front brace keeps the platform in one piece.

total) into the fence, and install the screws from the bottom side.

Before you can attach the rear fence permanently, make trial crosscuts and check the results. The position of the fence will almost certainly need fine-tuning. It's easy to rotate the rear fence back and forth a little with hammer taps or a bar clamp, even with the two screws snug. Keep making test cuts and adjusting as necessary.

Don't, however, cut all the way through the platform at this time. Leave just enough plywood at the rear of the platform to hold the sled together.

When the sled makes true 90-degree crosscuts, it's time to attach the rear fence permanently.

Lon Schleining teaches woodworking at Cerritos College in Norwalk, California.

From 90-degree to 45-degree cuts with a simple template

With this template, you'll be able to make accurate miter cuts on your tablesaw. The template is nothing more than a piece of Baltic birch plywood with two sides at 90 degrees to each other and a back side that registers against the rear fence of the sled. This template sits far enough forward so that long workpieces clear the ends of the rear fence.

There are any number of ways to make such a shape. I used the opportunity to test the accuracy of my sled. First I laid out and rough cut the template from a corner of a

sheet of plywood and got one of the sides straight on a jointer. This can also be done on the sled by aligning the edge over the saw kerf and nailing the template to the sled (don't let the nails go all the way through). I then cut the opposite side at 90 degrees to the first using the rear fence.

To cut the base at 45 degrees to the two sides, I cut to the layout line on the base by aligning it over the kerf and nailing the template to the sled. I've rarely gotten a base perfect the first time.

To find out which way it's out, I center the point of the template on the saw kerf and align the base against the rear fence. Then I scribe its outline on the sled. I flip it over

and check it against the scribe marks. If it sits perfectly between the lines, I'm on the money. If not, I recut the back of the template as required. Finally, I attach it to the sled with a few screws, make some trial miters and adjust accordingly. –L.S.

TABLESAW SLED CUTS BOX JOINTS

By Lon Schleining

Boxes of every imaginable size and material can be assembled with mechanically interlocking box joints that are nearly as strong as the material itself. Box joints are not only reliable and attractive but also can be easy to make. They can be cut by hand or with a router, but I prefer to use a simple jig that fits onto my tablesaw crosscut sled. With this easily made accessory, you'll be able to assemble a strong, useful box in as little as an hour.

The same basic jig can be adapted to cut box joints as narrow as ⅛ in. or as wide as ¾ in., but I'll concentrate on ½-in.-wide joints—a useful size for drawer boxes and small chests.

My crosscut sled is easily the most useful and frequently used jig in my shop. As long as the sled is accurately made and works smoothly, it can be modified to cut box joints.

The rear fence must be substantial, because it will provide a mounting surface for the box-joint jig. To support the jig adequately, the rear fence on your crosscut sled must be secure, at least 5 in. or 6 in. high and square to the sled.

For ½-in. box joints, the sled will wind up with a ½-in. slot in it, but attaching a plywood insert will return your sled to its more common uses, making it as good as new.

To make the jig, start by ripping a clear piece of hard maple for a spacer block. Initially, leave it ¹⁄₁₆ in. wider than the size of the joint you're going to make. In this case, the spacer block should be about ⁹⁄₁₆ in. square and long enough to run through a surface planer safely.

One of the critical adjustments is the width of the dado cut. For cutting box joints, you'll need a good stacked dado set—not the kind that wobbles—that can be reset to the same width easily.

Once the dado is set up, everything else will be adjusted

THE BASIC BOX-JOINT JIG

Adding a box-joint jig to a crosscut sled takes only a few bolts and scraps of plywood. This jig is set up to cut ½-in. joints, but the same methods can be used to make jigs for any joint size.

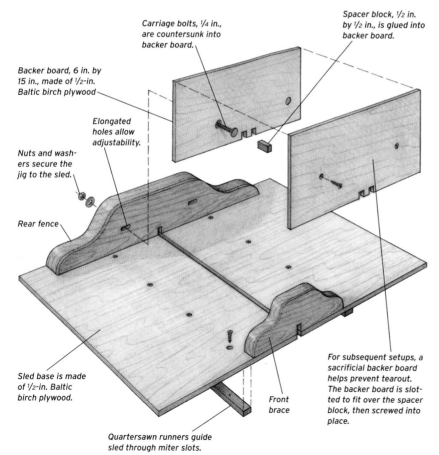

Carriage bolts, ¼ in., are countersunk into backer board.

Spacer block, ½ in. by ½ in., is glued into backer board.

Backer board, 6 in. by 15 in., made of ½-in. Baltic birch plywood

Elongated holes allow adjustability.

Nuts and washers secure the jig to the sled.

Rear fence

Sled base is made of ½-in. Baltic birch plywood.

Quartersawn runners guide sled through miter slots.

Front brace

For subsequent setups, a sacrificial backer board helps prevent tearout. The backer board is slotted to fit over the spacer block, then screwed into place.

to fit. The width of the dado determines the width of the box joint because both the pin and slot are the same size. As you set up the various blades to cut a ½-in. dado, mark which ones you use and how they are installed so you'll be able to use the same setup next time.

With the dado blades in place, make a new ½-in.-wide slot in the sled. Then you are ready to fit the spacer block. Using the sled, cut a slot in a piece of scrap with the dado, then surface plane the spacer block until it fits tightly in the slot. Next, you'll need a backer board that will bolt to the rear fence. Set the height of the dado above the sled base to match the thickness of the spacer block. Cut two pieces of ½-in. Baltic birch plywood or equivalent, about 8 in. by 14 in., and then cut ½-in.-deep slots with the dado in the center of both pieces on the longest side. Glue a 2-in. piece of the spacer block into the slot on one of the pieces, and set it aside to dry. Make sure the spacer block is square to the backer board, and remove any

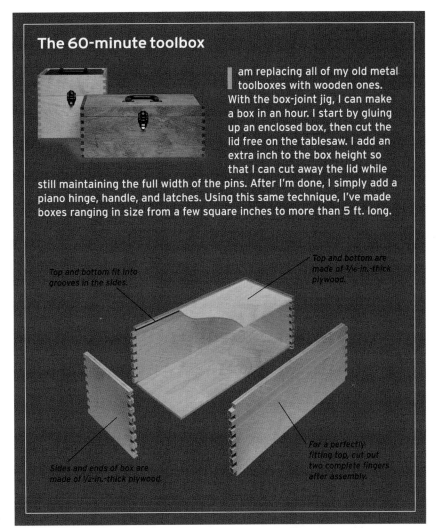

The 60-minute toolbox

I am replacing all of my old metal toolboxes with wooden ones. With the box-joint jig, I can make a box in an hour. I start by gluing up an enclosed box, then cut the lid free on the tablesaw. I add an extra inch to the box height so that I can cut away the lid while still maintaining the full width of the pins. After I'm done, I simply add a piano hinge, handle, and latches. Using this same technique, I've made boxes ranging in size from a few square inches to more than 5 ft. long.

Top and bottom fit into grooves in the sides.

Top and bottom are made of ¼-in.-thick plywood.

Sides and ends of box are made of ½-in.-thick plywood.

For a perfectly fitting top, cut out two complete fingers after assembly.

Attaching the jig to a crosscut sled

Set up the dado blade. Use a stacked dado the width of the box joints to cut through the sled. Run a slot through the backer board at the same time.

Glue the spacer block in place. Take light cuts on a surface planer until the spacer block fits into the slot in the backer board. Then glue a 2-in. length into place and set aside the assembly to dry.

Adjust the jig. To find a starting point, use the leftover length of spacer material to locate the spacer block ½ in. to the right of the dado blade, then tighten down the bolts.

Cut a Joint, and Check the Fit

1 Make the first cut. Hold the end piece against the spacer block and backer board, with the top edge facing the spacer block. Cut slowly, and remove the piece before returning the sled to the starting position.

2 Continue cutting the joint. For subsequent cuts, fit the slot over the spacer block, and proceed to the end of the piece.

3 Make the first cut on the side piece. Hold the end piece so that its top edge is against the top edge of the side piece. With the end piece fitted over the spacer block and with its top edge facing the dado blade, position the top edge of the side piece toward the spacer block, and continue cutting.

4 Check the fit; adjust the jig. The corner will be too loose, too tight, or possibly just right. If it's too loose, move the jig slightly to the left. If it's too tight, move it to the right. Tighten the bolts again, then cut another trial corner joint to make sure it's just right.

excess glue while it's still soft. Use ¼-in. carriage bolts to hold the backer board to the sled. Begin by recessing the heads into the birch plywood so they do not protrude. Then drill ¼-in. holes the rest of the way through the plywood.

Set the backer board onto the sled so that the spacer block is about ½ in. to the right of the dado blade, and clamp it in place. Mark the locations for the mounting holes in the sled fence by inserting a pencil through the holes in the backer board.

Unclamp the backer board, and lay out holes ¼ in. to the left and to the right of the marks. Drill two ⁵⁄₁₆-in. holes for each bolt, and chisel away the wood between the holes. Place flat washers under the nuts, then tighten the nuts just enough to draw the carriage bolts into the backer board.

The beauty of this jig is its adjustability. As a starting point, use a piece of the leftover spacer block to locate the pin exactly ½ in. to the right of the dado blade, then tighten down the nuts. A few test joints will lead you to the necessary adjustments.

Using the method in the sidebar at left, you should find the two test pieces fit together quite easily—neither too tightly nor too loosely—allowing enough room for glue. If your pieces fit together perfectly, congratulations. But chances are the joint will not fit perfectly at this point. Mark the position of the jig before making any adjustment so you know how far to move it. If the joint is too loose, back off the nuts and move the backer board and spacer to the left just a little. If the joints are too tight, move the spacer just slightly to the right.

Lon Schleining is a woodworker in Long Beach, California.

TENONING JIG FOR THE TABLESAW

By Brad Schilling

The mortise and tenon is one of the most common woodworking joints. So a good tablesaw tenoning jig is a valuable tool for the shop. But top-quality, commercially made jigs don't come cheap. When I was faced with cutting a bunch of tenons, I decided to build a jig that included all of the features found in a top-of-the-line model.

The jig has a tall fence to support the workpiece. And a heavy-duty hold-down keeps the stock securely in place. To minimize tearout, a narrow piece of scrap stock can be temporarily clamped in front of the workpiece. The jig slides smoothly along the table of the saw without side-to-side play. And a threaded rod with a crank allows easy and accurate adjustment of the workpiece relative to the blade.

Once I worked out the design and bought the parts, I put together the jig in only a few hours. My total cash outlay for everything was about $40*, inexpensive compared with a store-bought jig with the same features.

The jig is made of 3/4-in.-thick medium-density fiberboard (MDF), a smooth material that tends to stay flat and is reasonably inexpensive. Keep in mind that the jig is sized for my Delta® Unisaw®. However, it can fit almost any saw simply by adjusting the length of the base as needed.

One more point before starting. Most of the parts of this jig are cut on the tablesaw. That means the saw must be cutting accurately. If it isn't, the jig won't have the built-in precision that's needed to make perfect cuts. So, before you get going, make sure the blade and rip fence are parallel to the miter-gauge slot and that the blade is square to the table.

TABLESAW TENONING JIG

With a heavy-duty hold-down, an extra-tall fence and a large, stable base, the tenoning jig provides a good measure of control and safety during a cut. MDF parts (all 3/4 in. thick) are smooth and stay flat. Runners made from UHMW plastic slide smoothly.

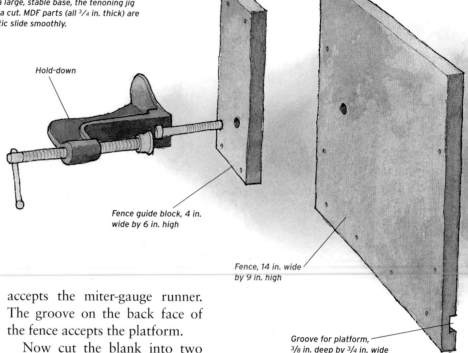

Hold-down

Fence guide block, 4 in. wide by 6 in. high

Fence, 14 in. wide by 9 in. high

Groove for platform, 3/8 in. deep by 3/4 in. wide

Rip the runners first

When the jig is in use, it's guided by an ultrahigh molecular weight (UHMW) plastic runner that travels along the saw's miter-gauge slot and fits in a groove in the jig's base. Cut the runner for a snug sliding fit in the slot. If the runner doesn't fit snugly, it can shift as it slides. While you're at it, cut the two plastic runners that mount to the platform. By the way, any good combination blade will produce a smooth cut in UHMW plastic.

Cut the MDF parts

With the runners cut, you can start working on the MDF base and platform. Because these two parts have a pair of parallel grooves that need to align when the jig is assembled, cut both parts from an oversize blank—a single piece of MDF, 14 in. wide by 24 in. long. That way the grooves in both parts can be cut at the same time to ensure alignment.

This is also a good time to cut the remaining grooves. The groove on the underside of the base

accepts the miter-gauge runner. The groove on the back face of the fence accepts the platform.

Now cut the blank into two parts: one 9¼ in. long for the platform and one 13 in. long for the base. The connecting block and the support block work together as part of the micro-adjust system. Both of these parts have a hole bored on one face, with each hole drilled just deep enough to accept a washer and nut. When the two parts have been assembled, the holes create a pocket that accepts both washers and nuts.

I used a router with an edge guide to cut the slot in the platform

for the carriage bolt. Before routing, I drilled a 5/16-in.-dia. hole to provide a starting point for a ¼-in.-dia. straight bit. The head of the carriage bolt is recessed in a counterbore in the underside of the base. Now add the threaded insert to the crank block. Drill a ½-in.-dia. hole, lubricate the outside threads of the insert with wax, and screw it in place.

Rip the plastic runners. *A combination blade makes a smooth cut in UHMW plastic.*

Cut some grooves. *A dado head plows a pair of parallel grooves in an oversized blank.*

Cut the blank in two. *Crosscutting the blank provides stock for the base and platform.*

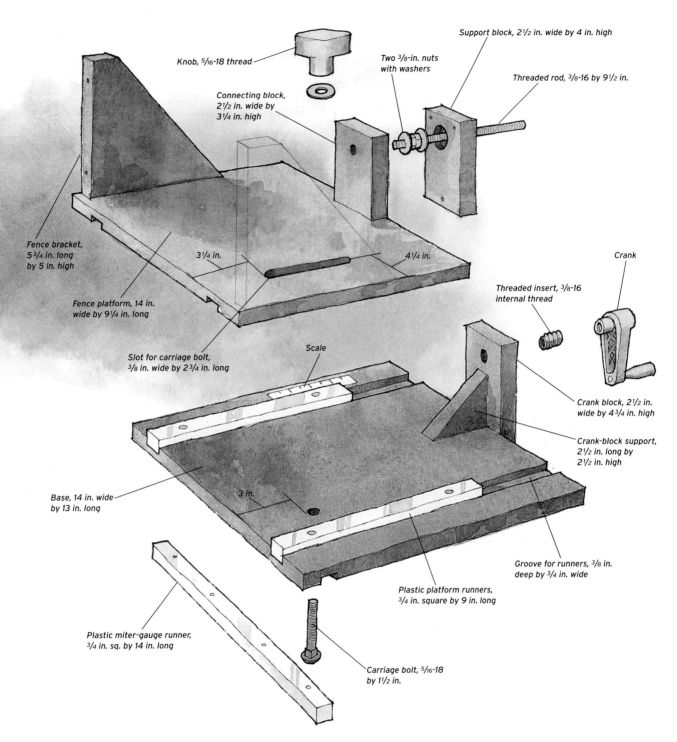

Knob, 5/16-18 thread

Support block, 2 1/2 in. wide by 4 in. high

Two 3/8-in. nuts with washers

Threaded rod, 3/8-16 by 9 1/2 in.

Connecting block, 2 1/2 in. wide by 3 1/4 in. high

Fence bracket, 5 3/4 in. long by 5 in. high

3 1/4 in.

4 1/4 in.

Fence platform, 14 in. wide by 9 1/4 in. long

Crank

Threaded insert, 3/8-16 internal thread

Slot for carriage bolt, 3/8 in. wide by 2 3/4 in. long

Scale

Crank block, 2 1/2 in. wide by 4 3/4 in. high

Crank-block support, 2 1/2 in. long by 2 1/2 in. high

Base, 14 in. wide by 13 in. long

3 in.

Groove for runners, 3/8 in. deep by 3/4 in. wide

Plastic platform runners, 3/4 in. square by 9 in. long

Plastic miter-gauge runner, 3/4 in. sq. by 14 in. long

Carriage bolt, 5/16-18 by 1 1/2 in.

Assemble and finish

At this point, all of the MDF parts can be screwed together. Keep in mind, though, that MDF tends to split, especially when screwing into an edge. So it's important to drill pilot holes before adding screws.

After that, cut the three runners to final length. Then drill, countersink and screw each runner in place.

The micro-adjust system comes next. Cut the threaded rod to length. Then add the crank, nuts and washers. To complete the system, it's just a matter of screwing the connecting block to the support block.

To add moisture protection to the jig, it's a good idea to apply a couple of coats of polyurethane

to the MDF parts. Mounting the hold-down completes the jig.

Note prices are from 2002.

Brad Schilling enjoys working wood in Fairview Heights, Illinois.

By William Krase

Angled tenons can be difficult to cut, especially if
they're compound. Krase's system greatly simplifies
the process. The workpiece seats securely against the
wedges at the juncture of the crossfeed and sliding
table, while the sliding table guides the whole affair
through the blade.

Lots of furniture—especially pieces intended to accommodate the human body—require joints that are not square. Chairs may have as many as 16 such joints, some of which are compound (angled in two planes). That's why chairs can be difficult. They don't have to be. With my addition of a crossfeed box to a standard crosscut sled and the use of purpose-made wedges, I can cut even compound-angled tenons quickly, accurately, time after time. The wedges establish the tenon angle while the crossfeed box positions the workpiece to get the correct length, width, and thickness of tenon.

I arrived at this method of cutting angled tenons because I wanted to make the stool in the photo at right. Since then, I've used it to make many pieces of furniture, and I've been completely satisfied with both the apparatus and results. Particleboard is what I had handy, but if I were to build another, I'd use meduim-density fiberboard (MDF) or a good-quality birch plywood instead.

To make the thumbscrews that fasten the crossfeed box to the sliding table, I bought a length of $1/16$-in. by $1/2$-in. brass strip, cut pieces to size, and soldered them into the head slots of slotted brass machine screws. The resulting homemade thumbscrews are oversize, so it's easy to tighten the crossfeed box in place.

The first thing I do when cutting angled tenons is to cut the end of the workpiece parallel to what will be the shoulder of the tenon, using the sliding table and wedges. (I make wedges for projects as I need them.) Then, when I position the wedge (or wedges), I make sure the end of the workpiece flushes up against the crossfeed box (for cutting shoulders) or the base of the sliding table (for the cheeks). Tenons angled in one plane require one wedge; compound-angled tenons require two. I use the same wedges for cutting both the shoulders and the cheeks.

William Krase is a retired aerospace engineer who builds furniture and boats in Mendocino, California.

Versatile joinery. *Angled tenons—some compound—were used almost exclusively in the construction of this walnut chair, stool, and side table. Legs on two of these pieces splay in two directions, requiring slightly angled tenons at both ends of apron pieces, stretchers and seat supports.*

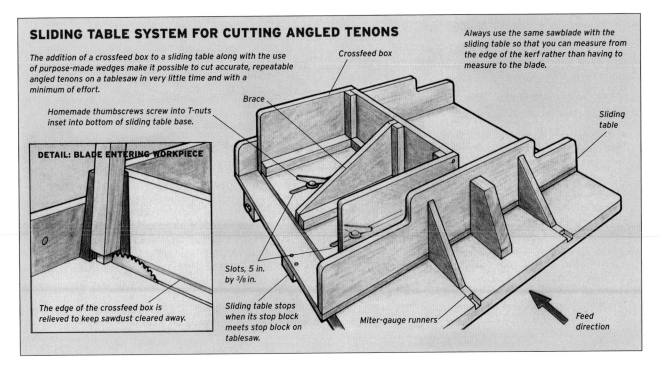

SLIDING TABLE SYSTEM FOR CUTTING ANGLED TENONS

The addition of a crossfeed box to a sliding table along with the use of purpose-made wedges make it possible to cut accurate, repeatable angled tenons on a tablesaw in very little time and with a minimum of effort.

Always use the same sawblade with the sliding table so that you can measure from the edge of the kerf rather than having to measure to the blade.

Crossfeed box

Brace

Homemade thumbscrews screw into T-nuts inset into bottom of sliding table base.

Sliding table

DETAIL: BLADE ENTERING WORKPIECE

The edge of the crossfeed box is relieved to keep sawdust cleared away.

Slots, 5 in. by $3/8$ in.

Sliding table stops when its stop block meets stop block on tablesaw.

Miter-gauge runners

Feed direction

DOVETAILING SLED FOR THE TABLESAW

By Jeff Miller

I like cutting dovetails by hand, but the nature of my business doesn't let me stay in practice. And I admit, I tend to lose a little accuracy when I'm out of shape. I've tried router jigs, but I've never found one I like. I find them fussy to set up, and to my eye, router-cut dovetails never look as good as those cut by hand.

Some years ago, a friend showed me a way to use my tablesaw and bandsaw to make dovetails that look hand cut. The jig is surprisingly fast to set up, and it lets me cut dovetails of any size and spacing. It's not a production jig, but it's fast enough to use in a professional shop, and it works well in limited production situations. Disadvantages? The quality of the fit will depend on your ability to cut accurately to a line. But I like that; I find it far more satisfying

than using a dovetail jig. In some ways, this is still a hand-cut procedure (I can hear the traditionalists howl). The finished joint certainly looks as if it's been hand-cut.

A Simple jig cuts the pins

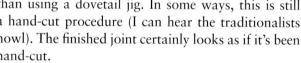

The key to this method is a table-saw jig for cutting the pins. Two fences angled to a narrow V-shape are mounted on a sled that runs in the miter-gauge slots of my tablesaw. I make the pins in two passes over a ½-in. dado cutter (see the photos on p. 96). With the first pass, I cut one side of each pin. Then I rotate the sled and cut the other side. I use the pins to mark the tails before cutting them on the bandsaw.

The base of the sled is made of ¾-in. plywood, 18 in. wide by 30 in. long (see the drawing on the facing

TABLESAW SLED FOR CUTTING DOVETAILS

This simple sled is the key to efficient machine dovetails that look hand-cut. Pins are cut in two passes on the jig, one on each side. The author cuts the tails on the bandsaw.

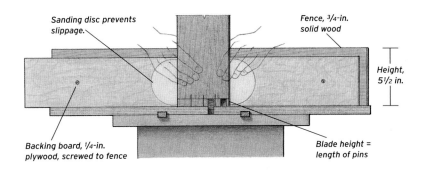

Sanding disc prevents slippage.

Fence, ³/₄-in. solid wood

Height, 5¹/₂ in.

Backing board, ¹/₄-in. plywood, screwed to fence

Blade height = length of pins

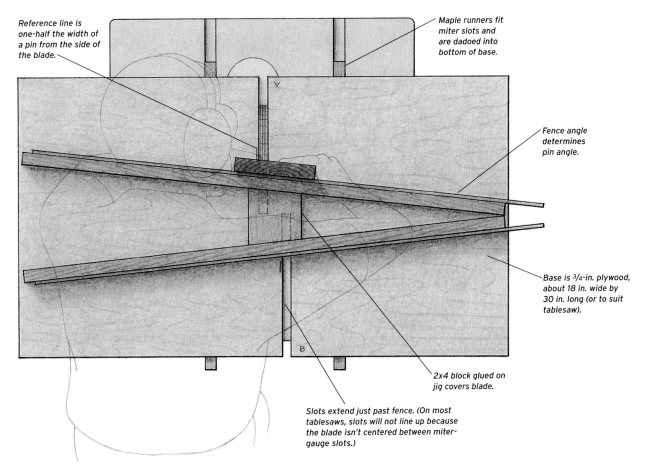

Reference line is one-half the width of a pin from the side of the blade.

Maple runners fit miter slots and are dadoed into bottom of base.

Fence angle determines pin angle.

Base is ³/₄-in. plywood, about 18 in. wide by 30 in. long (or to suit tablesaw).

2x4 block glued on jig covers blade.

Slots extend just past fence. (On most tablesaws, slots will not line up because the blade isn't centered between miter-gauge slots.)

page). The runners for the miter slots are glued into shallow dadoes on the bottom of the sled. To ensure the dadoes are parallel to one another, I run the same edge against the fence while cutting each dado.

The fences are set at 6 degrees off a line drawn perpendicular to the blade, which gives a pin angle of 6 degrees. This is a 9:1 ratio. I picked that angle simply because I think it looks best. I recently discovered the jig I had been using for years had one fence set at 6 degrees, the other at 8 degrees. I never noticed until I measured it for drawings. The lesson: Don't worry too much about the angle.

The fences are made of ³/₄-in. solid wood, 5³/₄ in. high and fastened from below with screws. Because the blade cuts through the sled between the fences, I glued a block into the space as a guard. After cutting a few dadoes of different widths and heights, the fence was chewed up in the area of the blade. So I mounted ¹/₄-in. plywood backing boards on the fences to prevent tearout. I move the backing boards each time I change the dovetail profile and replace them when necessary. Sanding discs glued to the backing boards keep the pin board from slipping. Just make sure that the discs are not in the path of the cut or sparks will fly.

Jig setup Is based on pin width

Laying out the dovetails is simple. As I do with hand-cut dovetails, I use a marking knife to scribe a line on both faces of the board to locate the bottoms of the

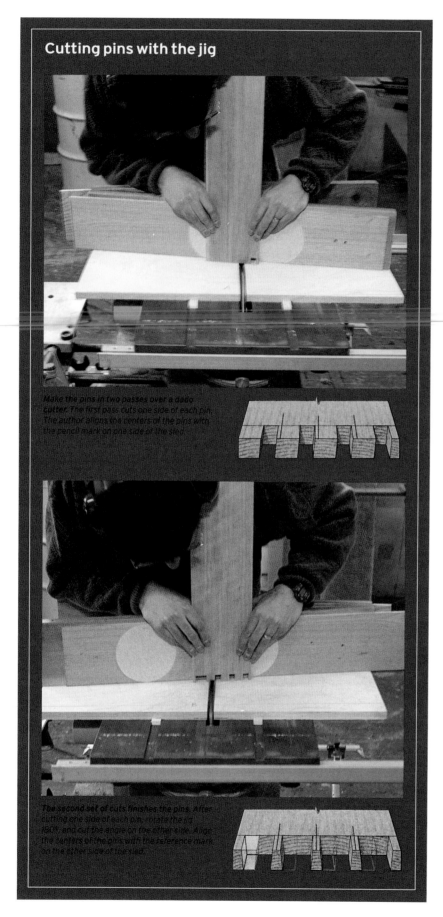

Cutting pins with the jig

Make the pins in two passes over a dado cutter. The first pass cuts one side of each pin. The author aligns the centers of the pins with the pencil mark on one side of the sled.

The second set of cuts finishes the pins. After cutting one side of each pin, rotate the jig 180°, and cut the angle on the other side. Align the centers of the pins with the reference mark on the other side of the sled.

pins and to help prevent tearout on the waste portion. I set the dado cutter so the depth of cut just touches the scribed line. On the outside face of the board, I mark the centerlines of the pins. I space them evenly, but you can space them any way you like. The angle of the cut is set by the angle of the fences; the width of the pins is up to you.

I made a pencil line on each side of the jig (see the top drawing on the facing page) to determine pin width. The distance from the pencil lines to the cutter is half the width of the pins. When cutting, I align each layout line on the pin board with the pencil line on the jig.

The first round of tablesaw cuts puts the angle on one side of the pins. I line up the reference marks, as shown in the top photo at left, run the sled through the blade and repeat at the next mark. I like the half-pins at each end to be close to full width, so I align the edge of the board with an imaginary line that's twice as far from the blade as the reference mark. When I've cut one side of all the pins, I turn off the saw and rotate the jig 180 degrees to cut the other side of the pins at the opposing angle (see the bottom photo at left). If there's any waste left between the two cuts, I scoot the board over and make another pass.

A bandsaw cuts the tails

The first step in laying out the tails is to scribe a baseline across both sides of the end of the board with a marking knife. Then the tails are scribed with a sharp awl. I do the marking on my jointer because it has a handy right-angle surface (see the top photo on the facing page). The outside face of the tailboard goes down on the jointer table, and the pin board stands on it with the marked face (outside)

Tails on the Bandsaw

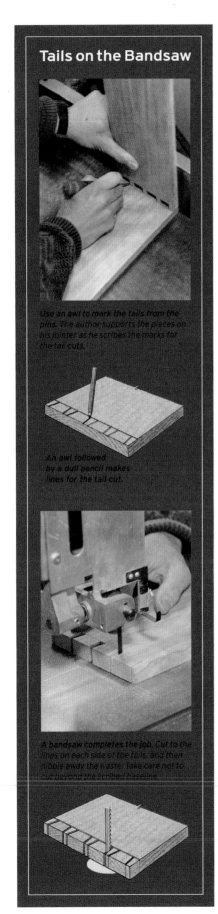

Use an awl to mark the tails from the pins. The author supports the pieces on his jointer as he scribes the marks for the tail cuts.

An awl followed by a dull pencil makes lines for the tail cut.

A bandsaw completes the job. Cut to the lines on each side of the tails, and then nibble away the waste. Take care not to cut beyond the scribed baseline.

The author gets an almost perfect mallet-tight fit right off the bandsaw. *With a little practice, anyone can have the same results.*

against the fence. Before I go any further, I label all the mating pieces to avoid confusion.

Cutting the tails is nothing more than cutting to the line on the bandsaw.

I cut the sides of the tails to the line and use the blade to nibble away the rest of the waste, being careful to stop at the scribed baseline (see the bottom photo at left). I rotate the piece 90 degrees and cut along the scribed line for the bottoms of the half-pins at the ends. Slightly ragged bottoms on the tail can be cleaned up with a chisel. After some practice, you can dispense with this step.

The first few times I cut dovetails this way, the fit was a little tight, and I had to pare the high spots with a chisel. If one section is loose, a small wedge glued in place can make an almost invisible repair. Sanding dust mixed with finish can make a good joint look almost perfect.

Jeff Miller's Chicago studio serves as shop, showroom, and classroom for his woodworking courses.

TABLESAW JIG CUTS SLIP JOINTS

by Frank Klausz

Some years ago, I went to see a show at the Metropolitan Museum. On display was a chair built around 1350 b.c.e., on which I could see a slip joint. There are reasons this joint has been in use for so long. Also called an open mortise and tenon, the slip joint is hard to beat for ease of assembly. And because of the large gluing area where the pieces meet, a slip joint holds up to a lot of stress.

What I really like about the slip joint is how fast it is to cut and assemble. I use a tablesaw jig that I designed several years ago. The beauty of this system is that you don't have to spend time marking all the pieces. The setup for the mortise is done by eye, and the tenon cuts are taken directly from the mortise.

I always make sure to keep some scrap pieces of wood on hand for setting up and testing the joints. Test pieces should be of the same thickness and width as the stock you'll use later.

I make the first setup by cranking the sawblade up to the width of the stile. I place the jig over the top of the saw fence and clamp in a piece of scrap. I adjust the saw fence so that it's cutting into the middle third of the thickness of the wood. Then I push the piece through, flip it in the jig, and push it through again. The first mortise is done.

After cutting all the mortises, I turn off the saw, leaving the last mortised piece clamped in the jig. I loosen the fence and tap it lightly toward the blade by the amount of the blade thickness. With this setup, the cheek line of the mortise is cut on the inside of the sawblade, closest to the fence; the cheek line of the tenon is cut on the outside of the blade. Then I remove the workpiece and clamp in a fresh piece of scrap for a test tenon. I run the piece through the saw, turn it around, and run it through again.

After these cuts have been made, the waste on either side of the tenon must be removed with the stock held flat on the table. A miter gauge works well for this operation.

Frank Klausz is a cabinetmaker in Pluckemin, New Jersey.

A JIG FOR MAKING SLIP JOINTS

This jig makes both mortises and tenons. A channel, sized to your tablesaw fence, keeps the jig running smoothly and safely.

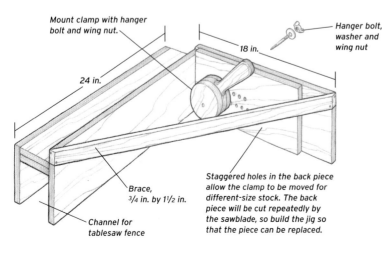

Mount clamp with hanger bolt and wing nut.

18 in.

Hanger bolt, washer and wing nut

24 in.

Brace, 3/4 in. by 1 1/2 in.

Channel for tablesaw fence

Staggered holes in the back piece allow the clamp to be moved for different-size stock. The back piece will be cut repeatedly by the sawblade, so build the jig so that the piece can be replaced.

QUICK CLAMP
The eccentric clamp holds any thickness of stock tightly. The offset hole makes the clamp act as a cam.

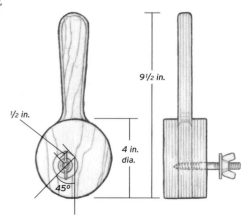

9 1/2 in.

1/2 in.

4 in. dia.

45°

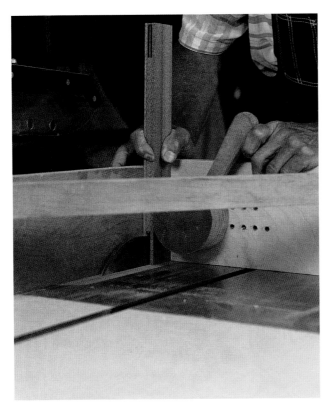

MORTISE

Cut the mortise first. With the clamp, secure the place of stock to be cut firmly into the back corner of the jig. Make the first cut. Remove the stock, flip it around, reclamp it, and make the next cut. Depending on the size of your slip joint, two passes are usually enough to complete the mortise. The one shown at left took three passes at two fence settings.

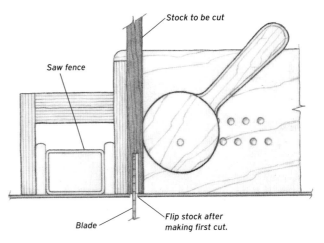

Stock to be cut

Saw fence

Blade

Flip stock after making first cut.

TENON

Change the setting from mortise to tenon. Use the mortised piece to reset the fence for the tenon cuts. Set the blade to cut on the other side of the thick line. Always use scraps to test this fit. Once the fence is set, cut one side of the tenon, flip the piece in the jig, and cut the other. Cut off the waste on the shoulder line later, using a miter gauge and a stop block.

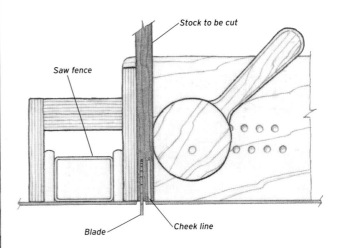

Stock to be cut

Saw fence

Blade

Cheek line

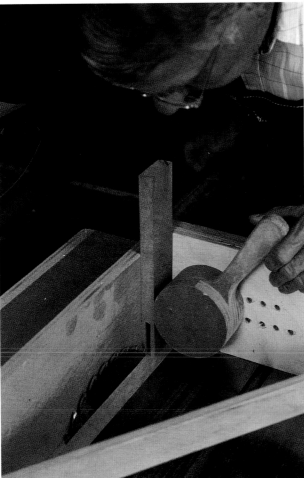

Check cuts for the tenon. To test the tenon setup, cut the checks first. The height of the sawblade off the table does not change. One pass per side is sufficient.

SHOP-BUILT ROLLER EXTENSION TABLE

by Bob Gabor

ROLLER EXTENSION TABLE

A shop-built extension table makes cutting large panels on the tablesaw a safer, easier operation.

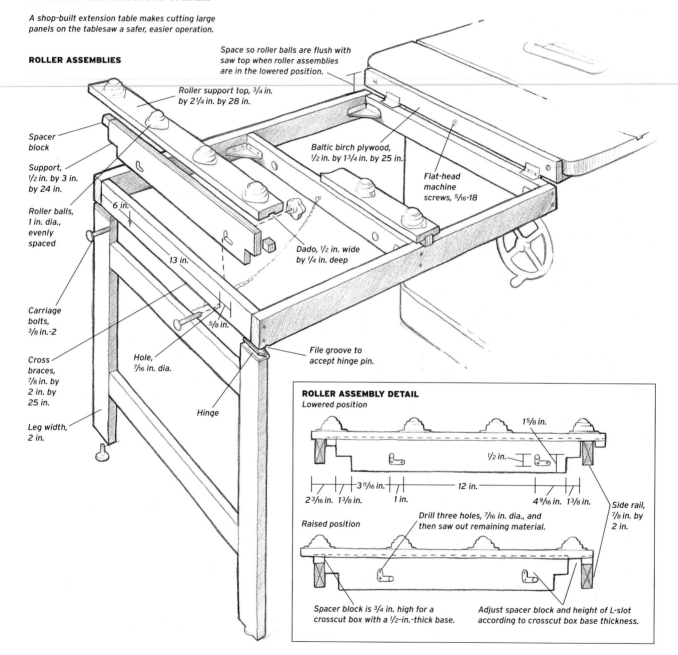

ROLLER ASSEMBLIES

Space so roller balls are flush with saw top when roller assemblies are in the lowered position.

Roller support top, 3/4 in. by 2 1/4 in. by 28 in.

Spacer block

Support, 1/2 in. by 3 in. by 24 in.

Roller balls, 1 in. dia., evenly spaced

6 in.

13 in.

5/8 in.

Carriage bolts, 3/8 in.-2

Cross braces, 7/8 in. by 2 in. by 25 in.

Leg width, 2 in.

Hole, 7/16 in. dia.

Hinge

Baltic birch plywood, 1/2 in. by 1 3/4 in. by 25 in.

Flat-head machine screws, 5/16-18

Dado, 1/2 in. wide by 1/4 in. deep

File groove to accept hinge pin.

ROLLER ASSEMBLY DETAIL
Lowered position

1 5/8 in.

1/2 in.

2 3/16 in. 1 3/8 in. 3 11/16 in. 1 in. 12 in. 4 9/16 in. 1 3/8 in.

Side rail, 7/8 in. by 2 in.

Raised position

Drill three holes, 7/16 in. dia., and then saw out remaining material.

Spacer block is 3/4 in. high for a crosscut box with a 1/2-in.-thick base.

Adjust spacer block and height of L-slot according to crosscut box base thickness.

I was tired of wrestling big sheets of plywood across the top of my tablesaw. I already had an outfeed table on the back of the saw, but what I really needed was a side extension table to support the heavy panels going into the saw. I didn't want to give up too much valuable floor space to an accessory that I wouldn't be using most of the time.

My solution was a fold-away extension table that uses rows of roller balls to support the workpiece. I chose roller balls instead of long, tube rollers because the balls won't pull stock off-line as it is fed through the saw. Normally, the roller balls are even with the saw's tabletop, but they also can be raised to support long panels that overhang the end of my crosscut box. This straight-forward shop fixture is easy to build and use. It sets up and drops back out of the way in a matter of seconds, and it makes cutting plywood on the tablesaw safer and more manageable.

Utility and economy in a shop tool

I'd rather make furniture than shop tools, so I designed the extension table to be as simple as possible. The top frame and the leg assemblies, as shown in the drawing on the facing page, are inexpensive and easy to assemble with a biscuit joiner. Yet they're light and strong. The length of the top-frame assembly and the leg assembly is determined by the distance between the floor and the top of the saw.

The top frame needs to be sized to just clear the floor in the folded position. The legs must be long enough to make the roller balls level with the saw top when the frame is in the raised position.

The extension table also supports long stock in my sliding crosscut box because the rollers are adjustable by the thickness of the crosscut box's bottom. Mounting the rollers on T-shaped assemblies, which adjust easily after loosening a few knobs, was a simple and reliable solution.

To fold the unit for storage (see the top photo at right), I hinged the legs to the top frame and also hinged the top frame to the tablesaw top. When folded down, the table doesn't take up much room in my shop. By adding adjustable levelers to the leg assemblies, I made it easy to fine-tune the height.

Finally, I added a piece of lightweight chain to limit the leg travel and a screen-door hook to keep the leg assembly folded for storage. I've been so pleased with the roller extension table that I've built another and attached it to the side of my outfeed table.

Bob Gabor is an amateur woodworker in Pittsboro, North Carolina, and a member of the Triangle Woodworkers Association.

Extension table stows away. *The extension table drops into its stored position in seconds and takes up no floor space. Adjustable roller assemblies can be raised so that the table also works with a sliding crosscut box.*

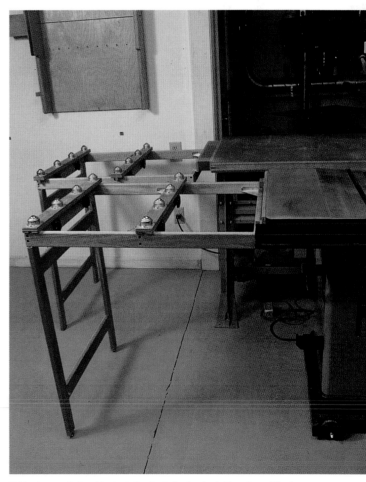

Fold out supports for wide stock. *A roller-ball extension table makes cutting large panels safer and easier. Unlike long tube rollers, roller balls won't pull stock out of line as it goes through the saw.*

TABLESAW DOVETAIL JIG

by Mark Duginske

Duginske's method produces machine-cut through dovetails with hand-cut accuracy. Both tails and pins are sawn using a shopmade jig on the tablesaw and trimmed with a narrow blade on the bandsaw. An ingenious system of spacer blocks and shims determines the layout of the joint and maintains a precision fit.

The dovetail is a classic joint that many craftsmen consider to be the hallmark of quality joinery. But the traditional method of cutting dovetails by hand requires skill and patience, and unless you're in practice and up to speed, all that sawing and chiseling is slow work. A router and jig is one alternative, but the monotonous look of most router-cut dovetails leaves something to be desired.

After years of experimentation, I developed a method for cutting through dovetails, which combines hand-tool flexibility with machine-tool speed and accuracy. It's a great system for the small-shop because it is fast, simple to use, and allows you to design the size and layout of dovetails to suit most applications.

How the system works

In a nutshell, the system employs two machine tools: the tablesaw and the bandsaw. A simple shopmade jig, shown in figure 1 on the facing page, mounted to the tablesaw's miter gauge supports the workpiece on edge for cutting both pins and tails with a standard sawblade. The blade is tilted for cutting the tails; for the pins, the miter gauge and jig are angled. While the jig maintains the angle of cut, a set of spacer blocks mounted to the jig spaces the sawcuts to produce a perfectly fitting joint without the need to mark the boards individually. After the tablesaw cuts are made, the waste is removed with a 1/8-in.-wide blade on the bandsaw using the saw's regular rip fence as a guide.

Although my system is straightforward, it involves quite a few steps that must be performed in order. The procedure is better illustrated with photographs and sketches than with a written description alone; therefore, I've included a step-by-step account in the sidebar on pp. 104–105 of how to cut a typical through dovetail joint.

Designing the joint and cutting the spacer blocks

The hinge pin of my entire dovetail system is the spacer block: Mounted to the tablesaw jig, the blocks

A handcut look by machine. The dovetail joints' precision fit can be fine-tuned by adding or subtracting paper shims when the pins are cut with the tablesaw jig.

provide a way to cut all pins and tails without having to mark out each board. Before cutting the blocks, you must design your dovetail layout, including the number, size, and spacing of the pins and tails. This will determine both the number of spacer blocks you'll need and their widths.

Following figure 2 on the facing page, you'll see that the number of spacer blocks needed equals the number of tails in the joint. In example 1, four blocks produce a joint with four tails, three full pins and two half pins. Once you've chosen the number of dovetails, you'll need to decide on their size and spacing. One of the advantages of my system is you can easily vary the sizes of pins and tails to make joints look more like they were hand cut. For the dovetail angle, I'd recommend 10 degrees, but avoid an angle outside the range of 8 degrees to 12 degrees.

My system allows you to alter the width of individual tails and the spacing of pins along a single

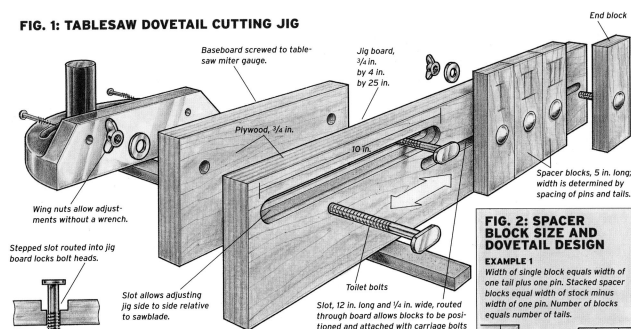

FIG. 1: TABLESAW DOVETAIL CUTTING JIG

End block

Baseboard screwed to table-saw miter gauge.

Jig board, 3/4 in. by 4 in. by 25 in.

Plywood, 3/4 in.

10 in.

Spacer blocks, 5 in. long; width is determined by spacing of pins and tails.

Wing nuts allow adjust-ments without a wrench.

Stepped slot routed into jig board locks bolt heads.

Slot allows adjusting jig side to side relative to sawblade.

Toilet bolts

Slot, 12 in. long and 1/4 in. wide, routed through board allows blocks to be posi-tioned and attached with carriage bolts and wing nuts.

FIG. 2: SPACER BLOCK SIZE AND DOVETAIL DESIGN

EXAMPLE 1
Width of single block equals width of one tail plus one pin. Stacked spacer blocks equal width of stock minus width of one pin. Number of blocks equals number of tails.

Half pin

Pin

Tail

4 1/4 in.

1 in.

1 in.   4 in.

1 in.

1 in.

1/4 in.

3/4 in.

1/4 in.

EXAMPLE 2
Making individual blocks different widths yields variable spacing of pins, width of tails.

4 3/16 in.

1 1/16 in.

1 5/16 in.

1 1/16 in.

1 1/4 in.

1 1/2 in.   4 in.

1 1/4 in.

3/16 in.

3/16 in.

Dovetail angle should be between 8° and 12°.

joint. In example 2 in figure 2, the center tail is wider than the tails on either side of it. You could just as easily make the outer tails wider or make two wide tails, two narrow tails, two wide, and so forth—as long as the resulting layout is symmetrical relative to the center of the joint. This last point is required for this cutting system to work correctly.

As you can see in figure 2, one block is equal to the width of one tail at its widest plus the width of one pin at its narrowest. Depending on your design, your spacer blocks may all be the same width or different widths, but in either case, the total width of the spacer blocks should equal the width of the stock minus the width of one pin.

The spacer blocks are made from scraps of 3/4-in. plywood. I cut two sets: One set is drilled for the bolts that mount the blocks to the jig board. The second set is left undrilled and used to mark the first tail board, which is necessary for setting the jig before cutting. If your joint has tails of various sizes, number your spacer blocks, so they can be kept in the correct order

Making the tablesaw jig

I made the tablesaw jig shown in figure 1 from 3/4-in. plywood. The jig, which mounts to the tablesaw's regular miter gauge, consists of two parts: a 4-in.-high baseboard that bolts through the gauge's head and a jig board that attaches to the baseboard. To allow the jig to be adjusted back and forth for setting different dovetail arrangements, the jig board is bolted through a 5/16-in.-wide slot. A pair of toilet bolts, or

closet bolts, connect the two parts of the jig. The slot is stepped (routed in two passes) to fit the toilet bolts' heads (see the detail in figure 1 above), allowing them to slide, yet not turn when the wing nuts, which lock the jig board to the baseboard, are tightened. Another slot routed through the jig board allows the spacer blocks to be positioned and bolted in place. You will need a 2-in.-long, 1/4-in. carriage bolt, with washers and a wing nut, for each block that you use.

It'll probably take some study and experimentation for you to master the process, so don't plan to make drawers from your precious stash of bird's-eye maple the first couple of times that you try the system. I am a real believer in practice makes perfect. The more you use this system, the better you will get at it.

Mark Duginske is a woodworker, teacher and author who lives in Wausau, Wisconsin.

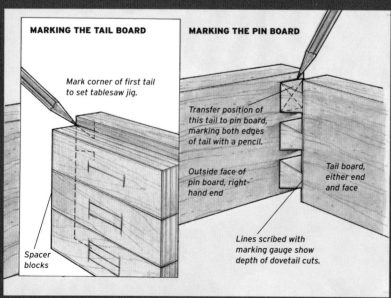

Step-by-step dovetails

Here are the steps you will need to follow for cutting out a set of through dovetails. The demonstration joint shown in these photos illustrates a typical joint, such as you might use for building drawers. Layout and dovetail size variations, and the construction of the tablesaw jig and spacer blocks needed to cut the joint are discussed in the main text.

Prepare the stock: Dress all stock to final dimensions with tail boards and pin boards of equal thickness; make sure ends are square and trimmed to final length. Set marking gauge to thickness of stock, which will equal the depth of the dovetails, and scribe both faces at each end of tail boards and pin boards. Stack dovetail spacer blocks and mark position of first tail's edge on one tail board (see the left drawing below).

THE TAILS

Cutting on the tablesaw: Set bevel of sawblade to desired dovetail angle (10 degrees) and square miter gauge to blade. Attach three spacer blocks and end block to the jig, squaring them to the saw table before bolting them on (see photo 1 at left). Lower sawblade slightly below depth of dovetail cuts. Now butt the edge of marked tail board up to third spacer block and slide the jig board until the mark aligns with sawblade, as shown in photo 2 at left. Tighten bolts that lock jig board to baseboard.

Place a tail board against jig, and take a trial cut on one side of the first tail. Set depth of cut by raising blade and recutting until cut reaches scribe mark on stock. Now flip the board end for end and take second cut. For third cut, rotate board edge for edge, then end for end for fourth cut. Remove spacer block one and repeat four cuts, flipping as before. Remove spacer two and repeat same sequence of cuts to complete tails. Now perform entire cutting sequence on each of the tail boards.

Bandsawing tail waste: Fit bandsaw with a 1/8-in. blade and adjust the rip fence so cutting depth to outside of blade equals depth of dovetails. Trim waste from between tails by sliding the stock into the blade via the sawkerfs cut on the tablesaw earlier, as shown in photo 3 at left. Flip stock over and bandsaw again to clean up corners between tails. Do this on all tail boards.

MARKING THE TAIL BOARD

Mark corner of first tail to set tablesaw jig.

Spacer blocks

MARKING THE PIN BOARD

Transfer position of this tail to pin board, marking both edges of tail with a pencil.

Outside face of pin board, right-hand end

Tail board, either end and face

Lines scribed with marking gauge show depth of dovetail cuts.

THE PINS

Sawing first side: Square tablesaw blade to table and lower blade height slightly. Set miter gauge to dovetail angle (10 degrees) with right side of jig board sloping away from blade and replace all spacer blocks. Transfer tail position to one pin board (see the drawing on p. 104) and then hold pin board (inside face toward jig) against first spacer block and adjust the jig board so the end mark lines up with the sawblade, as shown in photo 1 at right. Take a trial cut and adjust blade height as before. For second cut, flip board end for end, keeping same face against jig. Now repeat first two cuts on all pin boards. Remove spacer block one, take two cuts (flipping board end for end as before), and repeat on all pin boards (see photo 2 at right). Remove spacer block two, and repeat cutting sequence on all pin boards.

Sawing second side: Reset the miter gauge so that it angles (10 degrees) in the other direction. Reattach spacer block two, but before bolting, slip a stack of a dozen or more paper shims between end block and spacer three. Align mark to blade and set jig board, as shown in photo 3 at right. Cut only the marked pin board (keeping its inside face against the jig), and follow the sequence of taking two cuts, flipping board between cuts, removing a spacer block and cutting again until you've removed all three spacer blocks (see photo 4 at right).

Bandsawing pin waste: With the same bandsaw rip-fence setting as before, carefully tilt pin board at necessary angle and slip blade into a saw kerf; then lower board flat onto table and cut away waste (see photo 5 at right). Hold the board securely as the blade will want to grab and pull the board down as you begin each cut. After sawing each pin waste, move the small waste blocks away from the blade with the eraser end of a pencil, for safety sake. Repeat to saw away waste on first pin board. Now trial-fit a pin board with a tail board. If the fit is too tight, remove as many paper shims as necessary, replace spacer blocks two and three, and recut trial pin board. Recheck joint fit and remove more shims if needed until dovetail joint slides snugly together. Retaining this shim arrangement, cut and trim all remaining pin boards as you did with the trial board.

Roller-topped drawers increase outfeed table capacity. By extending the bottoms of two drawers at the back of his tablesaw, Vucolo created a place to mount outfeed rollers. Here, he opens one drawer to rip a piece of 6/4 mahogany.

Drawer slide alignment is important. With the outfeed table flipped, the author positions a slide before he screws it to the poplar rail. Precise alignment ensures smooth operation of the outfeed rollers. A leg socket is below the square.

SHOPMADE OUTFEED TABLE

By Frank A. Vucolo

In my small shop, ideal concepts are often compromised by the reality of limited space. My design for an outfeed table is a classic case in point. I started out thinking big. Ideally, I wanted the outfeed surface to extend 48 in. from the back of my table-saw, so I would no longer have to set up and then reposition unstable roller stands. My ideal was quickly squashed, however, when I realized I couldn't dedicate that much permanent floor space. I need the space behind the saw to store my planer and router table when I'm not using them.

After some careful measuring, taking into consideration where I would locate all the machines,

I concluded that the outfeed table should extend 30 in. from the back of the saw. But I still needed more support to rip long stock and to cut sheet goods.

While I was pondering possible solutions, I started to think about rollers that could extend off the back of the fixed table and then retract into it when they weren't needed. Then I remembered how amazed I was at the strength of Accuride®'s extension drawer slides (150-lb. capacity) when I had used them for file drawers in a desk pedestal. After a little more head scratching, nudged along by a couple of cups of coffee, I decided to incorporate the slides into a pair of drawers with rollers mounted on the front of them

OUTFEED TABLE ASSEMBLY

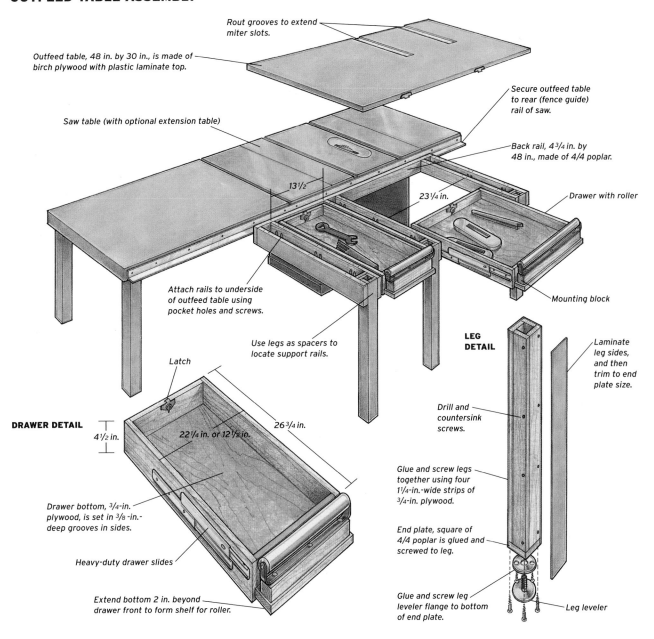

Rout grooves to extend miter slots.

Outfeed table, 48 in. by 30 in., is made of birch plywood with plastic laminate top.

Saw table (with optional extension table)

Secure outfeed table to rear (fence guide) rail of saw.

Back rail, 4¾ in. by 48 in., made of 4/4 poplar.

Drawer with roller

13½

23¼ in.

Mounting block

Attach rails to underside of outfeed table using pocket holes and screws.

Use legs as spacers to locate support rails.

LEG DETAIL

Laminate leg sides, and then trim to end plate size.

Drill and countersink screws.

Latch

DRAWER DETAIL

4½ in.

22¼ in. or 12½ in.

26¾ in.

Glue and screw legs together using four 1¼-in.-wide strips of ¾-in. plywood.

Drawer bottom, ¾-in. plywood, is set in ⅜-in.-deep grooves in sides.

End plate, square of 4/4 poplar is glued and screwed to leg.

Heavy-duty drawer slides

Glue and screw leg leveler flange to bottom of end plate.

Leg leveler

Extend bottom 2 in. beyond drawer front to form shelf for roller.

for the outfeed table (see the right photo on the facing page). Now I simply open a drawer to get an additional 24 in. of outfeed surface when I'm ripping long boards or cutting sheet stock.

Allowing an extra 1 in. for the extension rollers and the drawer slide action, the outfeed table is designed to support work up to 55 in. from the back of the saw table. With the drawers in the closed position, only 30 in. of floor space behind the tablesaw is committed. I made the drawers different widths so that I have various outfeed options, and I extended the drawer bottoms out in front of the drawers. This way, I have a place to mount the rollers (see the detail

drawing above). As a bonus, I get two drawers for storing saw accessories. And because the rollers are an integral part of the outfeed table, they are adjusted precisely in relation to the tabletop.

I constructed the outfeed table's top, legs, and drawer bottoms out of ¾-in. birch plywood. The under-table support rails are made from 4/4 poplar, as are the drawer sides, fronts, and backs. For added protection and to give a nice slick surface, I covered the legs and top with plastic laminate.

Frank A. Vucolo builds furniture for his home in East Amwell, New Jersey.

A BETTER TAPERING JIG

By Richard W. Beebe II

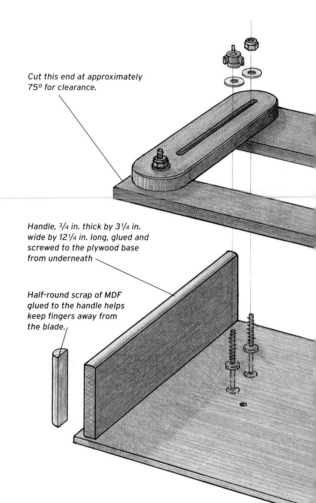

Cut this end at approximately 75° for clearance.

Handle, 3/4 in. thick by 3 1/4 in. wide by 12 1/4 in. long, glued and screwed to the plywood base from underneath

Half-round scrap of MDF glued to the handle helps keep fingers away from the blade.

I build a lot of Shaker-style furniture, and many of the pieces have tapered legs. There are numerous ways to taper a leg, and I tried them all before concluding that my preferred method is to use a tablesaw to cut off most of the waste and a jointer to make a light pass to clean up the surface of the sawcut. I tried one commercially available jig made of aluminum, but it felt terribly unsafe because it did not hold the workpiece firmly in place while I made the cut. So I set about making my own tapering jig.

The design shown here is the third generation of my attempts to make a jig that's easy and safe to use. I made the base of 1/4-in.-thick plywood, reasoning that a thinner base would allow the sawblade to cut through thicker stock. For all but the thickest legs, however, a 1/2-in.-thick base would make a sturdier

jig. I screwed a strip of UHMW (ultra-high molecular weight) plastic to the underside of the base so that the jig can ride in the miter-gauge slot with as little friction as possible.

I used 3/4-in.-thick medium-density fiberboard (MDF) for the fence, the cleat, the handle, the hold-down support, and the sliding braces because it's flat and stable and it machines well. I used a scrap of maple for the hold-down clamp because it's stiff and strong. The clamp applies pressure wherever needed, on any size workpiece that will fit on the jig. The sliding braces and the hold-down clamp are held in place with threaded knobs and carriage bolts. The adjustable fence is secured to the braces with carriage bolts and nylon locknuts.

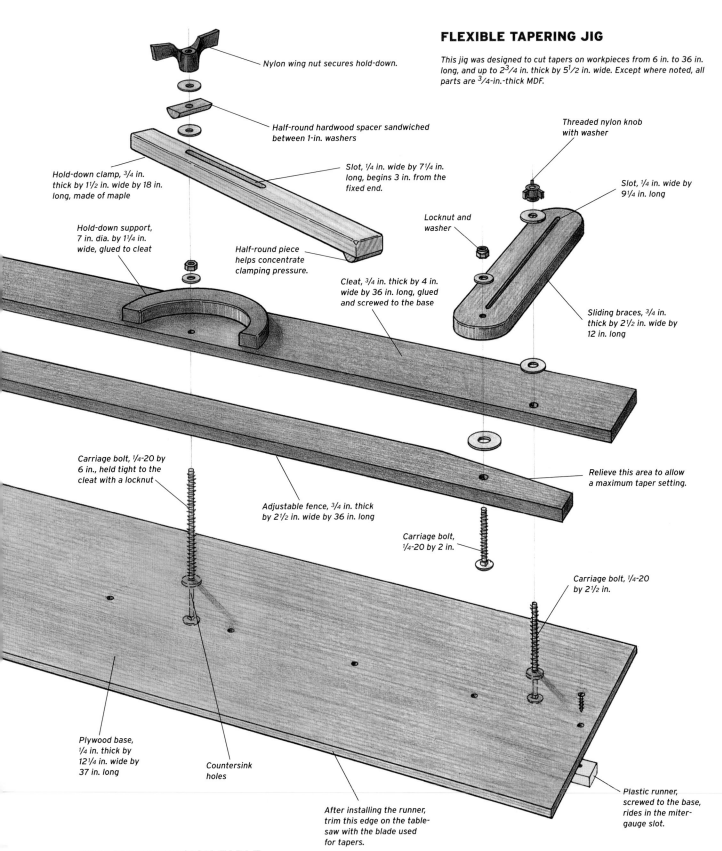

FLEXIBLE TAPERING JIG

This jig was designed to cut tapers on workpieces from 6 in. to 36 in. long, and up to 2³/₄ in. thick by 5¹/₂ in. wide. Except where noted, all parts are ³/₄-in.-thick MDF.

Nylon wing nut secures hold-down.

Half-round hardwood spacer sandwiched between 1-in. washers

Hold-down clamp, ³/₄ in. thick by 1¹/₂ in. wide by 18 in. long, made of maple

Slot, ¹/₄ in. wide by 7¹/₄ in. long, begins 3 in. from the fixed end.

Threaded nylon knob with washer

Slot, ¹/₄ in. wide by 9¹/₄ in. long

Hold-down support, 7 in. dia. by 1¹/₄ in. wide, glued to cleat

Half-round piece helps concentrate clamping pressure.

Locknut and washer

Cleat, ³/₄ in. thick by 4 in. wide by 36 in. long, glued and screwed to the base

Sliding braces, ³/₄ in. thick by 2¹/₂ in. wide by 12 in. long

Carriage bolt, ¹/₄-20 by 6 in., held tight to the cleat with a locknut

Adjustable fence, ³/₄ in. thick by 2¹/₂ in. wide by 36 in. long

Relieve this area to allow a maximum taper setting.

Carriage bolt, ¹/₄-20 by 2 in.

Carriage bolt, ¹/₄-20 by 2¹/₂ in.

Plywood base, ¹/₄ in. thick by 12¹/₄ in. wide by 37 in. long

Countersink holes

After installing the runner, trim this edge on the tablesaw with the blade used for tapers.

Plastic runner, screwed to the base, rides in the miter-gauge slot.

ROLLER EXTENSION TABLE

A shop-built extension table makes cutting large panels on the tablesaw a safer, easier operation.

Mark pencil lines to define the tapers

Before tapering the legs for a project, I always cut all of the mortises first because it's easier to do on square stock. For two-sided tapers, the mortises help me keep track of which sides of the legs will be tapered.

Using a pencil, mark the apron line, indicating where the taper starts on the leg, and then mark a line on the bottom of that same leg to define where the taper ends and how much material must be removed. Use those two lines to set up the jig, lining them up with the edge of the jig that will ride against the sawblade. Set the fence in place and clamp the leg firmly onto the jig.

Two-sided tapers are cut on the inside faces of each leg, which already have been mortised for the aprons. To prepare for the first cut, set up the leg in the jig with one of the mortises facing down. Make the first cut, unclamp and rotate the leg, clamp it back in place for the second cut, and then taper the second side.

To cut tapers on all four sides of a leg, I use a center-point attachment that slips over the jig's handle. The pivoting side of the attachment has a nail that engages and supports the leg as it's being tapered. Mark a center point on the bottom of the leg. Use an awl to punch the center point. When rotating the leg for all four tapers, it will revolve around this point.

Cutting two-sided tapers

Many furniture designs feature legs that are tapered on the two interior faces. When using the tapering jig, it's important to cut these tapers in the proper order (see drawing at right).

Mark the tapers. Scribe where the tapers begin and end, first on the faces of the leg (left), then on the bottom of the leg (right).

①

② *Position the workpiece in the jig. Line up the layout mark on the bottom of the leg with the edge of the jig's base (top), then lock down the sliding brace. Next, adjust the top end of the fence until the layout mark on the leg face aligns with the blade (bottom). Now lock down the top sliding brace.*

③ *Cut the tapers. Secure the leg in the jig with the hold-down clamp. Make the first cut, turn off the saw, then rotate the leg (see drawing) to make the second cut.*

TIP: CUT THE TAPERS IN THE PROPER ORDER
Start with the first side to be tapered facing the blade and the second facing down.

Sides to be tapered

Rotate for the second cut.

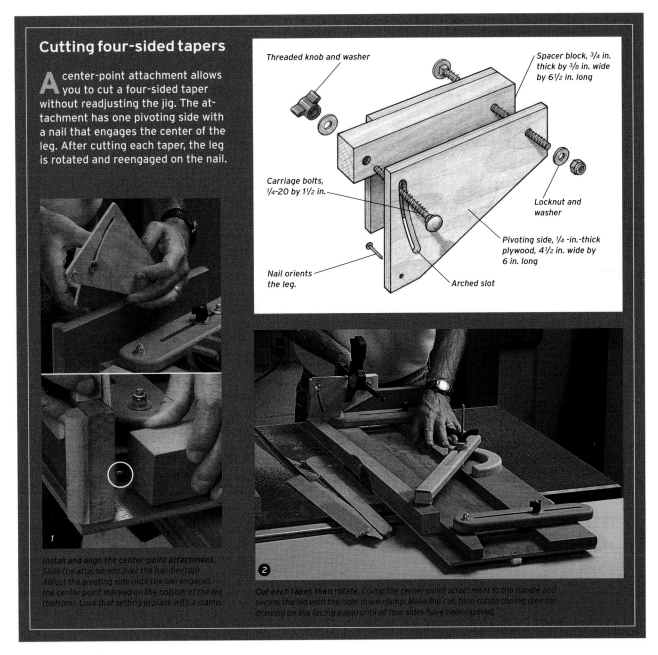

Cutting four-sided tapers

A center-point attachment allows you to cut a four-sided taper without readjusting the jig. The attachment has one pivoting side with a nail that engages the center of the leg. After cutting each taper, the leg is rotated and reengaged on the nail.

Threaded knob and washer

Spacer block, 3/4 in. thick by 3/8 in. wide by 6 1/2 in. long

Carriage bolts, 1/4-20 by 1 1/2 in.

Locknut and washer

Nail orients the leg.

Pivoting side, 1/4-in.-thick plywood, 4 1/2 in. wide by 6 in. long

Arched slot

1 Install and align the center-point attachment. Slide the attachment over the handle (top). Adjust the pivoting side until the nail engages the center point marked on the bottom of the leg (bottom). Lock that setting in place with a clamp.

2 Cut each taper, then rotate. Clamp the center-point attachment to the handle and secure the leg with the hold-down clamp. Make the cut, then rotate the leg (see the drawing on the facing page) until all four sides have been tapered.

When you're setting up a four-sided taper, you still have to follow the routine used on the two-sided tapers, marking pencil lines where the taper begins at the top apron line and where it ends on the bottom of the leg.

Now set up the center-point attachment so that the nail engages the center of the leg. From there, it's a matter of repetitive cutting: Clamp the leg in place, make the cut, unclamp, rotate and clamp it back in place, and so forth, until you've finished cutting tapers on all four sides. It's best to rotate the leg (see the drawing on the facing page) so that there's an untapered side against the base of the jig for all but the final cut.

Keep in mind that you don't need the center-point attachment to cut four-sided tapers. Instead, follow the steps for cutting two-sided tapers, then readjust the fence to cut the last two. When cutting the last two tapers, the flat of the apron surface is all that is riding against the fence, so be sure to place the hold-down clamp over that part of the leg.

Richard W. Beebe II manages the data network for the Yale School of Medicine. Away from work, he makes furnishings and cabinetry for his home in a small basement shop in Hamden, Connecticut.

FIVE ESSENTIAL BANDSAW JIGS

By Michael Fortune

The wall next to my bandsaw is festooned with jigs that expand the versatility of the basic machine. Though simple to build, each jig quickly and safely delivers the precise results I depend on. This chapter presents five of my favorites.

Build these jigs from Baltic birch plywood or medium-density fiberboard (MDF), and adjust dimensions to fit your bandsaw. For the jigs to work correctly, the bandsaw's blade must cut parallel to the fence. To achieve this, I check that the bandsaw's tires are in good shape (no grooves or ridges), then set the fence parallel to the miter-gauge slots. Next, I adjust the angle of the upper wheel. If the blade's centerline aligns with the centerline of the upper wheel, it will cut parallel to the fence.

Check by ripping some scrap. You'll know it's right when the back of the blade is centered in its kerf.

Michael Fortune designs and builds furniture in Lakefield, Ontario, Canada.

Rip tapers at any angle

A lot of woodworkers cut tapers on a tablesaw, but I think it's safer and just as fast on the bandsaw. And unlike a tablesaw, a bandsaw allows for stopped tapered cuts. My adjustable jig slides between the bandsaw's fence and a plywood guide, which is attached to the table and prevents the jig from wandering into the blade. Two similar jigs, one 24 in. long and one 48 in. long, accommodate different-size workpieces. Toggle clamps can be used to hold any length of workpiece securely.

When tapering four sides of, say, a table leg, always rotate the stock so that the newly tapered side faces up. This way, for the first two cuts, the workpiece's flat sides bear on the jig and its fence. Rotating the leg for the third cut places a taper against the fence, but an offcut between the two will keep the leg straight. For the fourth cut, an offcut at the fence and another placed between the leg and the bed of the jig will support the leg. The offcuts are taped into position slightly forward of the stop to accommodate the wood lost to the bandsaw kerf.

Threaded knob

Adjustable stop, 1/4 in. thick by 1 in. wide by 5 in. long

1/4-20 hanger bolt, 2 1/2 in. long

Adjustable fence, 3/4 in. thick by 3 in. wide by 25 in. long

Slot, centered, 1/4 in. wide by 11/8 in. long

Tenon, 1/4 in. thick by 1/4 in. deep, notched for hanger bolt

Pivot hole

Adhesive-backed sandpaper

Cutout for blade

Plywood base, 3/4 in. thick by 8 in. wide by 24 in. long

Slot, 1/4 in. wide by 6 1/4 in. long, recessed on the underside for carriage bolt

Plywood guide, 3/4 in. thick by 9 in. wide by 13 in. long

1/4-20 carriage bolt, 1 1/2 in. long

Cutout for tabletop adjuster

Rabbet, to fit table edge

Clamping block, 1 1/2 in. thick by 1 1/2 in. wide by 12 in. long

Jig setup. Adjust the rip fence so that the jig is almost touching the blade. Then clamp down the plywood guide, which should just allow the jig to slide.

Locate the taper's end. Marks on the stock align with the edge of the jig, which is the cut line. After fixing the outfeed knob, adjust the stop to clear the blade.

Locate the taper's start. Align the beginning of the taper with the edge of the jig and tighten the infeed knob.

Make circles of all sizes

This is a useful jig that's also fun. The workpiece turns on the jig's pivot point and cuts circles and arcs with a wide range of radii. I thread the jig with a ¼-20 tap, so it will accommodate any size pivot point I care to grind from a bolt. They can range from the full ¼-in. dia. for heavier pieces, to a needle point for delicate work. To avoid a center mark on the stock, attach a sacrificial surface to the underside of the workpiece with double-sided tape.

The pivot point is in a sliding arm dovetailed into the body of the jig. This arm can be moved gently forward while you rotate the stock into the blade, initially creating a spiral-shaped cut. A stop block clamped to the outboard end of the arm hits the body of the jig when you reach the correct radius, and only then does the blade begin to cut in a circle.

Make the track and sliding arm of a hard and stable wood. The sliding arm and track are dovetailed so that the arm does not tip out of the track, and the bearing surfaces are waxed. The track could be dovetailed directly into the body of the jig, but it is easier and will remain more accurate if a strip of hardwood is dovetailed, then set into a dado.

Keep in mind: The bandsaw blade must be narrow enough to cut the desired radius, and the cutting edge of the teeth must align with the centerline of the pivot point on the sliding arm. If the pivot is forward or back of the teeth, the blade will not cut freely and the circle will not be true.

Spiral into the circle. With the saw running, gently push the arm forward while rotating the stock into the blade (above right). Once the stop reaches the end of the guide track, the blade starts to cut the actual circle (right).

2 CIRCLE-CUTTING JIG

The sliding pivot arm on this jig allows cutting circles of any diameter your shop and your back can handle.

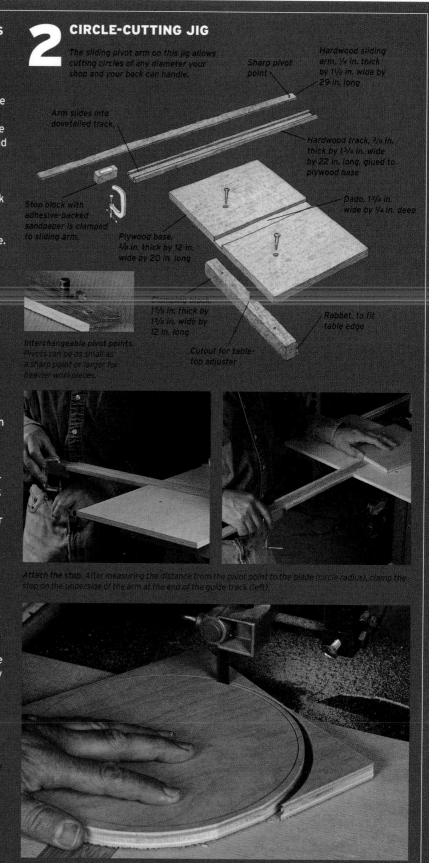

Sharp pivot point

Hardwood sliding arm, ¼ in. thick by 1⅛ in. wide by 29 in. long

Arm slides into dovetailed track.

Hardwood track, ⅜ in. thick by 1¾ in. wide by 22 in. long, glued to plywood base

Stop block with adhesive-backed sandpaper is clamped to sliding arm.

Dado, 1¾ in. wide by ¼ in. deep

Plywood base, ⅜ in. thick by 12 in. wide by 20 in. long

Clamping block, 1⅜ in. thick by 1⅝ in. wide by 12 in. long

Rabbet, to fit table edge

Cutout for tabletop adjuster

Interchangeable pivot points. Pivots can be as small as a sharp point or larger for heavier workpieces.

Attach the stop. After measuring the distance from the pivot point to the blade (circle radius), clamp the stop on the underside of the arm at the end of the guide track (left).

Cut small wedges safely

This simple and safe jig allows the cutting of identical wedges. The jig rides against the fence, which is set so that the blade just misses the jig. Notches the size and shape of the wedges are cut in the jig, and they hold the stock as it's cut. As a new size of wedge is needed, I add a new notch to the jig. For repeat projects, each notch is labeled with the project name and the dimensions of the wedge.

I start with a piece of stock that's crosscut to the length of the wedge, and flip the blank over with every cut. The MDF base serves as a zero-clearance throat plate that stops the wedges from binding in the bandsaw's more open throat plate. When the stock gets too small to handle safely, I switch to a new piece or use a push stick.

3 TENON WEDGE JIG

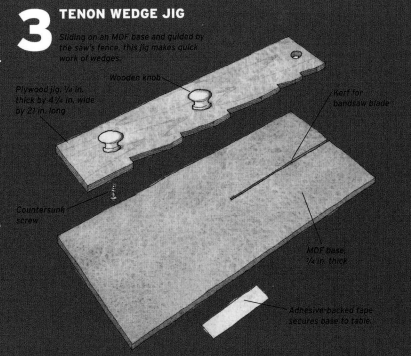

Sliding on an MDF base and guided by the saw's fence, this jig makes quick work of wedges.

Wooden knob

Plywood jig, ¼ in. thick by 4¼ in. wide by 21 in. long

Kerf for bandsaw blade

Countersunk screw

MDF base, ¼ in. thick

Adhesive-backed tape secures base to table.

Cut notches on the jig freehand. Draw the wedge on the jig, by tracing it or by determining its angle or its length and width. Clearly mark these measurements on the jig.

The wedge-o-matic. Place the long-grain end of the stock against the long edge of the notch. Flip the stock forward with each pass.

Small wedges require a zero-clearance throat plate. Attach a piece of ¼-in. MDF on the table with double-sided tape to prevent pieces from getting trapped in the throat plate.

Safely reproduce curved shapes

Finger jigs are used to guide carefully made patterns on the bandsaw. The finger spaces the pattern just slightly away from the bandsaw blade, leaving a small amount of material to be worked by hand, or as I frequently do, shaped by a router outfitted with a flush-trimming bit. The pattern works with both the bandsaw and the router. This is a great technique for making multiples of curved chair parts such as rails or stretchers.

The blade is positioned within the notch at the end of the finger. The distance the finger protrudes past the blade determines the amount of wood overhanging the edge of the pattern when the cut is complete. The ends of the finger should be curved slightly tighter than any curve on the pattern.

Simple, shallow curves can be bandsawn by clamping the finger jig directly to the table, and affixing the stock above the pattern (4). For complex curves, it is better to position the pattern and the finger jig above the stock so that the contact between the finger and pattern is visible (5). It's a little trickier to secure the stock to the pattern in this case. If you don't mind the holes, screws through the face of the stock can be used. If holes are a problem, hold the stock to the pattern with wedges or dowels, as shown on the facing page.

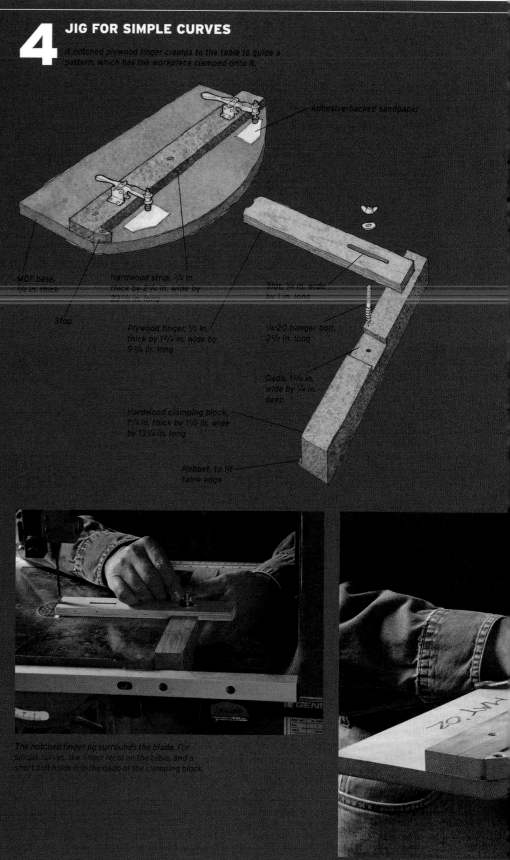

4 JIG FOR SIMPLE CURVES

A notched plywood finger clamps to the table to guide a pattern, which has the workpiece clamped onto it.

Adhesive-backed sandpaper

MDF base, ¾ in. thick

Hardwood strip, ¾ in. thick by 2¼ in. wide by 23¼ in. long

Stop

Slot, ¼ in. wide by 1 in. long

Plywood finger, ½ in. thick by 1¾ in. wide by 9¾ in. long

¼-20 hanger bolt, 2½ in. long

Dado, 1¾ in. wide by ¼ in. deep

Hardwood clamping block, 1¼ in. thick by 1½ in. wide by 13½ in. long

Rabbet, to fit table edge

The notched finger jig surrounds the blade. For simple curves, the finger rests on the table, and a short bolt holds it in the dado of the clamping block.

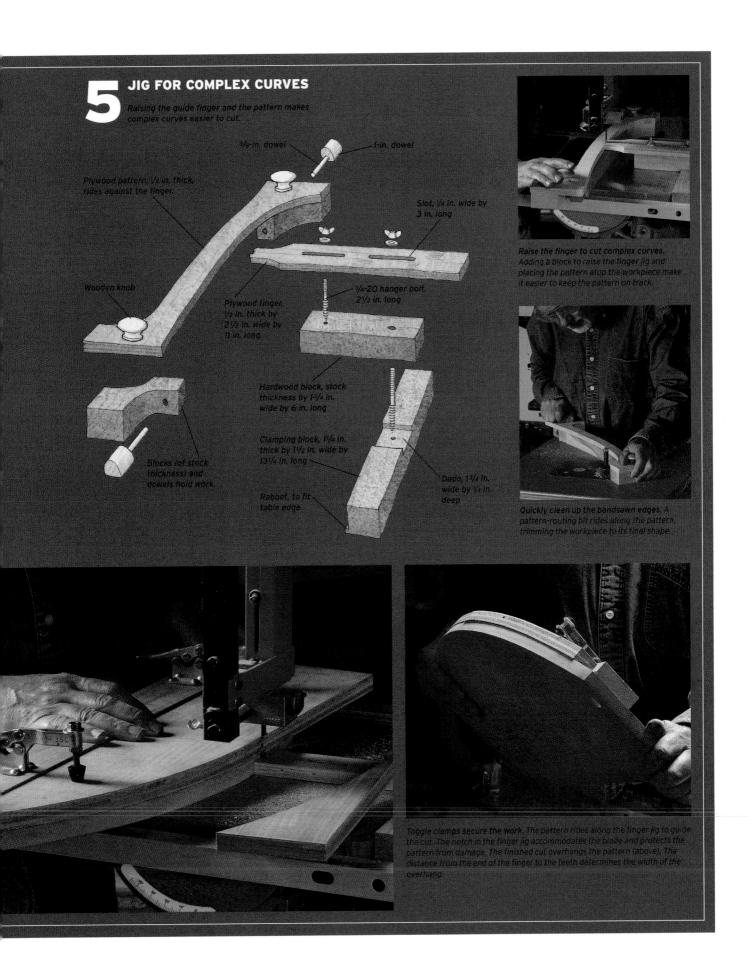

5 JIG FOR COMPLEX CURVES

Raising the guide finger and the pattern makes complex curves easier to cut.

³⁄₈-in. dowel

1-in. dowel

Plywood pattern, ½ in. thick, rides against the finger.

Slot, ¼ in. wide by 3 in. long

Wooden knob

Plywood finger, ½ in. thick by 2½ in. wide by 11 in. long

¼-20 hanger bolt, 2½ in. long

Blocks (of stock thickness) and dowels hold work.

Hardwood block, stock thickness by 1¾ in. wide by 6 in. long

Clamping block, 1¼ in. thick by 1½ in. wide by 13¼ in. long

Dado, 1¾ in. wide by ¼ in. deep

Rabbet, to fit table edge

Raise the finger to cut complex curves. Adding a block to raise the finger jig and placing the pattern atop the workpiece make it easier to keep the pattern on track.

Quickly clean up the bandsawn edges. A pattern-routing bit rides along the pattern, trimming the workpiece to its final shape.

Toggle clamps secure the work. The pattern rides along the finger jig to guide the cut. The notch in the finger jig accommodates the blade and protects the pattern from damage. The finished cut overhangs the pattern (above). The distance from the end of the finger to the teeth determines the width of the overhang.

BANDSAW BASE DESIGNED FOR RESAWING

By John White

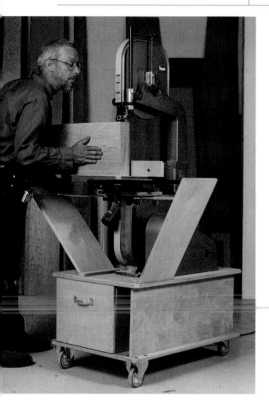

I recommend a serious upgrade for a bandsaw being used exclusively for resawing. It adds infeed and outfeed supports to make it easier to support wide and long boards. Also, the factory-supplied base is replaced with a shorter, shopmade base that lowers the saw table to a more comfortable resawing height. I also add a tall fence to help guide the stock through the blade.

Add the infeed and outfeed supports

The infeed and outfeed supports are simply ¾-in.-thick plywood panels that tip out from the top of the base. The panels are held in place by support rods made out of large turnbuckles. The rods attach to the saw by slipping around the shank of the knobs that lock the table trunnions. The turnbuckles make it easy to fine-tune the supports to the bandsaw's table height. The panels rest against stop blocks on the saw's base. Eyebolts screwed into the stop blocks help

position the piece on the base. And the support rods just hook over the knobs. Removing the panels takes only a few seconds.

To enlarge the stock steel base enough to accept the infeed and outfeed supports, add a piece of plywood between the steel base and the cast-iron frame.

To make a support rod, replace the right-hand threaded eyebolt on each turnbuckle with a longer bolt that has an eye large enough to slip around the shank of the trunnion lock-knob. Once the eyebolts have been adjusted, add nuts to lock them in place. Because one of the threads in each turnbuckle is left-handed, you'll need a left-handed nut to lock that side. I had no problem finding all of the hardware I needed at the local hardware store.

The infeed support should tilt at about a 45-degree angle. That way, the top end of the support can't be easily pushed and lifted by the board it's holding up. The outfeed support, however, should be installed at a more upright angle so that you can move the outfeed table's stop block away from the saw and clear the cover for the drive belt. The top end of the support cannot lift because, on the outfeed end, the drag of the board pulls against the support rod.

There's a simple way to determine the length of the supports. Make

them longer than necessary. Hold them in position against a straightedge placed across the saw table, mark, and cut. The top and bottom edges of the supports are rounded over with a ⅜-in.-radius router bit.

Make the base

For ripping and resawing, the table of a bandsaw should be close to the height of a tablesaw, not the 42-in. to 45-in. height typical of bandsaws on factory-supplied bases. A high table is fine for cutting small stock, but it's awkward for working with large boards being run against a fence. I made my new base as low as possible. The saw's table ended up just shy of 39 in. high, and now it's much easier to handle stock.

The base is a simple box made of Baltic birch plywood and assembled using butt joints and screws. A large drawer provides room for bandsaw blades and miscellaneous small parts. In addition to the drawer, a compartment on one side serves as a place to store the infeed and outfeed supports. The bolts mounting the casters thread into capped insert nuts. The 3-in.-wide gap above the back panel of the box allows access to the motor-mounting bolts.

The motor is simply bolted in place with its pulley in line with the pulley on the saw. The belt tension is adjusted by adding or removing

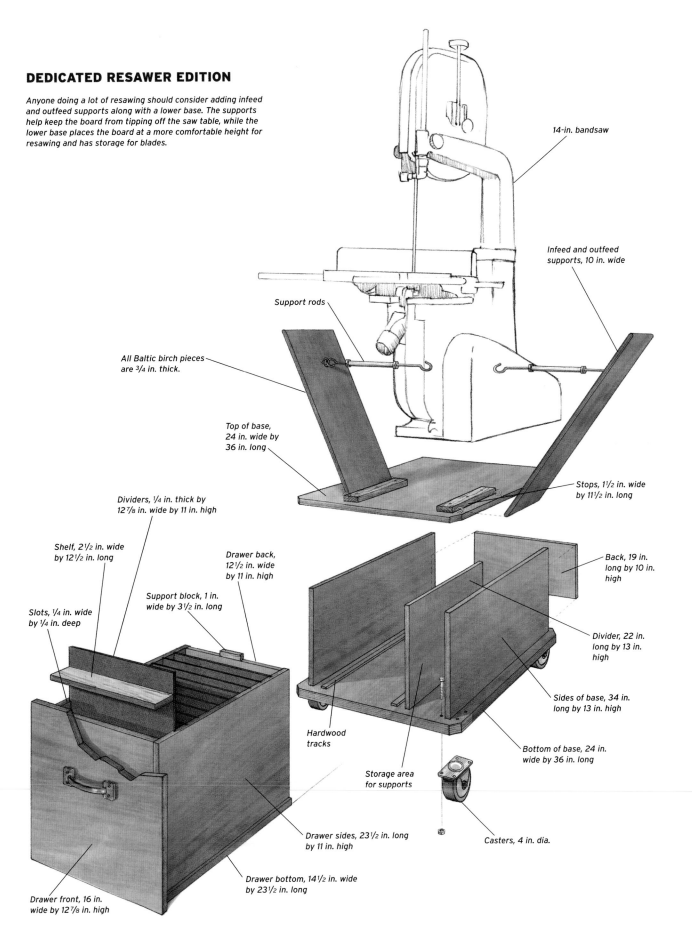

DEDICATED RESAWER EDITION

Anyone doing a lot of resawing should consider adding infeed and outfeed supports along with a lower base. The supports help keep the board from tipping off the saw table, while the lower base places the board at a more comfortable height for resawing and has storage for blades.

14-in. bandsaw

Infeed and outfeed supports, 10 in. wide

Support rods

All Baltic birch pieces are 3/4 in. thick.

Top of base, 24 in. wide by 36 in. long

Stops, 1 1/2 in. wide by 11 1/2 in. long

Dividers, 1/4 in. thick by 12 7/8 in. wide by 11 in. high

Shelf, 2 1/2 in. wide by 12 1/2 in. long

Drawer back, 12 1/2 in. wide by 11 in. high

Back, 19 in. long by 10 in. high

Support block, 1 in. wide by 3 1/2 in. long

Slots, 1/4 in. wide by 1/4 in. deep

Divider, 22 in. long by 13 in. high

Sides of base, 34 in. long by 13 in. high

Hardwood tracks

Storage area for supports

Bottom of base, 24 in. wide by 36 in. long

Drawer sides, 23 1/2 in. long by 11 in. high

Casters, 4 in. dia.

Drawer front, 16 in. wide by 12 7/8 in. high

Drawer bottom, 14 1/2 in. wide by 23 1/2 in. long

sections from a link belt. Using a link belt eliminates the need for a sliding motor mount. On my saw I was able to reuse the original belt guard. If that's not possible on your saw, make a simple plywood box to cover the belt and pulleys.

The drawer slides on hardwood tracks attached to the bottom of the base. A single hardwood block attached to the top back edge of the drawer prevents the drawer from tipping when extended. The block is slightly oversize and mounted with two recessed screws. Then, for a smooth sliding fit, trim it to size with a block plane.

Add an auxiliary fence

I also made a tall auxiliary fence to support a board during resawing (see the drawing and photos on the facing page). The fence is short in length but sturdy enough that it remains square to the table when pressure is applied. In addition, it is easy to adjust the fence angle to eliminate blade drift—the propensity for a bandsaw blade to wander from a straight line during a cut. One thing to note: If the factory-supplied fence on your bandsaw is of little value, you'll need to get a better fence before you can add this resaw fence.

My auxiliary fence extends to just past the trailing edge of the blade. There's a reason for this short length. Thick stock often has a fair amount of tension in the wood, even when carefully dried. When you're resawing, the tension in the wood is released, sometimes causing the offcut to bend or twist into the fence, which means you'll have to push pretty hard to keep the board against the fence. By using a fence that is short in length—much like that on a European-style tablesaw— you can keep the uncut portion of the board firmly against the fence

Supports assemble in seconds. Mounting the infeed and outfeed supports is simple. One end butts against a stop, and the other hooks to the underside of the saw table.

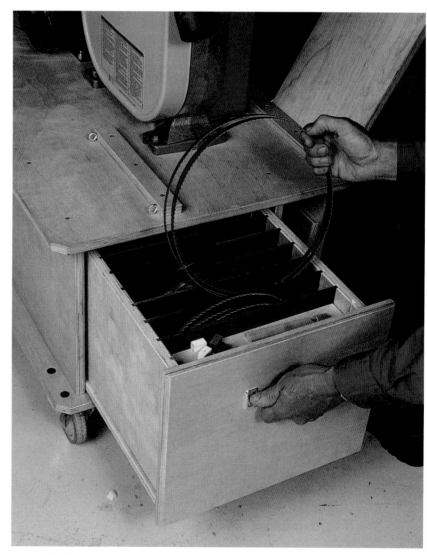

Drawer offers storage. The single drawer can hold several coiled bandsaw blades, while the shelf in front is a handy place for small parts. The supports slide into the compartment on the right.

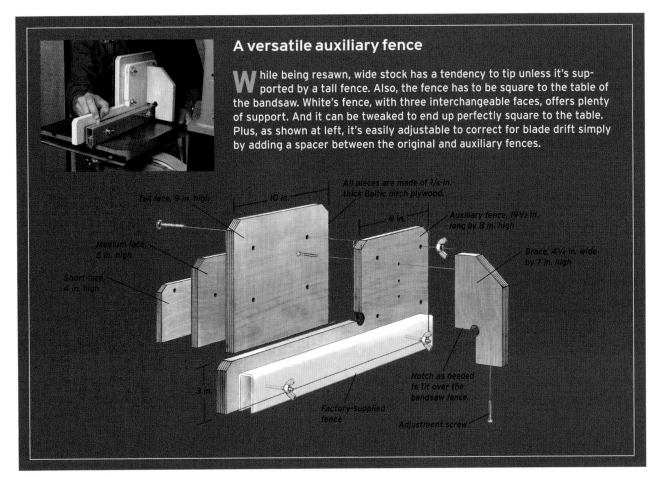

A versatile auxiliary fence

While being resawn, wide stock has a tendency to tip unless it's supported by a tall fence. Also, the fence has to be square to the table of the bandsaw. White's fence, with three interchangeable faces, offers plenty of support. And it can be tweaked to end up perfectly square to the table. Plus, as shown at left, it's easily adjustable to correct for blade drift simply by adding a spacer between the original and auxiliary fences.

Tall face, 9 in. high

10 in.

All pieces are made of ³⁄₄-in.-thick Baltic birch plywood.

8 in.

Auxiliary fence, 19½ in. long by 8 in. high

Medium face, 6 in. high

Short face, 4 in. high

Brace, 4¾ in. wide by 7 in. high

3 in.

Notch as needed to fit over the bandsaw fence.

Factory-supplied fence

Adjustment screw

while the offcut is free to bend or twist into the open air.

The fence I installed has two main components: a back piece with a brace that bolts to the original fence and a set of interchangeable faces, each one of a different height. The idea here is to use a face that is narrower than the board to be resawn but wide enough to support the board adequately during the cut. That way, both for safety and maximum blade support, the blade guard along with the upper blade guide can be lowered close to the top edge of the board.

With this fence, it's easy to adjust for blade drift by adding spacers between the original fence and the auxiliary fence, changing the angle of the fence relative to the blade. Dowels or small hardwood blocks work fine as spacers. On some blades, the drift can be considerable. One blade I use needs a ³⁄₄-in.-thick spacer before it cuts straight.

For accurate cuts, the auxiliary fence should be square to the table. Sometimes, however, a factory-supplied fence won't be quite as square as you'd like. To correct for this out of squareness, mount thin shims (I use strips of aluminum flashing attached with double-faced tape) to the back of the fence. The shims should be long enough to bear on any spacer that is added to correct for blade drift. Once the auxiliary fence has been squared to the table, adjust the screw on the bottom of the brace to give the fence added support.

John White is the author of Care and Repair of Shop Machines *(The Taunton Press, 2002).*

Smooth sawing. *The face of the fence extends just past the sawblade teeth. That way, should the cutoff piece curl outward, it can't push the board away from the fence during the cut.*

SHOPMADE PLANER TABLE

by Andy Beasley

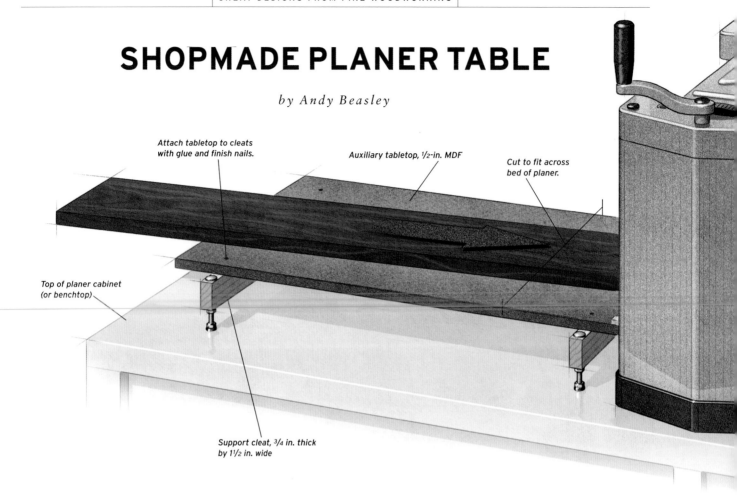

Attach tabletop to cleats with glue and finish nails.

Auxiliary tabletop, 1/2-in. MDF

Cut to fit across bed of planer.

Top of planer cabinet (or benchtop)

Support cleat, 3/4 in. thick by 1 1/2 in. wide

Benchtop thickness planers are compact workhorses that produce remarkably smooth wood surfaces. But, like any thickness planer, they often create snipe—that's the 2-in.-long (or so), slightly deeper cut at each end of a board. Granted, some newer models have made good strides at reducing the problem, but like the common cold, snipe defies eradication. Indeed, it's rare to find a thickness-planed board that's snipe-free.

However, adding an adjustable table to a benchtop thickness planer can help make snipe a non-issue—if not by eliminating the problem, then at least by keeping it to a bare minimum. Snipe that measures less than, say, 0.004 in. is rarely a problem.

This adjustable table has only a handful of parts. Four support cleats—two in front of the planer, two behind—mount under a length of 1/2-in.-thick medium-density fiberboard (MDF) that serves as the tabletop. The cleats attach to the top of the planer cabinet with a few carriage bolts and washers. The bolts allow me to elevate the ends of the tabletop slightly, giving it a subtle bow. This slight rise at each end is the secret to reducing snipe. Adjusting the outside support cleats is easy: After loosening the hex nuts adjacent to the cabinet, simply tighten the upper nut to raise the

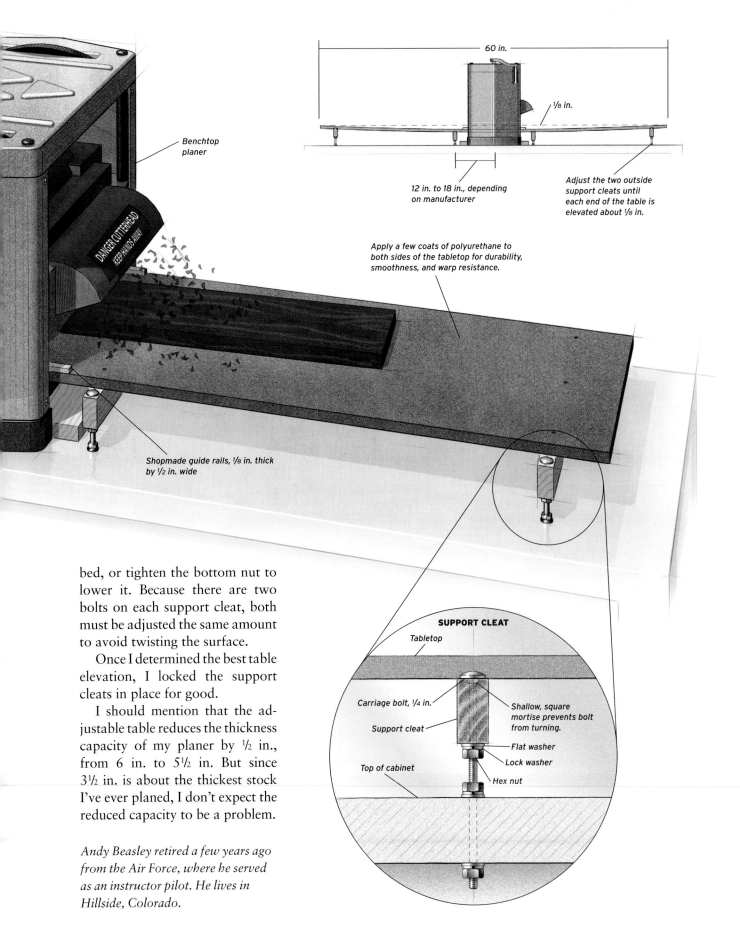

Benchtop planer

60 in.

1/8 in.

12 in. to 18 in., depending on manufacturer

Adjust the two outside support cleats until each end of the table is elevated about 1/8 in.

Apply a few coats of polyurethane to both sides of the tabletop for durability, smoothness, and warp resistance.

Shopmade guide rails, 1/8 in. thick by 1/2 in. wide

DANGER CUTTERHEAD KEEP HANDS AWAY

SUPPORT CLEAT

Tabletop

Carriage bolt, 1/4 in.

Support cleat

Shallow, square mortise prevents bolt from turning.

Flat washer

Lock washer

Top of cabinet

Hex nut

bed, or tighten the bottom nut to lower it. Because there are two bolts on each support cleat, both must be adjusted the same amount to avoid twisting the surface.

Once I determined the best table elevation, I locked the support cleats in place for good.

I should mention that the adjustable table reduces the thickness capacity of my planer by ½ in., from 6 in. to 5½ in. But since 3½ in. is about the thickest stock I've ever planed, I don't expect the reduced capacity to be a problem.

Andy Beasley retired a few years ago from the Air Force, where he served as an instructor pilot. He lives in Hillside, Colorado.

by *Greg Colegrove*

DANGER CUTTERHEAD
KEEP HANDS AWAY

A flat, stable planer bed reduces snipe. The author's height-adjustable feed table and platform, both made of Melamine, have practically eliminated the problem. Maple edging prevents boards from wandering off the table.

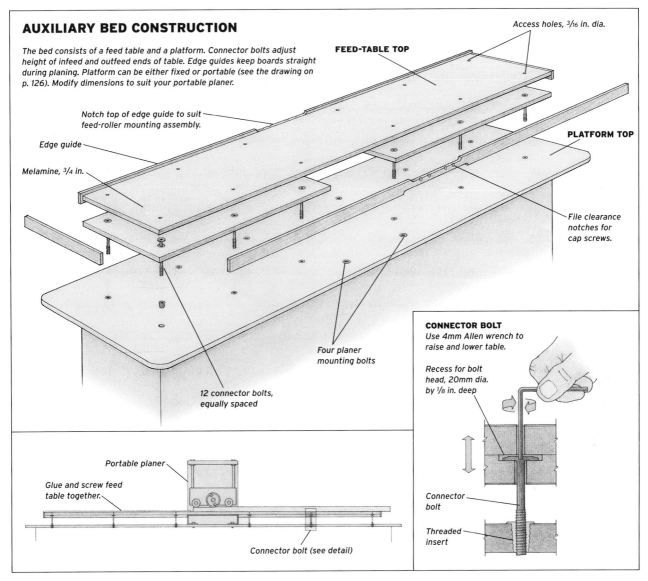

AUXILIARY BED CONSTRUCTION

The bed consists of a feed table and a platform. Connector bolts adjust height of infeed and outfeed ends of table. Edge guides keep boards straight during planing. Platform can be either fixed or portable (see the drawing on p. 126). Modify dimensions to suit your portable planer.

Access holes, 3/16 in. dia.

FEED-TABLE TOP

Notch top of edge guide to suit feed-roller mounting assembly.

Edge guide

Melamine, 3/4 in.

PLATFORM TOP

File clearance notches for cap screws.

Four planer mounting bolts

12 connector bolts, equally spaced

CONNECTOR BOLT
Use 4mm Allen wrench to raise and lower table.

Recess for bolt head, 20mm dia. by 1/8 in. deep

Connector bolt

Threaded insert

Portable planer

Glue and screw feed table together.

Connector bolt (see detail)

Portable thickness planers that I've used have an annoying habit of sniping the ends of boards. My 12-in. Delta planer is no exception. I initially accepted that I'd have to scrap 2½ in. on both ends of every board I planed. But soon my conscience and checkbook convinced me there had to be a better way. Because I really am a rocket scientist, I figured I should be able to cure this otherwise fine machine of its hiccups.

Snipe is a deep cut, like a divot, in one or both ends of a planed board (see the inset photo on the facing page). Snipe occurs when the end of the board tilts upward into the cutterhead. Portable planers are known to be snipers because of their short, rollerless beds. Planers that are adjusted for depth of cut by raising and lowering the head are particularly susceptible.

This problem is hard to correct on many small planers because they don't have large, stable beds. A machinery engineer I spoke with confided that the best I could expect with a planer like mine, without any modifications, was about .005 in. of snipe. I knew I could do better, so I started looking for ways to improve support for the workpiece as it passed through the planer.

Designing a rigid, height-adjustable auxiliary bed

My first effort consisted of extension rollers, which required far too much fiddling, and the rollers had no guides to keep stock moving straight. Then I saw a planer auxiliary bed at a local woodshop that went right through the mouth of the planer. I went back to my shop and adapted the idea, making a table that was stiff but adjustable in height.

The adjustable bed has reduced my planer's snipe to between .002 in. and .003 in. Such a small discrepancy in thickness is easy to sand or handplane out. And with the long bed, I don't have to feed and retrieve one board at a time. Stock up to about 4½ ft. long is supported at the far end, so I can plane several in a bunch, left to right, or in succession, end to end. Gang-feeding eliminates snipe altogether.

The auxiliary bed reduces my planer's depth-of-cut capacity by ¾ in., but I rarely plane anything thicker than 4 in. anyway. If I'm planing large, heavy planks, I put blocks under both ends of the table to avoid damaging or moving them.

Choose from two different support platforms

I've built two different versions of the auxiliary bed: one in which the feed table sits on a dedicated base and one that can be moved. The only difference between the feed tables is length. The first bed, which sits on a cabinet platform, is designed for stock up to 6 ft. long.

The second bed, which I built for a cabinetmaker friend, is 8 ft. long and has a more compact platform. It must be placed on a stable bench or work table (see the photo at right), but it will handle longer stock and is more portable. With the help of a buddy, you could stand the unit—with the planer attached—against a wall, store it overhead or transport it in a truck or van. Most portable planers don't come with stands, so it's nice to have the planer at a comfortable operating height.

You should be able to build either one of these planer auxiliary beds for less than $75. I made both units primarily out of white Melamine, which provides a flat, low-friction surface for the feed table. And with Melamine, it's easy to spot and remove wood chips and debris. For a rigid table, I fastened two layers of ¾-in. Melamine together.

You will need a bit of hardwood to make edge guides for the tables. I used ¼-in.-thick maple strips that extend ¼ in. above the surface. I also covered the Melamine ends with maple trim, this time flush with the tabletop. Not too long ago, I added a planer hood that's connected to a dust collector. The table should be kept free of chips; otherwise, boards will plane inconsistently.

I can adjust the flatness of the feed table with 12 connector bolts that join the table to its support platform. To reduce friction, I periodically spray the feed table with TopCote®, a dry lubricant.

Greg Colegrove is a rocket-launch countdown specialist. He runs a part-time furnituremaking business in Aurora, Colorado.

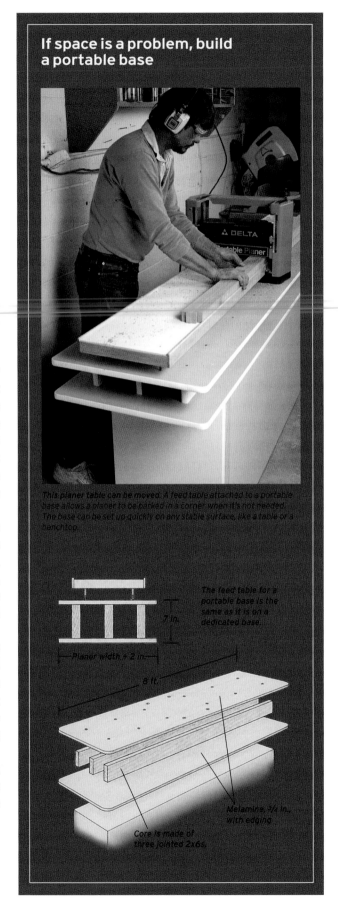

If space is a problem, build a portable base

This planer table can be moved. A feed table attached to a portable base allows a planer to be parked in a corner when it's not needed. The base can be set up quickly on any stable surface, like a table or a benchtop.

The feed table for a portable base is the same as it is on a dedicated base.

7 in.

Planer width + 2 in.

8 ft.

Melamine, ¾ in., with edging

Core is made of three jointed 2x6s.

ADJUSTABLE PLANER SLED
SURFACES WARPED STOCK

By Keith Rust

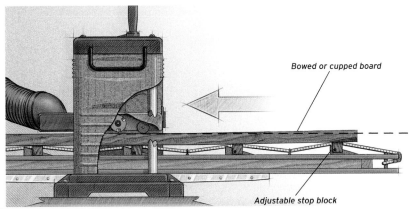

THE SLED SUPPORTS WARPED BOARDS

A jointer is the proper tool for flattening a single face of a board. But many woodworkers lack a jointer that can handle wide boards. This sled supports a cupped or bowed board so the planer can act like a jointer, producing a flat and straight surface. The board then can be flipped over and planed conventionally to mill it to final thickness.

Bowed or cupped board

Adjustable stop block

Working with wide lumber is a joy: The figure and color are seamless, just as it came off the log. But many woodworkers face a problem when it comes to flattening one side of a wide board. We can rip the board into narrower pieces, use a 6-in. or 8-in. jointer, and then rejoin the parts, but a perfect match is not always possible. The alternative is to handplane one side flat, a laborious process.

Now, I like handplaning as much as the next guy, but I prefer to save my energy and let machines dimension lumber. To this end, I designed an adjustable sled that allows me to face-joint lumber with a thickness planer. The sled

JOINTER SLED FOR THE PLANER

The body of the sled must be rigid, dead flat, and not too heavy, which makes a torsion-box design the best choice. The rough board that needs flattening rests on a series of supports that are adjusted to fit the board using sliding wedges.

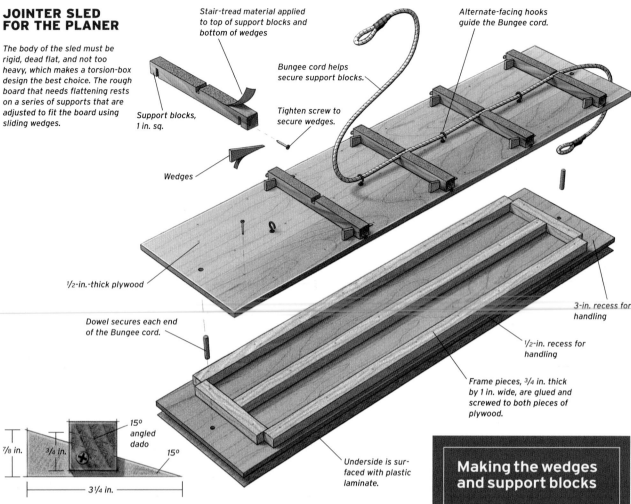

Stair-tread material applied to top of support blocks and bottom of wedges

Bungee cord helps secure support blocks.

Tighten screw to secure wedges.

Support blocks, 1 in. sq.

Wedges

Alternate-facing hooks guide the Bungee cord.

1/2-in.-thick plywood

Dowel secures each end of the Bungee cord.

3-in. recess for handling

1/2-in. recess for handling

Frame pieces, 3/4 in. thick by 1 in. wide, are glued and screwed to both pieces of plywood.

Underside is surfaced with plastic laminate.

15° angled dado

7/8 in.   3/4 in.   15°

3 1/4 in.

is reliable and quick to set up and adjust without using any tools. To make it, you first need to determine the maximum width the bed of your planer will accept and how long a sled you want. My 12 1/2-in. portable planer could handle a sled of the same width, but to avoid having too tight a fit, I opted for a 12-in.-wide sled.

The top of the sled has a series of stock supports made of hardwood milled to 1 in. square. To determine their length, measure your planer's inside clearance, keeping in mind that the supports will have about 1/2 in. of a drywall screw sticking out each end. My planer allowed for 11 1/2-in.-long supports with no danger of a screw head touching anything on the way through.

In use, the supports—held in place by a Bungee® cord—are raised or lowered using 15-degree wedges made from 1/4-in.-thick medium-density fiber-board (MDF).

In use, the supports adjust to stabilize warped stock. Once the stock is secure in the sled, I simply run the assembly through the planer.

I recently built a chest of drawers with bent-laminated drawer fronts and had no trouble using this sled to flatten 11-in.-wide hard maple to make drawer-front plies. This is a jig (unlike some I've attempted) that has proven to be worth far more than the original time invested in designing and building it.

Keith Rust lives in Arlington, Texas.

Sled setup

Place the board on the sled. If it is cupped, rest it with the concave side facing down. Rock the board to locate high spots.

Adjust the support blocks. Slide the wedge until the block just touches the board. Then tighten the drywall screw by hand to lock the wedge in place.

Using the sled

Flatten one side. With the planer turned off, slide the sled through to check for obstructions and to determine the highest point on the board. After the first pass, check and adjust the wedges, if necessary. Once you have flattened one surface of the board, you can dispense with the sled and run the other side of the board through the planer to thickness it.

Using the jig

Once the jig is made, it takes little time to rout a mortise. A standard straight bit works just fine, although a spiral upcut bit does a better job clearing chips from the mortise.

Clamp the workpiece to the workbench. A pair of hold-downs anchors the workpiece to the jig.

Set the bit depth. With the desired mortise depth marked on the workpiece, adjust the bit depth on the router.

Center the bit. After marking the location of the mortise, adjust the edge guide to center the bit in the mortise.

Stop blocks establish the mortise length. Stop blocks on each side of the router base limit the travel of the base.

VERSATILE MORTISING JIG

by Jeff Miller

A plunge router, rather than a fixed-base router, is pretty much a must to cut mortises. Any effort to tip the bit of a fixed-base router into a workpiece to create a mortise is not only dangerous, but it's also likely to produce an inaccurate cut. A midsize (1½ hp to 2½ hp) plunger is sufficient, as this technique creates mortises by making lots of light cuts.

The diameter of the router bit determines the width of the mortise. For example, a ¼-in.-wide mortise is cut with a ¼-in.-dia. bit; and a ¾-in.-wide mortise is cut with a ¾-in.-dia. bit. You also could choose a mortise width that requires moving the router over and taking extra passes to widen the opening. But because straight bits are available in so many sizes, you can usually find one to match the mortise width you need.

It's important to support and guide the plunge router as it cuts. A jig goes a long way toward providing the necessary support, ensuring a well-cut mortise. The jig I use is very simple (see the drawing on the facing page), with just three wooden parts: a body, a spacer strip, and a guide strip.

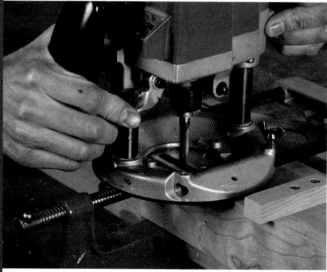

Take light cuts until you reach the final depth. To produce smooth, straight-sided mortises, make multiple passes with the router, with each pass removing no more than 1/32 in. of stock.

A pair of hold-downs are used to secure the workpiece to the body. With the hold-downs in place, the jig accepts stock up to about 2¾ in. wide. To work with wider stock, simply remove the hold-downs and secure the workpiece with a couple of C-clamps.

You'll also need to make a wooden auxiliary fence to attach to the edge guide of the router. The auxiliary fence offers two benefits. It increases the length of the edge guide, providing extra support during a cut. And because the auxiliary fence fits into a groove created by the spacer and guide strips, it prevents the edge guide from shifting away from the body, and that means the router can't wander from a straight-line cut.

In use, the fence slides back and forth in the groove. The clearance between the fence and the groove should be no more than the thickness of a sheet of paper. To help the parts slide easily, I like to add a thin coat of wax to both the groove and the auxiliary fence.

Jeff Miller builds furniture in his Chicago shop (www. furnituremaking.com). He also teaches and writes about woodworking.

A stop block for multiple mortises

When several identical workpieces require mortises, Miller adds a stop block to the front of the mortising jig (see the bottom left photo on the facing page), allowing him to position each piece quickly.

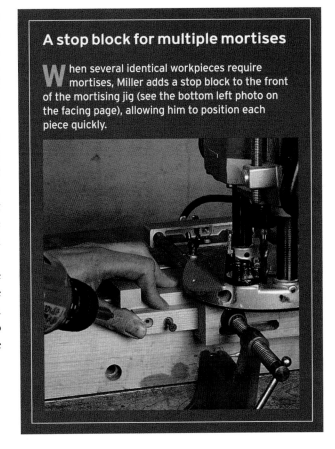

A SIMPLE MORTISING JIG

A sturdy jig, used with a plunge router and edge guide, ensures well-cut mortises. An auxiliary fence, mounted to the edge guide, slides in a groove to keep the router bit running dead straight.

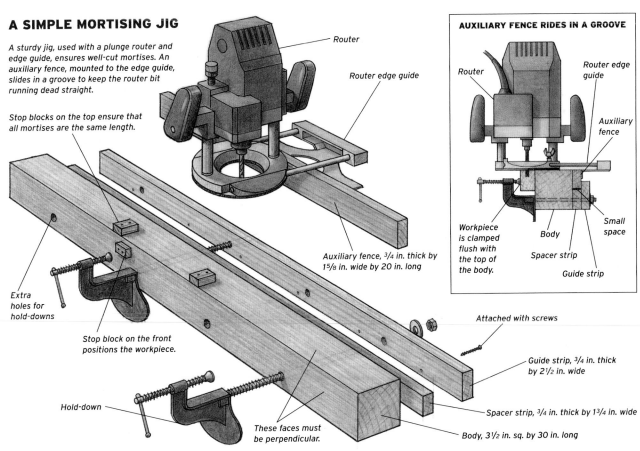

Router

Router edge guide

Stop blocks on the top ensure that all mortises are the same length.

Auxiliary fence, ¾ in. thick by 1⅝ in. wide by 20 in. long

Extra holes for hold-downs

Stop block on the front positions the workpiece.

Hold-down

These faces must be perpendicular.

Attached with screws

Guide strip, ¾ in. thick by 2½ in. wide

Spacer strip, ¾ in. thick by 1¾ in. wide

Body, 3½ in. sq. by 30 in. long

AUXILIARY FENCE RIDES IN A GROOVE

Router

Router edge guide

Auxiliary fence

Workpiece is clamped flush with the top of the body.

Body

Spacer strip

Guide strip

Small space

by Bill Ewing

A customer recently asked me to build a round column to support a peninsula countertop that he was adding to his kitchen. The 10-in.-dia., 30-in.-high column would be capped on each end. I knew there would be some difficulty building a round column out of wood, but as I do so often, I took the job with only a general idea of how to proceed.

A round wood column is typically made by joining several straight boards together in a circle, creating a multisided column. The outside of this column is then shaped into a cylinder. I could see two problems with this project: How would I glue all of the sides together? And I do not own a lathe, so how would I turn a multisided column into a smooth cylinder?

Laying out the column

My first steps were to determine the number of sides required and to check the stock thickness. Eight sides seemed about right, and I had ¾-in.-thick maple. I have learned that time spent at the drawing board pays huge rewards in the shop, so I begin by making a scale drawing of the column cross section.

The edge bevel angle needed to join the eight sides is 22½ degrees, and the side width measured about 4⅛ in. I took special notice of

the remaining stock thickness at the completed column joints (about ⅜ in.).

A holding fixture ensures precise alignment during glue-up

The challenging part of making columns this way is gluing up all eight sides at once. Looking at the cross-section drawing, I reasoned that by creating a fixture to hold every other side in a fixed position, the remaining four sides would float, or slide, into place, creating tight joints. The holding fixture is simply two plywood octagons separated by a 2×4. The octagons are designed to support every other column side, providing a hard registration surface for clamping. The other four sides of the octagon do not contact the remaining column sides.

Circle-cut the fixture support

Now to the matter of turning this eight-sided column into a cylinder: I knew I could make circular discs with a router. Because a disc is the end view of a cylinder, I guessed there would be a way of generating a cylinder using discs as a guide. With a 10-in. plywood disc mounted at each end of the column as the reference surface, a carriage could span the length of the column and ride on these discs. Traversing along the carriage, the router could then mill the faceted column into a cylinder.

Bill Ewing is a custom cabinetmaker in Girard, Ohio.

TWO-PIECE ROUTER JIG

CARRIAGE

Rail, 13/16 in.

Slot for router bit

End stop, 1/2 in. by 9/16 in.

Cap, 1/4-in. plywood

Base, 1/2-in. plywood

End piece, 3/4-in. plywood

SUPPORT FIXTURE

Workpiece

Disc, 3/4-in. plywood

Workpiece rotates on 3-in. screw.

3/4-in. plywood

2x4 leg attached to plywood with two screws

1 1/4-in. screw holds workpiece in place while routing.

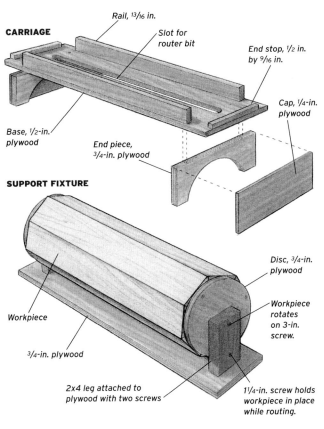

USING THE JIG

Make one left-to-right pass, return the router to the left, nudge the carriage slightly around the column, then make another pass.

When the carriage reaches the point where it will soon slip off the column, stop and reposition the column.

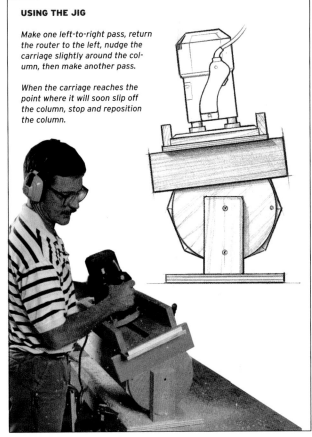

Simple jig aids glue-up

This holding fixture helps the author glue up the column sides. The fixture is simply two plywood octagons separated by a length of 2x4. The plywood octagons support every other column side, providing a hard registration surface for clamping.

Clamp four sides. Every other side of the column is clamped to the holding fixture. The remaining sides float into position.

Add tape. The tape temporarily holds the nonclamped sides in place.

Add more clamps and tie it off. The combination of clamps and rope holds the assembly solidly together.

BENCH-MOUNTED ROUTER TABLE STORES EASILY

By Paul Manning

I was getting ready to make grandfather clocks—one for each of my three children and I needed a router table. The clocks entailed routing lots of curved moldings, raised panels, and long boards; and their imminence finally forced me to think about designing a router table that would suit my needs. Because of the limited floor space in my basement shop, I hesitated to build a freestanding unit. And I discarded the idea of building a table where the router would sit on my workbench because it would make the work surface too high to work at comfortably.

It occurred to me that I could make a suitable router table that took advantage of the features of my very sturdy 8-ft.-long cabinetmaker's workbench, if I could design the table so that the router hung below the workbench surface. In effect, my router table is really only a router tabletop in that it has no legs and gets its sturdiness from being clamped to the bench. The table has three parts: the main table, which is the center section that holds the router and fence, and infeed and outfeed extension wings, which are clamped in the tails and side vises, respectively. Best yet, when I'm not using the table, the whole thing hangs on hook eyes from my basement ceiling joists, freeing up valuable floor space.

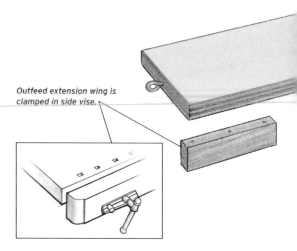

Outfeed extension wing is clamped in side vise.

Buy the fence and build the table from scraps

I bought a phenolic-resin router-base insert and a cast-aluminum router fence for about $120. I had been thinking about building a fence, and while toying around with a design idea, I came across what I thought was a perfectly adequate system that has 14-in.-long adjustable fences and a dust-collection port that plugs right into my shop vacuum.

My bench is very heavy. Even with the weight of the router and the 13-in. cantilever of the router table, the bench is sturdy enough that it won't tip forward, and thus no supporting legs are needed under the front edge of the table.

My main table is 30 in. wide and 24 in. deep, but obviously you'll have to size your table to fit the size and shape of your workbench. The most important dimension

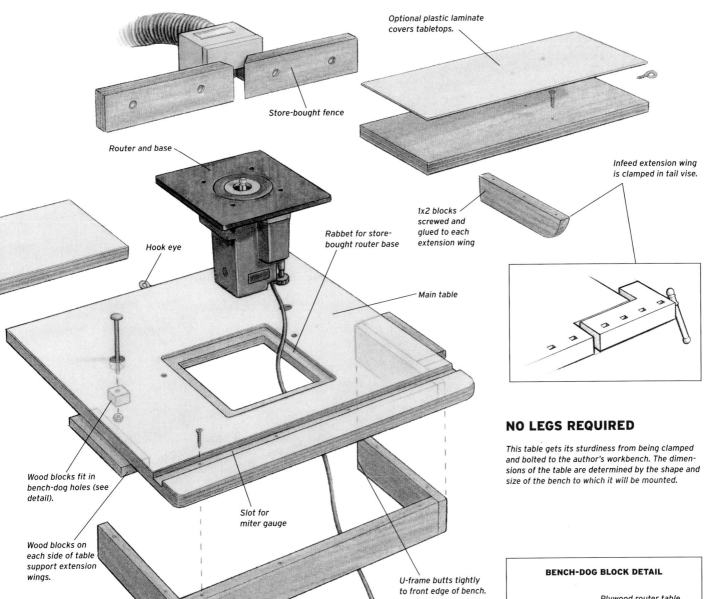

Optional plastic laminate covers tabletops.

Store-bought fence

Router and base

Infeed extension wing is clamped in tail vise.

Hook eye

Rabbet for store-bought router base

1x2 blocks screwed and glued to each extension wing

Main table

Wood blocks fit in bench-dog holes (see detail).

Wood blocks on each side of table support extension wings.

Slot for miter gauge

U-frame butts tightly to front edge of bench.

NO LEGS REQUIRED

This table gets its sturdiness from being clamped and bolted to the author's workbench. The dimensions of the table are determined by the shape and size of the bench to which it will be mounted.

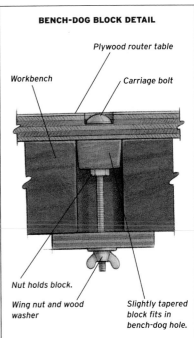

BENCH-DOG BLOCK DETAIL

Plywood router table

Workbench

Carriage bolt

Nut holds block.

Wing nut and wood washer

Slightly tapered block fits in bench-dog hole.

is the location of the router itself. It should be mounted as close as possible to the front edge of the workbench. The extension wings can be of any length and width, but I made mine 6 in. narrower than the front edge of the main table so that I can stand close to the working router bit.

The tabletop extends beyond the U-frame, permitting the use of clamps for featherboards and hold-downs and making room for a miter-gauge slot. The extensions have short pieces of hardwood underneath for insertion into the bench vises.

The table is well sealed with polyurethane, and the top surfaces are covered with plastic laminate. The plastic laminate is not an absolute necessity; a table that is well sealed and sanded smooth should be satisfactory. The grandfather clocks, by the way, turned out great.

Paul Manning lives in North Andover, Massachusettes.

STOW-AWAY ROUTER TABLE

By Jim Wright

AN EFFICIENT WORKSTATION

This router table clamps to your workbench in seconds. Measurements are guidelines; size parts to fit your bench for secure mounting.

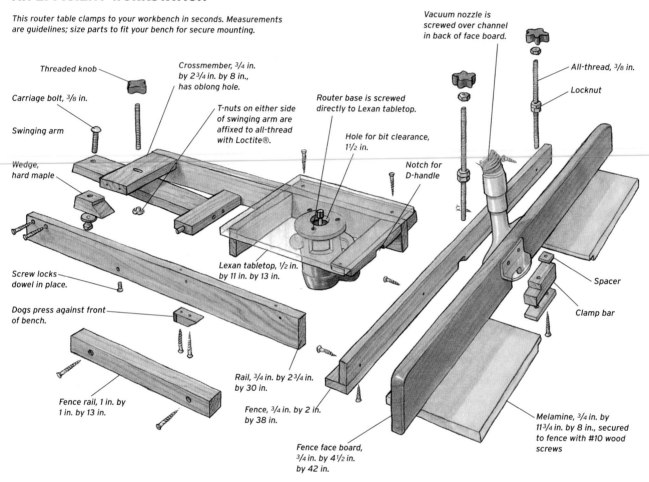

Threaded knob

Carriage bolt, 3/8 in.

Swinging arm

Wedge, hard maple

Screw locks dowel in place.

Dogs press against front of bench.

Fence rail, 1 in. by 1 in. by 13 in.

Crossmember, 3/4 in. by 2 3/4 in. by 8 in., has oblong hole.

T-nuts on either side of swinging arm are affixed to all-thread with Loctite®.

Lexan tabletop, 1/2 in. by 11 in. by 13 in.

Rail, 3/4 in. by 2 3/4 in. by 30 in.

Fence, 3/4 in. by 2 in. by 38 in.

Fence face board, 3/4 in. by 4 1/2 in. by 42 in.

Router base is screwed directly to Lexan tabletop.

Hole for bit clearance, 1 1/2 in.

Notch for D-handle

Vacuum nozzle is screwed over channel in back of face board.

All-thread, 3/8 in.

Locknut

Spacer

Clamp bar

Melamine, 3/4 in. by 11 3/4 in. by 8 in., secured to fence with #10 wood screws

---

DETAIL: ADJUSTABLE FENCE

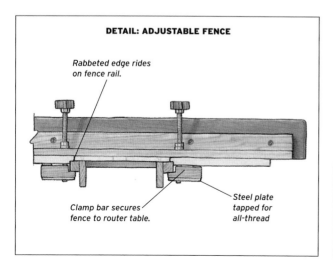

Rabbeted edge rides on fence rail.

Clamp bar secures fence to router table.

Steel plate tapped for all-thread

DETAIL: BENCH-FRAME CONNECTION

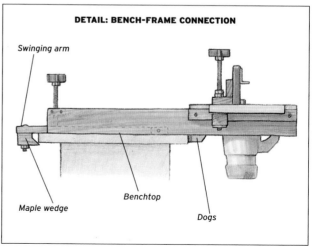

Swinging arm

Maple wedge

Benchtop

Dogs

Big router-table performance in a benchtop package. This shop-built router table sets up in seconds and stores easily when not in use. Securely clamped to your benchtop, it can do most anything more conventional router tables can.

I am afraid my early attempts at making a router table were nothing to write home about. The first three designs—a table with legs, a cabinet base, and a table attached to my tablesaw—all ended up on the scrap heap. They were just too bulky, a fatal flaw when it came to my small shop and lack of storage space.

It finally occurred to me all I really needed was a simple router table that could be clamped to my workbench. Here's how it works: I attach my router to a plastic insert and drop it into the frame of the table; the router hangs over the front edge of my bench. A sliding fence rides on top of the frame and adjusts easily. The mass of the bench keep the router table from vibrating, but best of all, the whole assembly is compact and easy to store (see the drawings on the facing page).

The key was in finding a way to clamp the assembly to my bench, so it wouldn't move. I did that by sizing the frame of the router table, so it spanned my bench exactly. Then I held the frame in place with a simple clamp made of a wooden wedge and a length of all-thread.

Build to fit

The first step is to decide how large a tabletop you need for your miter. I have a D-handle on my router, so I had to cut a relief in the framing to accommodate it. I made the frame for my router table of hard maple. The corners are fastened with #10 wood screws, so assembly is easy.

The router table stays in place because it grabs both the front and the back edge of my workbench. Attached to the rear of the router-table frame is a maple wedge that hooks over the back edge of my bench. Screwed into the bottom of the frame near the front of the table are two dogs that press against the front edge of the bench. When I tighten the knob at the back of the frame, the wedge pulls up against

the bottom of the bench and locks the frame into place. Because the dogs on the front of the frame are tight against the front of the bench, my router table really can't go anywhere.

The fence is made to slide on the frame. Two clamps lock it in place. Attached to the right and the left sides of the fence are two pieces of Melamine, which support the work as it's fed past the bit. The fence slides on or off in seconds. Once the router is mounted to the table, the table itself can be mounted or removed from the bench in 15 seconds—without changing the position of the fence.

The fence has a face board screwed to it with a channel in the back to create a duct for dust collection, as shown in the drawing. I added a plastic finger guard for safety. As a bonus, I find that the guard helps control the dust.

Jim Wright is an amateur wood-worker in Berkley, Massachusetts.

ADJUSTABLE ROUTER JIG CUTS ARCHES

by Bill Ewing

THE RADIUS ARM

The radius arm consists of a piece of hardwood, a wooden circle and a piece of Masonite. Slots in the arm, which accept the adjustable pivot point, are cut on a router table. A tenon at the end of the arm fits into a mortise in the wooden circle. Stick-on measuring tape measures the distance between the pivot point and the router bit. The Masonite backing adds strength and provides a base for the router.

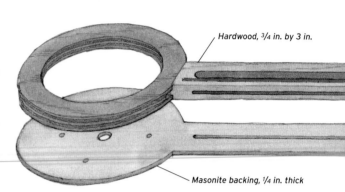

Hardwood, 3/4 in. by 3 in.

Masonite backing, 1/4 in. thick

THE BASE

The main body of the jig base is made of 3/4-in. plywood with routed slots that house the sliding pivot point. The 4-in.-wide recessed template well is as deep as the template material is thick—1/4 in. on this jig. Rail templates butt the top of the well; panel templates butt the bottom. The bottom of the base is covered with Masonite.

Butt panel template here when cutting.

Butt rail template here when cutting.

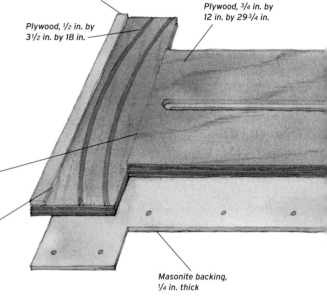

Hardwood stop, 3/4 in. by 1 in.

Plywood, 1/2 in. by 3 1/2 in. by 18 in.

Plywood, 3/4 in. by 12 in. by 29 3/4 in.

Masonite backing, 1/4 in. thick

In woodworking, as in architecture, arches can be both decorative and functional. Positioned below the main structure, an arch adds strength without the visual weight of heftier underpinnings. Placed higher up, such as in the upper rail of a bookcase, an arch lends a bit of elegance. Adding an arch to the upper rail of a cabinet door is also an easy way to refine the sometimes boxy look of frame-and-panel construction.

I wanted to find a quick way to cut arched doors so that I could offer this design option to my clients. After a little planning and experimentation, and in one quick afternoon, I was able to make an adjustable jig that allows me to cut arched raised-panel doors of almost any size. The few hours spent building the jig proved worth the time; over the last four years I've used it to make countless doors for the kitchen cabinets that are the mainstay of my business.

The only way to get uniformly fair arches is to work from two accurate templates—one for the rail and one for the panel. Each door width also requires a different set of templates. Using the two-piece jig shown here, I can quickly and efficiently cut a set of panel and rail templates to fit a wide range of cabinet-door sizes. By using these templates in conjunction with rail-and-stile-cutting bits, you can cut the door parts for a whole set of kitchen cabinets in a day.

The key to this jig is that it can be adjusted in two different ways. The radius arm of the jig (the top

SLIDING PIVOT POINTS

The sliding pivot points in the base and the radius arm must fit snugly into their corresponding slots. The author puts a 5/32-in. brass rod in the radius arm's pivot point and a mating brass tube in the base's pivot point. The rod and tube provide a smooth, precise connection between the radius arm and the jig base. Rod and tubing can be found at most hobby shops.

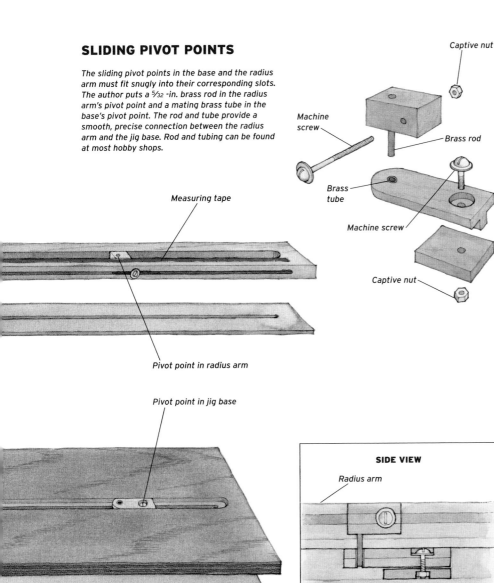

Captive nut

Machine screw

Brass rod

Brass tube

Machine screw

Captive nut

Measuring tape

Pivot point in radius arm

Pivot point in jig base

SIDE VIEW

Radius arm

Jig base

Drywall screw

piece in the drawing) allows you to make arcs of different radii. The sliding pivot point in the base (the bottom piece) allows you to move the center point of the arc's radius to accommodate varying widths of door rails. Another great thing about this jig is that it can be adjusted while the router is in place. To cut out the panel and rail templates, I always use a plunge router with a ¼-in. straight bit. Of course, this jig can be used for building more than cabinet doors—it comes in handy any time a piece of furniture needs an arch.

Bill Ewing is a cabinetmaker in Girard, Ohio.

A JIG FOR CUTTING CURVED AND TAPERED REEDS

By John Van Buren

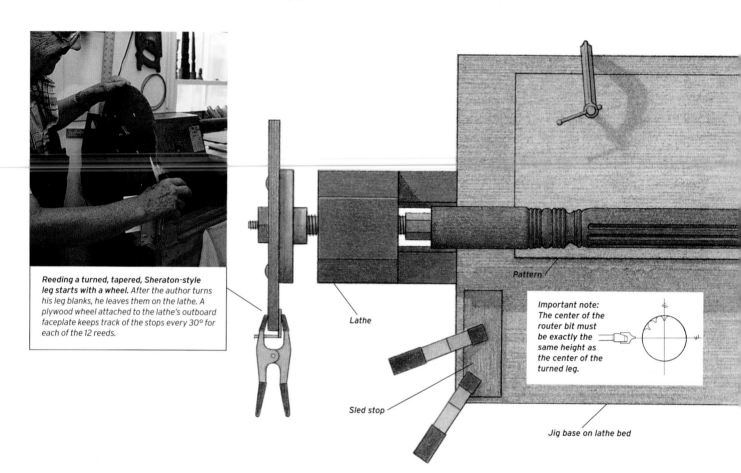

Reeding a turned, tapered, Sheraton-style leg starts with a wheel. After the author turns his leg blanks, he leaves them on the lathe. A plywood wheel attached to the lathe's outboard faceplate keeps track of the stops every 30° for each of the 12 reeds.

Lathe

Pattern

Sled stop

Jig base on lathe bed

Important note: The center of the router bit must be exactly the same height as the center of the turned leg.

I have never been satisfied with any of the methods I've seen for cutting reeds on a turned and tapered leg. The problem is that the variable depth of the reed cannot be adjusted with precision. Obviously, for the reed to stay properly proportioned in the lower, narrower sections of the turning, the router bit must make a shallower cut so that the size of the reed diminishes with the size of the leg. This can be done with a lathe and two simple shopmade jigs: a horizontal router sled and a pattern made of 1/4-in. plywood.

A sled for the router

The sled holds the router bit in a horizontal position and has two bearing surfaces cut out of one piece of wood screwed to the vertical face of the sled. The

top bearing surface rides against the surface of the turning and limits the maximum depth of the reeding cut. The bottom bearing surface rides against the edge of the pattern and controls the depth of cut when maximum depth is not desired—for example, at the narrow end of the leg. I use a 3/16-in. radius point-cutting roundover bit.

The pattern guides the sled

After turning the leg blanks but before cutting the pattern, clamp or bolt a jig base to the lathe bed. The base is a piece of 3/4-in. plywood with a smooth surface for the router sled to ride on and broad enough to hold the pattern and the sled. The height of the jig base is adjusted with shims so that the tip of

First, drop a line, but make sure it is true. Using a square, drop a perpendicular repeatedly from the turning to the pattern blank. Connect the points and bandsaw carefully so that the pattern profile is the same as the turned leg.

Next, check and clamp the pattern. After the bandsawn pattern has been filed smooth, clamp it exactly under the leg. To make shallower reeds at the bottom of the leg, move the end of the pattern slightly toward you.

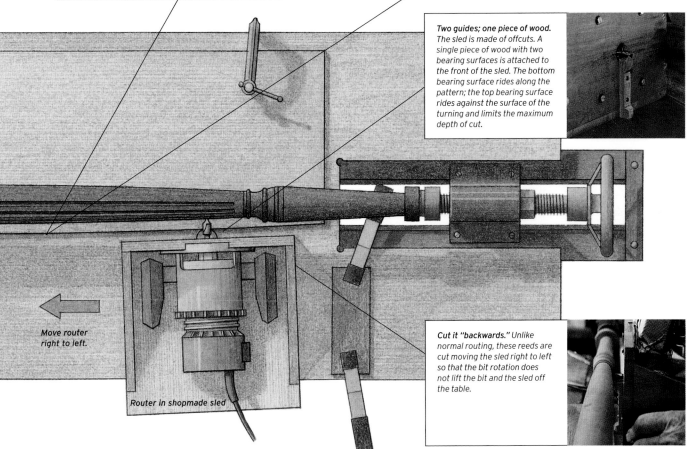

Two guides; one piece of wood. The sled is made of offcuts. A single piece of wood with two bearing surfaces is attached to the front of the sled. The bottom bearing surface rides along the pattern; the top bearing surface rides against the surface of the turning and limits the maximum depth of cut.

Move router right to left.

Router in shopmade sled

Cut it "backwards." Unlike normal routing, these reeds are cut moving the sled right to left so that the bit rotation does not lift the bit and the sled off the table.

the router bit in the sled is exactly the same height as the lathe centers.

The pattern is simply a piece of ¼-in. plywood cut in the same profile as the turned leg. You have to make a decision about where you want less or more cutter depth. Filing away the pattern edge allows deeper cutter penetration. In the case of a uniform taper, you only need to slide the pattern toward the sled at the narrow end of the leg to move the cutter away from the piece for the shallower cut. Lateral stops for the router sled are clamped to the jig base to limit the length of the reed.

Usual routing routine would suggest that you move the router from left to right. In this case, such movement might cause the bit to ride up and ruin the adjacent reed. Instead, move the bit from right to left, because the rotation of the horizontal bit tends to hold the cutter down. This method can also be used to cut flutes or facets rather than reeds. All that's left in any case is some hand sanding.

John Van Buren is a retired neurosurgeon in Herndon, Virginia.

MICRO-ADJUSTABLE JIG SPEEDS TENONING

By Patrick Warner

Most of the furniture making I do is experimental. Nothing in the design is standard. Consequently, when making tenons for joinery, I want a jig that will accommodate a wide range of sizes. Some adjustable woodworking jigs use the tap-and-clamp method. That works, but it's simply not very handy when you're making lots of different-sized tenons.

The jig I use to make tenons is nowhere near as sophisticated as some screw-driven woodworking machinery, but with a slight turn of the adjusting handle, I can dial in tenons to within 0.001 in. and cut 2-in.-long tenons in under a minute. The range of travel allows for shoulder widths up to ⅝ in. A straight bit in a router does the cutting. The jig works with either a template guide bushing or a bearing-guided pattern bit.

Although only one face is machined at a time, the work can be flipped, remounted, and milled in fewer than 10 seconds. The jig shown here will cut only two-faced tenons or four-faced tenons on narrow stock (approximately less than 1½ in.). For four-faced tenons on wider boards, you can (1) expand the size of the travel mechanism and clamp base to accommodate all four cuts, (2) cut the two short tenon faces by hand, or (3) build another similar jig for wider stock so that it will handle the other two faces.

Cutting a stack of tenons in under three minutes. Precise adjustments and fast-acting toggle clamps on this jig allow you to make uniform router-cut tenons in quantity.

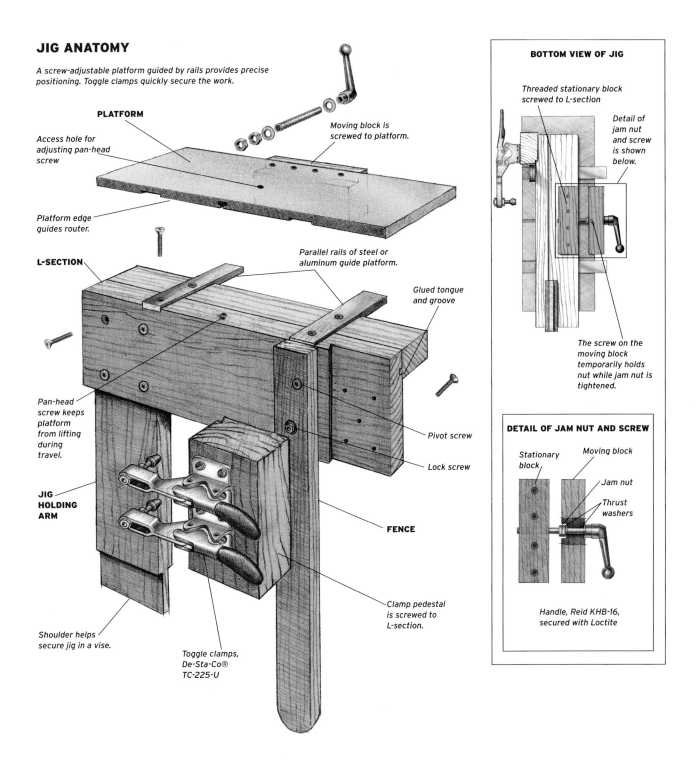

JIG ANATOMY

A screw-adjustable platform guided by rails provides precise positioning. Toggle clamps quickly secure the work.

PLATFORM

Access hole for adjusting pan-head screw

Moving block is screwed to platform.

Platform edge guides router.

L-SECTION

Parallel rails of steel or aluminum guide platform.

Glued tongue and groove

Pan-head screw keeps platform from lifting during travel.

JIG HOLDING ARM

Pivot screw

Lock screw

FENCE

Shoulder helps secure jig in a vise.

Toggle clamps, De-Sta-Co® TC-225-U

Clamp pedestal is screwed to L-section.

BOTTOM VIEW OF JIG

Threaded stationary block screwed to L-section

Detail of jam nut and screw is shown below.

The screw on the moving block temporarily holds nut while jam nut is tightened.

DETAIL OF JAM NUT AND SCREW

Stationary block

Moving block

Jam nut

Thrust washers

Handle, Reid KHB-16, secured with Loctite

Making the jig

A simple L-section forms the backbone of this jig (see the drawings above). An adjustable platform above the work supports and guides the router, controlling the tenon size. This platform is positioned by a threaded rod (or lead screw) and held in alignment with metal guide rails. Toggle clamps secure the work in place, while a holding arm allows the jig to be secured in a vise or clamped to a bench. This jig will hold stock up to 8/4 thick and 10 in. wide and of any length.

The jig is made mostly of wood, but for many parts I used metal joinery methods, which produce rugged, accurate jigs. Rabbets or grooves align parts, and machine screws hold them together. I cut threads directly into the mating wooden part using machinist's taps. You could also use wood screws, carriage bolts, and threaded inserts for the assembly.

Use a template to build a jig. To cut matched tail slots, align the front edge of the template with the L-section. Repeating this operation on the platform ensures that the rails stay in alignment and that the jig operates smoothly. The cuts are made with a top-bearing pattern bit.

Dialing in the perfect tenon. If the test cut results in too big a tenon, adjust the jig and cut again. The author has made a number of jigs based on the same basic design. The top surface of the platform is a handy place for notes and reference lines for cutting multiples or to repeat a setup at a later time.

For strength, most of the wood used in this jig is red oak. The adjustable platform, however, is medium-density fiberboard (MDF) because I wanted a smooth, flat, stable material to guide the router.

Making tenons with the jig

I prefer using a fixed-base router when I make tenons with this jig. A plunge router may be better for multiple-depth cuts, but it's difficult to plunge one safely along an edge because of the small footprint and high center of gravity.

Install the cutter and guide collar on your router, and set the depth of cut. Adjust the toggle clamps to the stock thickness. Very large work may require the addition of a C-clamp. Be sure to position the work against both the fence and the underside of the platform. Routing in this orientation, across the grain, quickly peels away material. Nevertheless, deep cuts should be done in multiple passes.

Position the platform at your best first guess and rout the first cheek of the tenon. I usually climb-cut (moving along the edge right to left) because there is so little resistance to the cut. When climb cutting, take light cuts to avoid a runaway router. Reposition the work and cut the opposite cheek without moving the platform. Test the tenon in its mortise. If it's too big, determine by how much and divide by two. Then move the platform back by that amount and repeat the cut.

Patrick Warner lives in Escondido, California. He has written three books on routing and even has a website on the subject. Visit the site at www.patwarner.com.

ROUTER FIXTURE
TAKES ON ANGLED TENONS

by Edward Koizumi

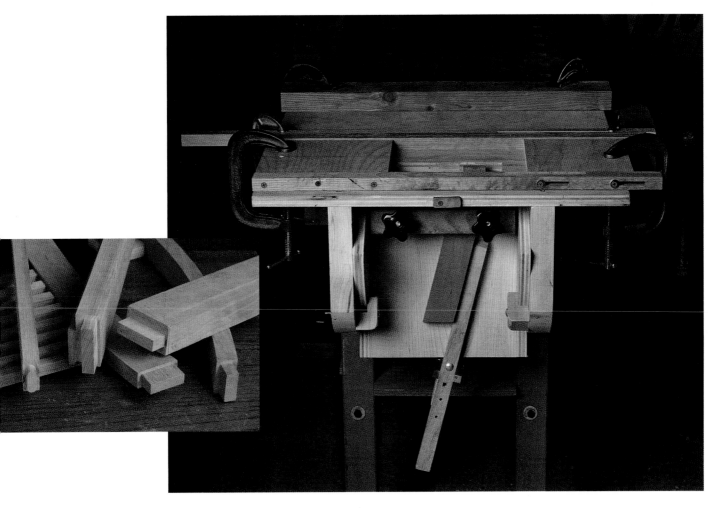

We live in a turn-of-the-century Arts and Crafts house, so it seemed quite natural to furnish it with pieces from that era. My wife bought a pair of Mission armchairs a couple of years ago to go with a 9-ft.-long cherry table I'd built for our dining room. Six months later, she bought two side chairs. It would be a while before we could afford a full set. Within earshot of my wife, I heard myself say, "How hard could it be to make these?"

"Oh, could you?" she asked.

"Sure," I said. The chairs looked straightforward enough, just a cube with a back. Upon closer examination, I realized that the seat was slightly higher and wider in the front than in the back. For the first time, I was faced with compound-angled joinery. I thought about dowels, biscuits, and loose tenons, so I could keep the joinery simple, but I wasn't confident in the strength or longevity of these methods.

I wanted good, old-fashioned, dependable mortise-and-tenon joints. After some thought, I decided an adjustable router fixture would be the simplest solution that would let me make tenons of widely varying sizes and angles.

The fixture I came up with is as easy to set up as a tablesaw. In fact, there are some similarities. The workpiece is held below a tabletop in a trunnion-type

TENON-ROUTING FIXTURE FOR COMPOUND ANGLES

This fixture, adjustable in two planes, is designed to let you rout compound-angled tenons consistently and accurately. The tenons can be either squared or rounded, depending on which guide frame you use.

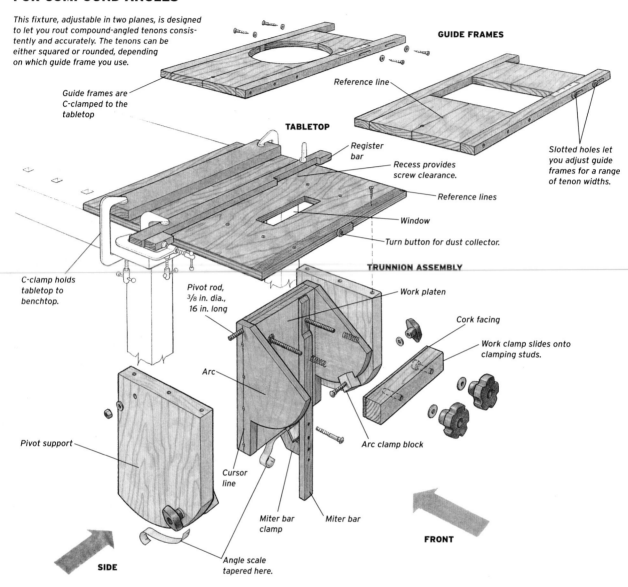

GUIDE FRAMES

Guide frames are C-clamped to the tabletop

Reference line

Slotted holes let you adjust guide frames for a range of tenon widths.

TABLETOP

Register bar

Recess provides screw clearance.

Reference lines

Window

Turn button for dust collector.

C-clamp holds tabletop to benchtop.

Pivot rod, 3/8 in. dia., 16 in. long

TRUNNION ASSEMBLY

Work platen

Cork facing

Work clamp slides onto clamping studs.

Arc

Arc clamp block

Pivot support

Cursor line

Miter bar clamp

Miter bar

FRONT

SIDE

Angle scale tapered here.

assembly that adjusts the tilt angle. For compound angles, a miter bar rotates the workpiece in the other plane. The fixture can handle stock up to 2 in. thick and 5 in. wide (at 0 degree–0 degree) and angles up to 25 degrees in one plane and 20 degrees in the other. This is sufficient for chairs, which seldom have angles more than 5 degrees.

To guide the router during the cut, I clamp a guide frame to the fixture over the window in the tabletop. And I plunge rout around the tenon on the end of the workpiece. The guide frame determines the tenon's width and length as well as whether the ends will be square or round. I made two frames, both adjustable, one for round-cornered tenons, the other for square tenons.

The fixture and guide frames took me just over a day to make, once I'd figured out the design. Then I spent about an hour aligning the fixture and making test tenons in preparation for routing the tenons on the chair parts. The fixture worked just as planned and allowed this relatively inexperienced woodworker to produce eight chairs that match the originals perfectly.

Making the fixture and guide frames

The fixture is simple to build. It consists of only two main parts, the trunnion assembly and the tabletop. The trunnion assembly is essentially a pair of arcs nestled between two pivot supports. Between the

ANGLES IN ONE PLANE (SIDE VIEW)

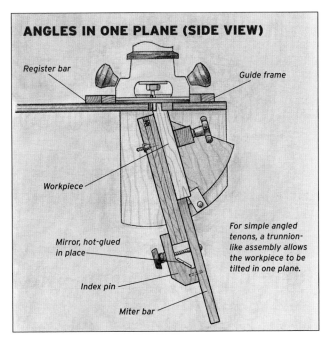

Register bar

Guide frame

Workpiece

Mirror, hot-glued in place

Index pin

Miter bar

For simple angled tenons, a trunnion-like assembly allows the workpiece to be tilted in one plane.

COMPOUND ANGLES (FRONT VIEW)

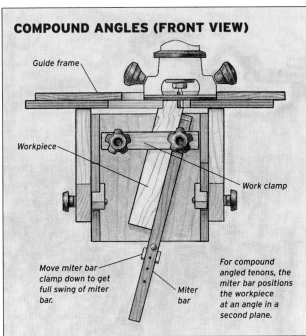

Guide frame

Workpiece

Work clamp

Move miter bar clamp down to get full swing of miter bar.

Miter bar

For compound angled tenons, the miter bar positions the workpiece at an angle in a second plane.

two arcs is a work platen, or surface, against which I clamp the component to be tenoned. There are other parts, but basically, the fixture is just a table to slide the router on and a movable platen to mount the workpiece on.

Edward Koizumi is a professional model maker in Oak Park, Illinois.

Using the jig

Mark out the tenon on a test piece. The test piece should be the same thickness and width as the actual components, but length isn't important.

Make the workpiece flush with the tabletop. The author uses a piece of milled steel, but the edge of a 6-in. ruler would work as well.

Make a pattern. An outline of the tenon traced on acetate helps align the guide frame for cutting any tenons of the same size.

Guide frame determines thickness and width of tenons. The author keeps the router's base against the inner edges of the guide frame and routs clockwise to prevent tearout. Guide frames can produce round-cornered or square-cornered tenons.

Set correctly, the fixture will yield tight joints, whether the tenons are straight, angled or compound-angled. Here, the author tests the fit of a seat-rail tenon into a leg mortise.

END-WORK ROUTER FIXTURE FOR TENONS AND MORE

by Patrick Warner

An end-work platform. This jig holds workpieces vertically for cutting tenons or rounding the ends of frame members with a router. The slats attached to the bottom of the router keep it from tipping as the router passes over the window in the top of the fixture.

Routing or shaping the end of a board can be a tricky proposition. Even on a router table fitted with a fence, the small amount of surface area on the end of a board doesn't provide much stability when you try to run the piece vertically past the bit. And if the stock is very long, the task is simply impossible because of the difficulty of handling a long piece on end, even if your shop's ceiling is high enough to allow it. My router end-work fixture provides a safe and simple solution for routing tenons as well as other joints or shapes on the end of a board.

How the fixture works

Basically, this is the way the fixture works: A frame member or other workpiece is clamped to the fixture, which references it for the desired cut. The fixture's large platform top provides a stable support for the handheld router, and a window cutout in the platform allows access for the bit to shape the narrow end of the workpiece, as shown in the photo above. The fixture features an indexing fence that's adjustable to facilitate angled tenons, such as those used to join seat rails to the rear leg of a chair. The method of guiding the bit depends on the job. Some joints, such as stub tenons, can be done with a piloted rabbeting bit that

Joinery options. A variety of joints can be routed with the end-work platform, including all kinds of square or angled tenons and sliding dovetails. Tenons can even be routed on the ends of round stock.

rides the faces of the stock. An auxiliary router fence can be used to create more complicated tenons, sliding dovetails or other shapes on the end of stock, including roundovers or chamfers. The stock can be any shape—square, rectangular or even round, as shown in the photo below. Practically any bit normally used on the edge or face of a board can be used with this fixture. Because the router bit slices the wood fibers parallel to the grain when shaping the end of a board, the fibers are effortlessly peeled away rather than sheared, as is the case with cross-grain router cuts.

Building the fixture

The parts for the fixture can be made from any hardwood; beech, maple and birch are good choices (I built mine from birch), or you can use a good-grade of ¾-in. or 1-in. medium-density fiberboard (MDF). The fixture consists of a router platform with a rectangular window cutout for the router bit; a workpiece clamping board, joined at 90 degrees to the platform with a tongue and groove and reinforced by two corner braces; and an adjustable indexing fence (see the drawing).

I use a tongue-and-groove joint to accurately register the clamping board to the platform, but I screw all the parts together instead of gluing them, so it's easier to disassemble and realign the parts later if necessary.

A threaded hand knob on the locking bolt makes fast fence adjustments without a wrench.

End routing stock

To use the fixture for routing basic tenons, I first set the indexing fence precisely 90 degrees to the router platform. Then, I set the fixture upside down on the bench, position the stock to be tenoned against the indexing fence with the stock's end flat on the bench, and secure it to the clamping board with a couple of C-clamps. This indexes the workpiece square to, and flush with, the top surface of the platform. I flip the entire assembly over and clamp the workpiece in the bench vise so that the router platform is at a comfortable working height.

To eliminate any chance that the router will tip as it passes over the window in the fixture's platform, I screw a couple of ½-in.-thick strips of wood to the router base. If the desired cut can be made at a single pass, such as for a stub tenon, any standard router will do. Simply chuck up a piloted bit, set the cutting depth (which determines the tenon's length) and guide the bit around the stock. Rabbet bits and pilot bearings of various diameters can be mixed or matched to produce tenons with shoulders from ¹⁄₁₆ in. wide to ⁹⁄₁₆ in. wide. I fit the router with an auxiliary guide that runs along the platform's edge when unpiloted cutters are used.

For deep cuts, like tenons that are longer than the cutting depth of the bit, a plunge router is my tool of choice. I set my plunge router's rotary depth stop to three different cutting heights and then shape each tenon in three passes, resetting the stop to take a deeper cut each time. By changing bits and cutting heights, tenon shoulders can be cut at different heights and can be centered or offset.

Patrick Warner is a woodworker, author and instructor who lives in Escondido, California.

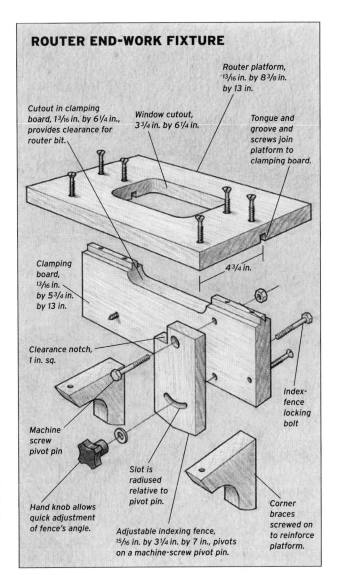

ROUTER END-WORK FIXTURE

Router platform, ¹³⁄₁₆ in. by 8³⁄₈ in. by 13 in.

Cutout in clamping board, ¹³⁄₁₆ in. by 6¹⁄₄ in., provides clearance for router bit.

Window cutout, 3³⁄₄ in. by 6¹⁄₄ in.

Tongue and groove and screws join platform to clamping board.

Clamping board, ¹³⁄₁₆ in. by 5³⁄₄ in. by 13 in.

4³⁄₄ in.

Clearance notch, 1 in. sq.

Machine screw pivot pin

Index-fence locking bolt

Slot is radiused relative to pivot pin.

Hand knob allows quick adjustment of fence's angle.

Adjustable indexing fence, ¹⁵⁄₁₆ in. by 3¹⁄₄ in. by 7 in., pivots on a machine-screw pivot pin.

Corner braces screwed on to reinforce platform.

Positioning the workpiece. After setting the adjustable indexing fence for shaping either a square or angled tenon, the fixture is held upside down on a flat surface, and the workpiece is clamped in place with its end flush with the top of the router platform. The fixture is then flipped over and clamped in a bench vise for routing.

Shaping tenons with a piloted rabbet bit is simple. The pilot bearing rides on the face of the workpiece as the short tenon is cut.

SHOP-BUILT HORIZONTAL MORTISER

By John F. Matousek

My wife and I had just transformed our basement into a sitting area, home office, alcove and bar, but it was clear to me that we weren't finished. I envisioned three major furniture projects I'd have to complete. We needed a built-in storage cabinet in the sitting area for a television and VCR; base cabinets in the office, and shelf units in the alcove for books, albums, and assorted art objects. I could foresee dozens—if not hundreds—of mortise-and-tenon joints, and I began to question my plan to tackle all of these projects.

I had read an article about mortise-and-loose-tenon joints, and I remembered that loose tenons are simple to make. If I could speed up the mortising process, I could complete my three projects in a reasonable amount of time. So I began to design a machine to make mortises.

I wanted a system that could be set up easily and be operated safely and that could accurately duplicate a mortising operation. Also, I needed a machine that could raise or lower the cutting bit as necessary for precise adjustments. But I wasn't sure that my scheme would work, and I didn't want to spend a lot of money on a failed experiment, so I built this setup with scraps and hardware left over from previous projects. The design I finally built was that of a horizontal compound-mortising table. As designed, it is meant to mortise mostly ¾-in.-thick lumber workpieces, using a solid-carbide, ¼-in. spiral upcut bit, powered by a standard 1½-hp router, which I mounted on a vertical back panel.

One turn of the threaded bolt can raise or lower the router. The author rigged up the adjusting device shown here to enhance his ability to fine-tune the height of the router bit in relation to the workpiece.

The machine has two movable tables. The top table moves at right angles to the bit, and the bottom table moves parallel to it. I mounted two drawer slides (Accuride model No. C-1029 center-mount slides) under the tables to provide for the side-to-side and front-to-back movements of the tables. Movable stops at each end of the bottom table can be set to control the distance the top table can move and thus the length of the mortise.

A mortiser and a conventional router table

After setting up the machine to cut a mortise, it's best to plunge the workpiece repeatedly into the cutting bit, drilling a series of holes, by moving the bottom table in and out and adjusting the top table a little for each plunge.

After that, clean up the sidewalls of the mortise by moving the top table left to right between the stops Also, by clamping a fence on the top table 45 degrees to the back panel, you can drill mortises into the ends of a 45-degree miter using essentially the same procedure.

By bolting the top table to the back panel—using two brackets on the underside—you can turn this machine into a router table, good for any number of shaping tasks.

As a mortiser, this machine is quite specialized, and I don't have to use it very often; but when I do, it saves me a bundle of time.

John F. Matousek lives in Englewood, Colorado, and is retired from his career as an information systems engineer.

A MORTISE-MILLING MACHINE

The author designed this setup primarily as a router-based mortiser. By being able to adjust the cutting edge in relation to the workpiece in three dimensions—up and down, in and out, side to side—he ended up with a rig that is as easy to use as it is accurate. By bolting the top table to the back panel that holds the router, he also uses it for other tasks, such as shaping the edges of raised panels.

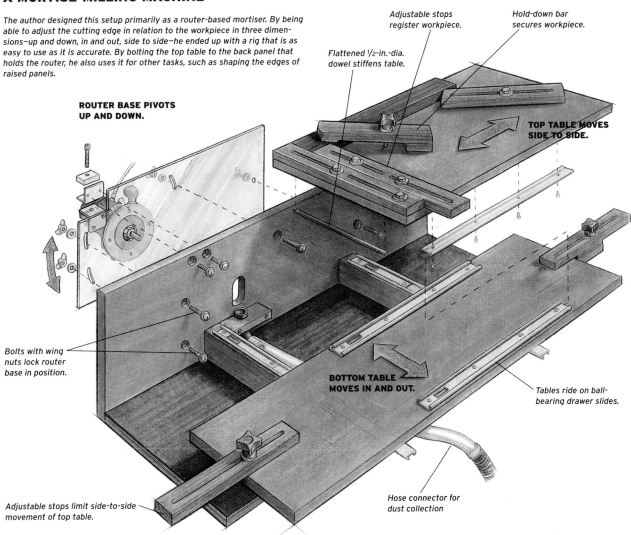

ROUTER BASE PIVOTS UP AND DOWN.

Adjustable stops register workpiece.

Hold-down bar secures workpiece.

Flattened 1/2-in.-dia. dowel stiffens table.

TOP TABLE MOVES SIDE TO SIDE.

Bolts with wing nuts lock router base in position.

BOTTOM TABLE MOVES IN AND OUT.

Tables ride on ball-bearing drawer slides.

Hose connector for dust collection

Adjustable stops limit side-to-side movement of top table.

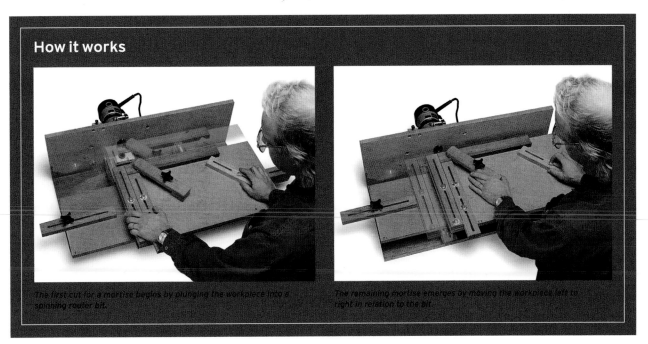

How it works

The first cut for a mortise begins by plunging the workpiece into a spinning router bit.

The remaining mortise emerges by moving the workpiece left to right in relation to the bit.

SHOPMADE SLOT MORTISER

By Gregory Paolini

As a member of a professional guild, I make a lot of Arts and Crafts style furniture, and I cut countless mortise-and-tenon joints. I used to cut the joints with a combination of hand and power tools, but I quickly realized that I had to find a more efficient way if I was going to keep the price of my furniture out of the stratosphere. I tried many different methods, but when I saw furniture maker and teacher Gary Rogowski using a slot mortiser, I was sold on the idea.

A slot mortiser basically is a table with a horizontally mounted router equipped with a spiral bit. The mortise is cut by plunging the workpiece into the bit while moving the workpiece from side to side to bore its width. Slot mortisers are the choice of production shops because they are very fast, accurate, and work well with integral or loose tenons.

I went shopping for a slot mortiser and found some machines that could do everything I needed—except fit into my budget. Prices for joint-making machines and commercial slot mortisers ranged from about $450 to $2,600*, and in some cases I still had to supply my own router. Talk about sticker shock. I figured, for that much money, why not try to make my own.

Like the commercial machines, mine had to be reliable and accurate. It needed to incorporate a horizontally mounted router, a table that could move on both *x*

and *y* axes, stops to control mortise width and depth, and a system to index and secure my work.

I achieved the *x*–*y* movement I was after by making two platforms, each of which moves along a different axis, with aluminum T-tracks riding in dadoes. The table also had to be stable and strong, as well as a little weighty, to resist jumping or jerking when cutting. Three stacked layers of 3/4-in.-thick medium-density fiberboard (MDF) provided both the weight and the stability I needed.

Keeping the router from deflecting while in use is critical,

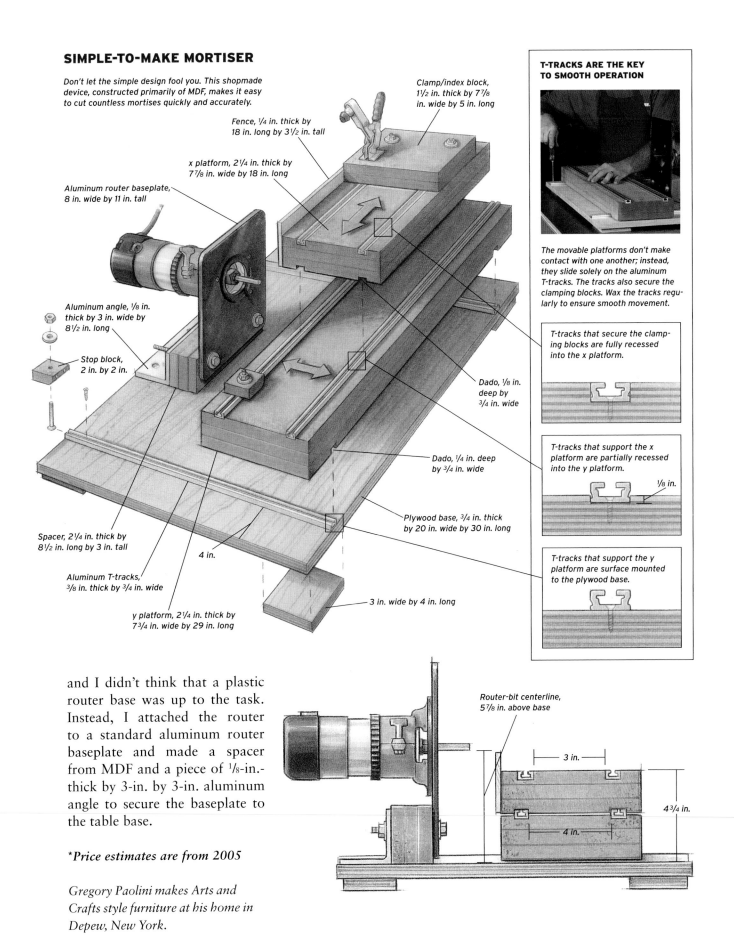

SIMPLE-TO-MAKE MORTISER

Don't let the simple design fool you. This shopmade device, constructed primarily of MDF, makes it easy to cut countless mortises quickly and accurately.

Clamp/index block, 1½ in. thick by 7⅞ in. wide by 5 in. long

Fence, ¼ in. thick by 18 in. long by 3½ in. tall

x platform, 2¼ in. thick by 7⅞ in. wide by 18 in. long

Aluminum router baseplate, 8 in. wide by 11 in. tall

Aluminum angle, ⅛ in. thick by 3 in. wide by 8½ in. long

Stop block, 2 in. by 2 in.

Spacer, 2¼ in. thick by 8½ in. long by 3 in. tall

Aluminum T-tracks, ⅜ in. thick by ¾ in. wide

4 in.

y platform, 2¼ in. thick by 7¾ in. wide by 29 in. long

3 in. wide by 4 in. long

Dado, ⅛ in. deep by ¾ in. wide

Dado, ¼ in. deep by ¾ in. wide

Plywood base, ¾ in. thick by 20 in. wide by 30 in. long

T-TRACKS ARE THE KEY TO SMOOTH OPERATION

The movable platforms don't make contact with one another; instead, they slide solely on the aluminum T-tracks. The tracks also secure the clamping blocks. Wax the tracks regularly to ensure smooth movement.

T-tracks that secure the clamping blocks are fully recessed into the x platform.

T-tracks that support the x platform are partially recessed into the y platform.

⅛ in.

T-tracks that support the y platform are surface mounted to the plywood base.

and I didn't think that a plastic router base was up to the task. Instead, I attached the router to a standard aluminum router baseplate and made a spacer from MDF and a piece of ⅛-in.-thick by 3-in. by 3-in. aluminum angle to secure the baseplate to the table base.

***Price estimates are from 2005**

Gregory Paolini makes Arts and Crafts style furniture at his home in Depew, New York.

Router-bit centerline, 5⅞ in. above base

3 in.

4 in.

4¾ in.

THE ULTIMATE ROUTER TABLE

By John White

The ultimate router table should be as convenient as a shaper or tablesaw—all of the common tasks and adjustments are done from above or outside the unit. It would also have the dust-collecting ability and vibration-dampening mass of a cabinet-mounted tool.

I came up with a router cabinet that meets all of the above criteria and is super-quiet to boot. The design relies on the JessEm Rout-R-Lift,® a screw-driven mechanism that allows you to raise and lower the router and bit by cranking a handle inserted from above. The JessEm unit is also sold by Jet® as the Xacta Lift®, for the same price—around $200* in many catalogs. By adding a shopmade mounting block to the lift, I was able to raise the router high enough to allow bit changes from above the table as well.

Eliminating the need to reach underneath the top let me mount the table on a cabinet, which could enclose a shop vacuum and muffle its sound and the roar of the router itself. A dust-collection manifold fits under the tabletop and behind the lift unit. A fence system with a dust port ties into the system below.

I mounted a switched outlet for the router and vacuum unit outside the cabinet. Just for fun, I threw in racks for bit and tool storage. Casters under one end of the cabinet make it mobile—like a wheelbarrow—but still stable on the floor.

The entire unit—cabinet, table and fence—is made of ¾-in.-

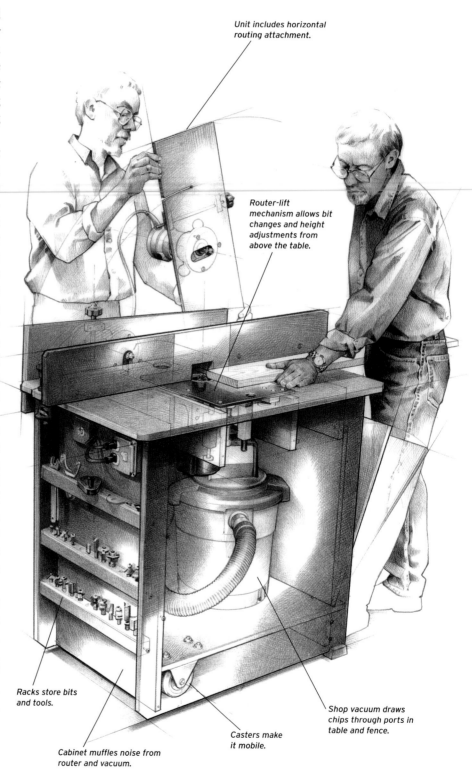

Unit includes horizontal routing attachment.

Router-lift mechanism allows bit changes and height adjustments from above the table.

Racks store bits and tools.

Cabinet muffles noise from router and vacuum.

Casters make it mobile.

Shop vacuum draws chips through ports in table and fence.

Router lift is the heart of the table

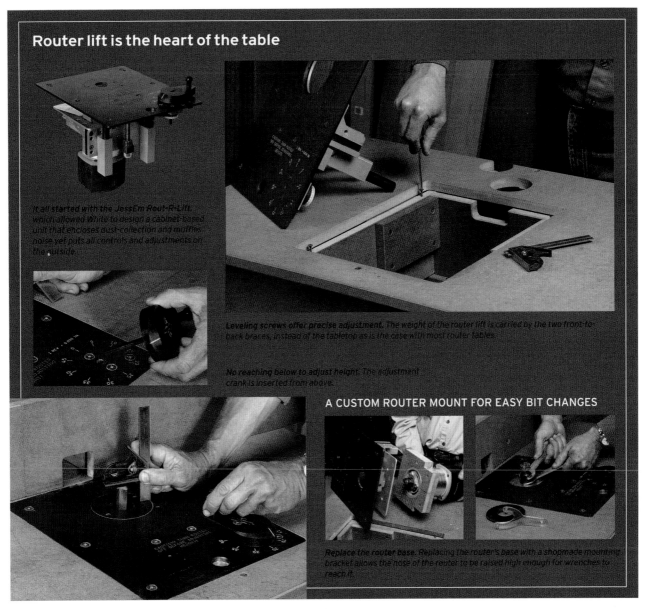

It all started with the JessEm Rout-R-Lift, which allowed White to design a cabinet-based unit that encloses dust-collection and muffles noise yet puts all controls and adjustments on the outside.

Leveling screws offer precise adjustment. The weight of the router lift is carried by the two front-to-back braces, instead of the tabletop as is the case with most router tables.

No reaching below to adjust height. The adjustment crank is inserted from above.

A CUSTOM ROUTER MOUNT FOR EASY BIT CHANGES

Replace the router base. Replacing the router's base with a shopmade mounting bracket allows the nose of the router to be raised high enough for wrenches to reach it.

FOLLOW THE AIRFLOW

The vacuum draws air and chips through the bit openings in the table and fence; into the dust manifold; and down the hose into the vacuum, where the dust and chips are filtered out. An angled flap of sheet metal deflects the router's exhaust blast away from the bit opening and into the cabinet.

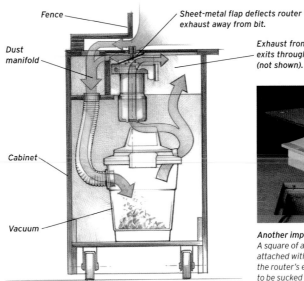

Fence

Dust manifold

Sheet-metal flap deflects router exhaust away from bit.

Exhaust from vacuum and router exits through the power-cord port (not shown).

Cabinet

Vacuum

Another important modification to the router lift. A square of aluminum flashing—bent slightly and attached with double-stick tape or screws—deflects the router's exhaust into the cabinet, allowing chips to be sucked past the bit.

SIMPLE PARTS, SMART FUNCTION

The cabinet is made entirely from ¾-in.-thick MDF joined with knockdown fasteners. The front-to-back braces below the tabletop support the router plate and double as the sides of the dust manifold. Two filler blocks close the gap around the lift mechanism, which makes for efficient dust collection.

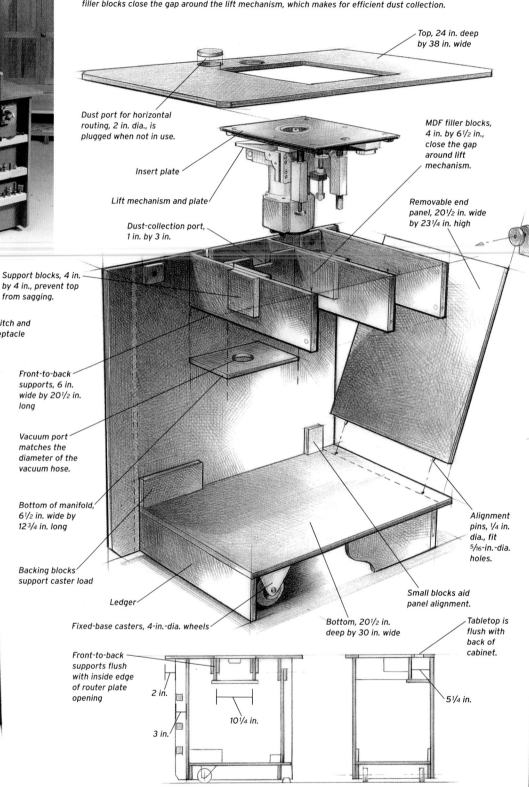

Top, 24 in. deep by 38 in. wide

Dust port for horizontal routing, 2 in. dia., is plugged when not in use.

MDF filler blocks, 4 in. by 6½ in., close the gap around lift mechanism.

Insert plate

Lift mechanism and plate

Removable end panel, 20½ in. wide by 23¼ in. high

Dust-collection port, 1 in. by 3 in.

Port for router and vacuum exhaust; cords also pass through here.

Support blocks, 4 in. by 4 in., prevent top from sagging.

20-amp switch and duplex receptacle

Front-to-back supports, 6 in. wide by 20½ in. long

Vacuum port matches the diameter of the vacuum hose.

Alignment pins, ¼ in. dia., fit 5/16-in.-dia. holes.

Bottom of manifold, 6½ in. wide by 12¾ in. long

Small blocks aid panel alignment.

Backing blocks support caster load

Ledger

Fixed-base casters, 4-in.-dia. wheels

Bottom, 20½ in. deep by 30 in. wide

Tabletop is flush with back of cabinet.

Racks for bit and tool storage, 1¾ in. sq.

Front-to-back supports flush with inside edge of router plate opening

2 in.

10¼ in.

3 in.

5¼ in.

End panel, 20½ in. wide by 33 in. high

FRONT VIEW

SIDE VIEW

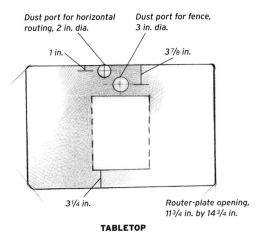

Dust port for horizontal routing, 2 in. dia.

Dust port for fence, 3 in. dia.

1 in.

3⁷⁄₈ in.

3¹⁄₄ in.

Router-plate opening, 11³⁄₄ in. by 14³⁄₄ in.

TABLETOP

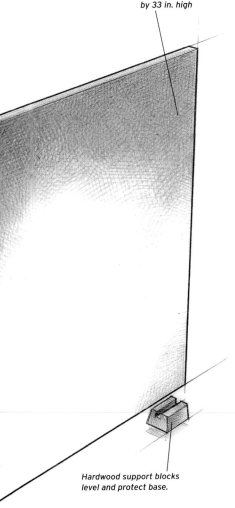

Latch assembly, made of MDF, bolt, nut, washer and rubber O-ring

Cabinet front and back, 34 in. wide by 33 in. high

Hardwood support blocks level and protect base.

A basic fence Is effective

The fence features a removable insert, a dust manifold that ties into the one below the table, and modified pipe clamps that grab the table edges.

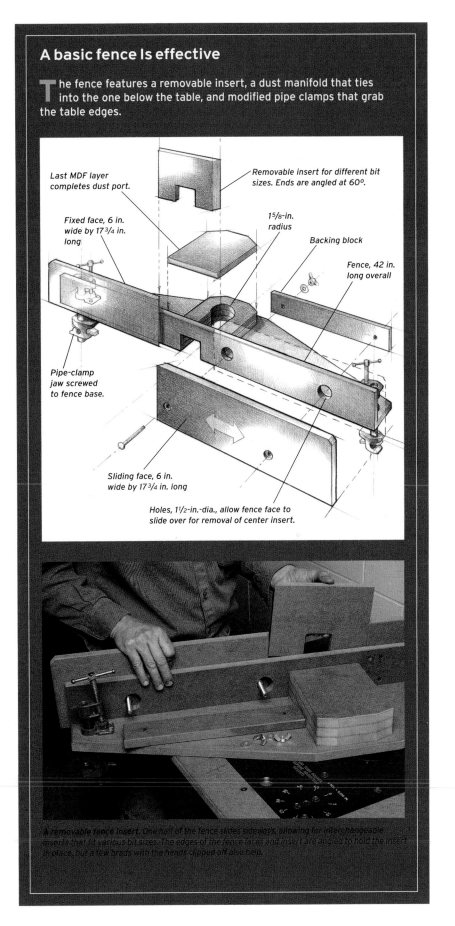

Last MDF layer completes dust port.

Removable insert for different bit sizes. Ends are angled at 60°.

Fixed face, 6 in. wide by 17³⁄₄ in. long

1⁵⁄₈-in. radius

Backing block

Fence, 42 in. long overall

Pipe-clamp jaw screwed to fence base.

Sliding face, 6 in. wide by 17³⁄₄ in. long

Holes, 1¹⁄₂-in.-dia., allow fence face to slide over for removal of center insert.

A removable fence insert. One half of the fence slides sideways, allowing for interchangeable inserts that fit various bit sizes. The edges of the fence faces and insert are angled to hold the insert in place, but a few brads with the heads clipped off also help.

thick medium-density fiberboard (MDF), with two coats of Watco oil for added durability. To make sure the cabinet would remain sturdy, I opted for cross-dowel knockdown fasteners over glue and screws.

One end panel is removable so that you can open the cabinet and empty the shop vacuum.

The large hole in the tabletop connects the fence's dust port with the dust-collection system below. Another one is necessary if you opt for the horizontal router attachment.

Fine-threaded drywall screws in the support braces act as levelers for the insert plate.

The fence is joined with long drywall screws but incorporates a dust box that ties into the dust-collection manifold through a hole in the tabletop. Also, a sliding face allows the fence to have an interchangeable center insert. Creating this "ultimate router table" takes some time and money, but the added precision and ease of use will reward you many times over.

Please note prices are from 2001.

John White is the shop manager for Fine Woodworking.

Horizontal routing attachment

The back of the table is flush with the cabinet so that White could include a horizontal routing attachment—useful for making tenons, raised panels, and sliding dovetails, among other operations.

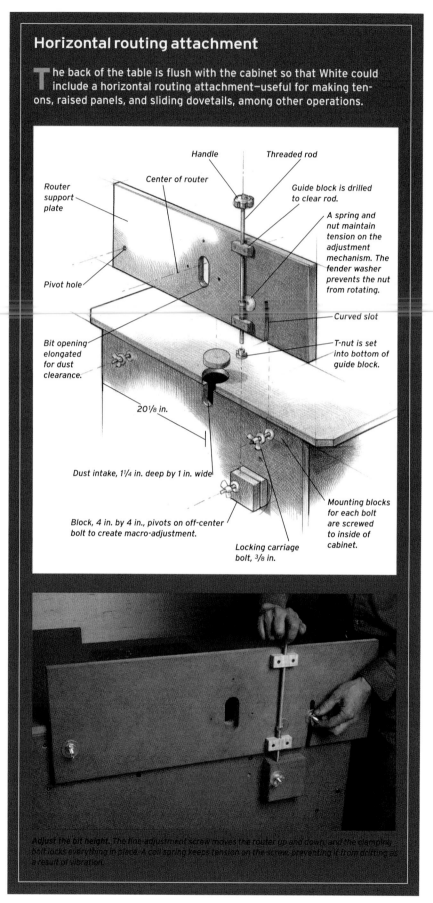

Handle • Threaded rod

Center of router

Router support plate

Guide block is drilled to clear rod.

A spring and nut maintain tension on the adjustment mechanism. The fender washer prevents the nut from rotating.

Pivot hole

Curved slot

Bit opening elongated for dust clearance.

T-nut is set into bottom of guide block.

20⅛ in.

Dust intake, 1¼ in. deep by 1 in. wide

Block, 4 in. by 4 in., pivots on off-center bolt to create macro-adjustment.

Locking carriage bolt, ³/₈ in.

Mounting blocks for each bolt are screwed to inside of cabinet.

Adjust the bit height. The fine-adjustment screw moves the router up and down, and the clamping bolt locks everything in place. A coil spring keeps tension on the screw, preventing it from drifting as a result of vibration.

SHOPMADE TRIMMER FOR FLUSH CUTS

By Jim Siulinski

Applying and trimming solid-wood edgebanding can be difficult and time-consuming. After applying an oversize strip to the edge, you have to trim it flush with the face of the panel. I find it difficult to balance a router or laminate trimmer on a panel edge, and I immensely dislike sanding out the inevitable snipe and chatter marks. I looked for a way to improve the process.

My solution was to make a carriage for a trim router with an extended base and fence and handles like those on a handplane (see the drawing on p. 161). The trim router is mounted in the fence and attached to the base at 90 degrees. The base rides on the face of the panel, and the fence rides along the edge. The 15-in. by 5-in. base significantly increases the surface area of the tool. It's stable and wobble free. An adjusting knob set into the top of the plane body allows precise alignment of the trimming bit with the bottom of the base for a perfectly flush cut.

I scrounged most of the materials from a junk pile at my workplace and from a friend's woodshop. I

A simple tool for cleaning up banded plywood edges. The author devised a carriage that improves stability for his trim router and makes flush cuts a breeze.

used Melamine with a medium-density fiberboard (MDF) core for the base and fence because it's stable, durable, and slides well over the work. The wood in the plane body is jarrah, though any stable hardwood will do. The only uncommon part is a scrap of anodized-aluminum angle bar I used for a bracket to house the adjusting knob. If I hadn't found the angle bar, I probably would have made some kind of bracket out of wood. Like many shopmade jigs, this one is fast, easy, and inexpensive to build. The whole jig took four hours to five hours, start to finish.

With the edge-banded plywood lying flat on a workbench, I use the carriage much like a handplane. To avoid tearout, the trimmer should be used with the bit turning into the cut, in the same direction as the trimmer's movement. This means that the carriage must be used in a left-handed fashion. (Lefties should appreciate this.) Facing the work on a bench, start at the left, and move to the right. The mass of the carriage and the sure grip of the planelike handles make it easy to keep the bit from self-feeding and clogging or skating down the workpiece. Be sure to clamp your work to the bench. A few test-cuts should ensure proper bit alignment with the base.

One of the trimmer's major advantages is its ability to trim directly over dadoes. I think it is easier to cut a dado before edge-banding, thus avoiding a more complex stopped dado cut. Using a trim router with just a bearing for a guide would ruin the edge as the bit turned into the dado.

The trimmer carriage works best when edge-banding sheet material at least as large as the carriage. I typically use it when making bookcases and shelves. Because the essential use of the fence is to make a stable cut, the carriage may be adapted to many other applications. I sometimes use it to trim the edge of a face frame on a finished case. By adjusting the bit, you can use it to cut rabbets. By changing bits, you can apply different molding profiles—and not just to edgebandings.

Jim Siulinski is an applications engineer at National Semiconductor and runs a small woodshop business on the side in Westbrook, Maine.

CARRIAGE FOR TRIMMING SOLID WOOD EDGE-BANDS

This carriage was designed to improve the stability of a trim router while cutting solid-wood edgebandings flush with panels. The base rides on the face of the panel. The plane body and handles make a sure and comfortable grip. The fence guides the trimmer along the edge of the panel. An adjusting knob and bracket allow fine adjustments to the depth of the cut.

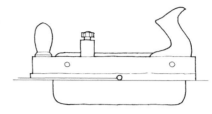

CUTTING DIRECTION
Use the trimmer with the bit turning into the cut to avoid tearout. Go slowly and steadily because the bit can self-feed.

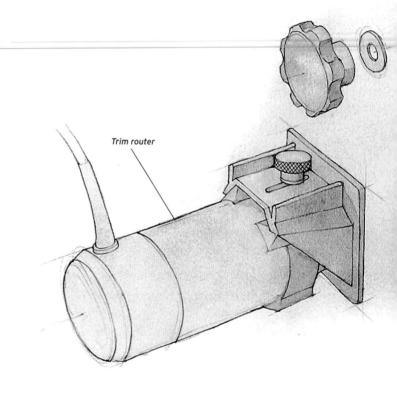

Trim router

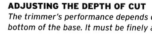

ADJUSTING THE DEPTH OF CUT
The trimmer's performance depends on how evenly the bit cuts with the bottom of the base. It must be finely adjustable.

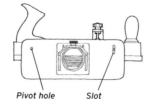

Pivot hole   Slot

Laminate trimmer's depth adjustment works to set trimmer's width of cut.

Slot in fence allows the base to travel up and down, pivoting on the opposite carriage bolt.

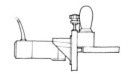

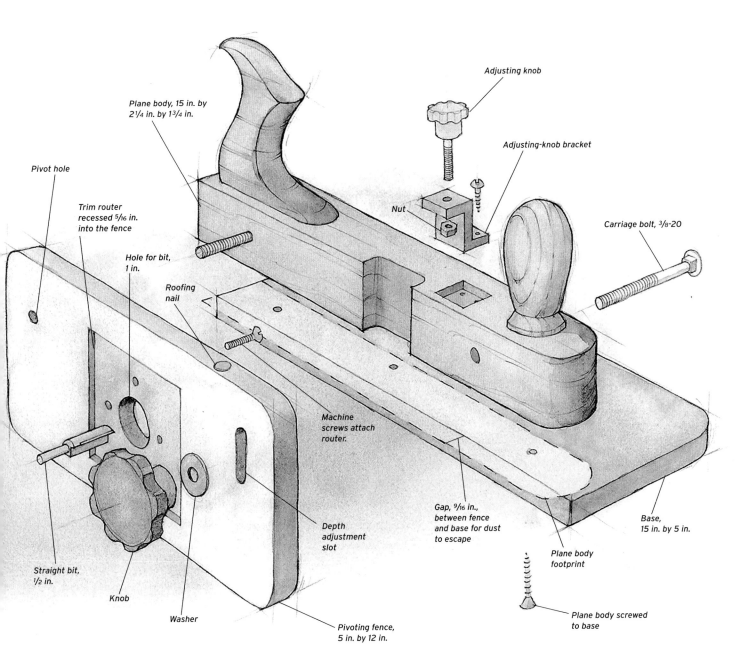

Adjusting knob

Plane body, 15 in. by
2¼ in. by 1¾ in.

Adjusting-knob bracket

Nut

Pivot hole

Carriage bolt, ³/₈-20

Trim router
recessed ⁵/₁₆ in.
into the fence

Hole for bit,
1 in.

Roofing
nail

Machine
screws attach
router.

Gap, ⁹/₁₆ in.,
between fence
and base for dust
to escape

Base,
15 in. by 5 in.

Plane body
footprint

Straight bit,
½ in.

Knob

Washer

Depth
adjustment
slot

Plane body screwed
to base

Pivoting fence,
5 in. by 12 in.

Easy design and assembly from odd materials. *The trimmer is mounted in a fence and attached to a base at 90 degrees.*

Adjusting knob sets cutting height. *A roofing nail makes a resilient contact point, reducing wear on the fence.*

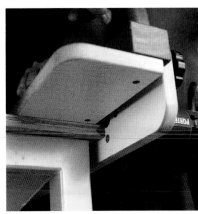

Gap between base and fence avoids obstacles. *The trimmer won't hang up on glue squeeze-out or oversize edge trim.*

HORIZONTAL ROUTER TABLE

By Ernie Conover

Being a traditionalist, I favor using mortise-and-tenon joints in all frame construction. For years I have cut tenons on the tablesaw with a tenoning jig, and I still favor this method for large tenons. For 3/4-in. stock, I became convinced that it would be child's play to build a simple table that would effectively cut tenons in almost all situations. This table, designed and made with the help of my friend Dave Hout, can be built in about two hours, works better than commercial tables of a similar ilk, and is small enough to be stored out of sight when not needed.

I made the table of medium-density fiberboard (MDF), but good-quality veneer-core plywood would work, too. Simple biscuit joints hold the table together. I used 3/4-in. material for the bottom and sides and a double thickness for the top. The same material can be used if you wish to construct a miter gauge. The swing arm was made of 1/2-in. veneer-core plywood, as were the front and back ends; the adjusting screw block can be made from any hardwood. While it is tempting to cover the table with plastic laminate, a couple coats of white shellac will give plenty of wear resistance.

Any 1 1/2-hp router that handles 1/2-in. bits will work in the table. The router does not have to be super-adjustable. Because the majority of tenons cut by my machine are 3/4 in. long, the router-bit depth is seldom changed. The adjustment that controls tenon thickness is tweaked frequently, but it's done using the screw in the screw block,

not the router itself. In short, when it comes to routers, an old clunker will do.

The table is easy to use. A 1/4-in. tenon is correct for 3/4-in. stock, yielding approximately a 1/4-in. shoulder, depending on the stock thickness. In most situations the shoulder dimension can be carried all the way around the tenon. This works splendidly because four quick cuts yield a perfect tenon. With a narrow rail (1 in. or less), a smaller shoulder at the top and bottom is desirable. In this case, you can either move out the 1/8-in. spacer below the adjusting screw to reduce the shoulders by the same amount or place a 1/8-in.-thick shim under the rail while cutting. For a haunched tenon, a spacer block of the same thickness as the groove in the adjoining post is interposed between the stock and the swing arm before starting the cut where the haunch is desired.

By plunging the bit through the swing arm after mounting the router, you get a zero-clearance opening that prevents small tenons from dropping into a void around the cutter. Most shavings end up under the table, but to ensure this you may have to widen this opening below the surface. By closing the open ends of the box with 1/2-in. plywood, a shop vacuum or dust collector can be connected to the table to minimize dust. **Safety Note:** When working with most table-mounted routers, stock is fed from right to left. But because the router for this table is mounted horizontally, stock must be fed from left to right, as in the photo above.

Ernie Conover runs Conover Workshops in Parkman, Ohio.

SIMPLE TO BUILD, EASY TO USE

This horizontal router table is made of ³/₄-in.-thick MDF and ½-in.-thick plywood joined with biscuits. Almost any type of non-plunging router is suitable, and depth and height adjustments are easily made.

Depth adjustment. *The depth of the cut is controlled using the adjustment gauge on the router.*

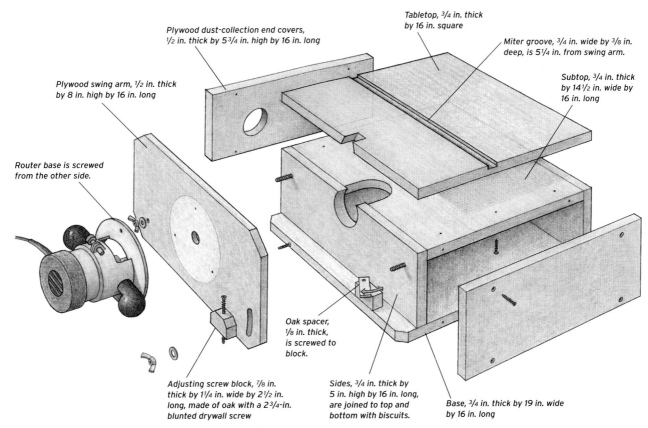

Plywood dust-collection end covers, ½ in. thick by 5³/₄ in. high by 16 in. long

Tabletop, ³/₄ in. thick by 16 in. square

Miter groove, ³/₄ in. wide by ³/₈ in. deep, is 5¼ in. from swing arm.

Plywood swing arm, ½ in. thick by 8 in. high by 16 in. long

Subtop, ³/₄ in. thick by 14½ in. wide by 16 in. long

Router base is screwed from the other side.

Oak spacer, ⅛ in. thick, is screwed to block.

Adjusting screw block, ⅞ in. thick by 1¼ in. wide by 2½ in. long, made of oak with a 2³/₄-in. blunted drywall screw

Sides, ³/₄ in. thick by 5 in. high by 16 in. long, are joined to top and bottom with biscuits.

Base, ³/₄ in. thick by 19 in. wide by 16 in. long

Accurate results

By turning the wood in a clockwise motion away from you, the breakout is confined to the initial cut. The author follows the sequence in the photos below to maintain consistent height and depth though all four cuts.

Height adjustment. *Fine-tune the height of the router bit by turning the screw in the screw block. When correct, tighten the wing nuts on the swing arm.*

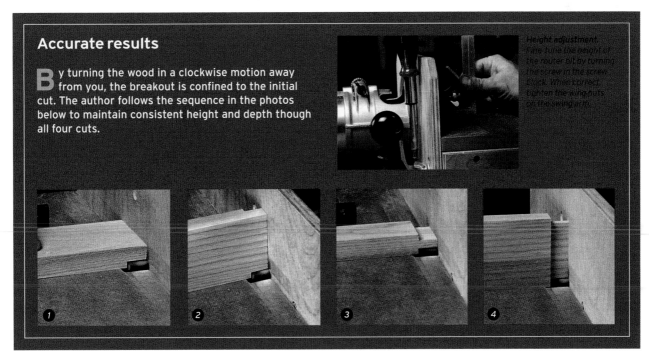

FIVE SMART ROUTER JIGS

By Yeung Chan

Few woodworkers enjoy the luxury of a spacious shop, and I'm no exception. Lacking the space for many large machines, I rely on my router when building furniture. However, used on its own, the router is limited in its abilities. More often than not, I use it in conjunction with various shopmade jigs that increase its ability to quickly and accurately cut circles, make edge profiles, cut dadoes, trim edge-banding, and even substitute for a lathe.

The five jigs illustrated here are all made from cheap and stable plywood or medium-density fiberboard (MDF) and require only a few pieces of hardware, available through Lee Valley Tools (www.leevalley.com; 800-871-8158) or Rockler™ (www.rockler.com; 800-279-4441). These router jigs are as easy to use as they are to make.

Yeung Chan builds custom furniture in Millbrae, California.

Cut perfect circles

This jig can be used to rout a circle with a maximum diameter of 72 in., but the design can be modified for other diameters. First, drill a ¼-in.-dia. hole, ¼ in. deep, in the middle of the workpiece. If you don't want the hole to show, work on the underside. Next, mark a point on the desired edge of the circle, place the sled over the base, and fit the jig's pin in the center hole. Move the base in or out until the bit is on the mark, then lock the sled.

Turn on the router and plunge down to start the initial cut, which should be less than ⅛ in. deep, just enough to define the circle. Use a jigsaw to cut away the outside pieces, leaving about ⅛ in. outside the final size of the circle. This method enables you to support the corners as they are cut off so that they won't damage the finished workpiece. Once the bulk of the waste has been removed, the router has to make only a light final cut. If you're working with solid wood, pay attention to the grain's orientation and the bit's rotation. Climb-cut when necessary to avoid tearout.

Make a shallow cut to define the circle. The initial cut made with the router should be only about ⅛ in. deep.

Remove the waste. Following the track left by the router, saw away the waste.

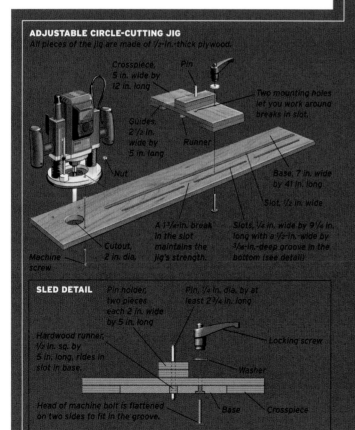

ADJUSTABLE CIRCLE-CUTTING JIG
All pieces of the jig are made of ½-in.-thick plywood.

Crosspiece, 5 in. wide by 12 in. long

Pin

Two mounting holes let you work around breaks in slot.

Guides, 2½ in. wide by 5 in. long

Runner

Nut

Base, 7 in. wide by 41 in. long

Slot, ½ in. wide

A 1¾-in. break in the slot maintains the jig's strength.

Slots, ¼ in. wide by 9¼ in. long with a ½-in.-wide by ³⁄₁₆-in.-deep groove in the bottom (see detail).

Cutout, 2 in. dia.

Machine screw

SLED DETAIL

Pin holder, two pieces each 2 in. wide by 5 in. long

Pin, ¼ in. dia. by at least 2¾ in. long

Hardwood runner, ½ in. sq. by 5 in. long, rides in slot in base.

Locking screw

Washer

Head of machine bolt is flattened on two sides to fit in the groove.

Base

Crosspiece

The final cut. The router now has to remove only a small amount of material, creating less dust and leaving a clean cut.

Trim or cut large panels

It is a difficult job to cut a large panel on a tablesaw that's not equipped with a sliding table. So I made a simple jig that can be used to cut out a section from a full sheet of plywood or to clean up a rough cut made by a jigsaw or a circular saw.

Once you've assembled the jig, run the router along the straight edge of the fence to create a matching straight edge on the base. To use the jig, clamp it at both ends of the workpiece with the edge of the jig aligned with the desired cut. As the router rides along the jig, it leaves a perfectly straight, clean cut.

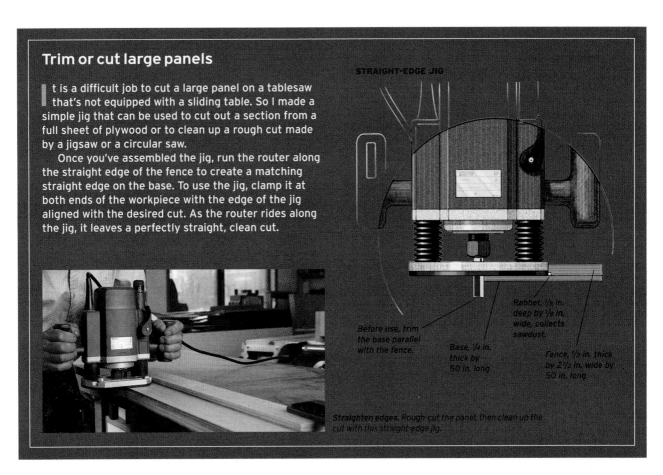

Before use, trim the base parallel with the fence.

Base, 1/4 in. thick by 50 in. long

Rabbet, 1/8 in. deep by 1/8 in. wide, collects sawdust.

Fence, 1/2 in. thick by 2 1/2 in. wide by 50 in. long

Straighten edges. Rough-cut the panel, then clean up the cut with this straight-edge jig.

Cut dadoes at any angle

I reach for this jig when I have to cut multiple parallel dadoes on a panel. Most of the time these grooves are perpendicular to the short fence of the jig, but they can be cut at different angles. Like the straight-edge jig, this one needs to be clamped at both ends during use. As long as you use the same size bit each time, and the same angle, the entry cut on the jig's short fence will show the location of the dado. Use an up-cut spiral bit, which will prevent chips from jamming in the dado. For deep dadoes, make several passes.

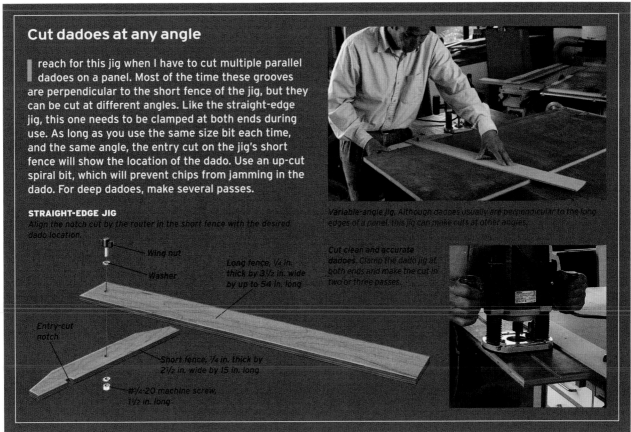

Variable-angle jig. Although dadoes usually are perpendicular to the long edges of a panel, this jig can make cuts at other angles.

STRAIGHT-EDGE JIG
Align the notch cut by the router in the short fence with the desired dado location.

Wing nut

Washer

Long fence, 1/4 in. thick by 3 1/2 in. wide by up to 54 in. long

Entry-cut notch

Short fence, 1/4 in. thick by 2 1/2 in. wide by 15 in. long

#1/4-20 machine screw, 1 1/2 in. long

Cut clean and accurate dadoes. Clamp the dado jig at both ends and make the cut in two or three passes.

Trim edgebanding quickly and cleanly

Flush-cut edgebanding. This jig allows you to cleanly cut solid-wood edgebanding flush with the plywood panel.

One of the hardest parts of using solid wood to edge plywood or laminate panels is trimming the edgebanding flush with the plywood. If you use a plane, you risk cutting through the thin plywood veneer, and sanding can leave cross-grain scratches on the plywood. This router jig enables you to trim the banding flush, quickly and flawlessly.

Mount the router on the jig, and set the depth of the bit so that it just clears the plywood surface. A router with micro-adjustment comes in handy. Adjust the guide block to align the bit so that the carbide tips extend just a hair over the plywood. Clamp the guide block tight, and you're ready to go.

Pay attention to the router bit's rotation and the direction you move the router. To avoid tearout, you want the leading edge of the bit to enter the wood first. Known as climb cutting, this method can be dangerous if the bit pulls the router forward uncontrollably. Because the amount of wood being removed is so small, you should be able to control the router easily.

EDGEBANDING TRIMMING JIG
The router bit should be positioned a hair above the plywood surface. The spacer/guide block is clamped to the jig to steer the router along the edging.

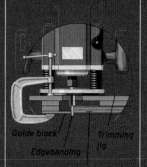

Guide block

Trimming jig

Edgebanding

Plywood panel

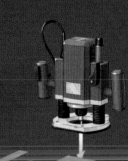

Top and bottom, 1/2 in. thick by 7 1/2 in. wide by 17 in. long, overlap by 11 in.

Cutout, 2 in. dia.

Guide block, 1/4 in. thick by 2 1/2 in. wide by 7 1/2 in. long, with spacer, 1 in. thick by 1 1/2 in. wide by 7 1/2 in. long

Make turnings with a router

This jig allows you to "turn" round columns and posts using a router. To use the jig, first drill a 5/16-in.-dia. hole, 1 1/2 in. deep, in each end of the workpiece, then insert a steel rod to hold the workpiece inside the jig. Lock a drill stop on each end of the rod where it enters the jig to prevent the workpiece from shifting during the turning. Clamp two wood guide pieces to the edges of the router subbase to restrict the router's side-to-side movement.

Turn on the router, slowly plunge down, and move the router halfway up and down the jig as you slowly rotate the workpiece. As you increase the depth of cut, you'll create a cylinder. Then repeat the process on the other half of the workpiece. Throughout the process, make small cuts for a better finish and a safer operation.

You can adapt this jig to create different turnings. Offset the hole at one end of the jig to make tapered turnings, or clamp blocks to the long sides of the jig to produce stopped turnings. If you design the jig with gently curving sides, the workpiece will become football shaped as it is turned.

TURNING JIG
The dimensions of this jig will vary based on the size of the blank to be turned. The four sides of the jig can be screwed together or clamped for greater flexibility. Steel rods passing through each end of the jig hold the blank.

Drill stop is tightened with hex key.

Steel rod, 5/16 in. dia.

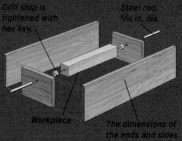

Workpiece

The dimensions of the ends and sides will vary according to the diameter and length of the turning.

Router-cut turnings. By guiding the router back and forth while turning the workpiece, a square blank gradually becomes a cylinder.

Tapered turnings. Lower the hole at one end of the jig to taper the turned workpiece.

Stopped turnings. Clamp blocks to the side of the jig to leave a square section on the turning.

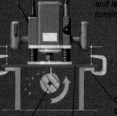

Guide pieces, clamped to subbase

Workpiece

Router subbase

COMPACT TOOL MAKES DADOES A SNAP

by Skip Lauderbaugh

Wall-mounted panel router is ideal for making quick dadoes. *Knowing his panel router had to save space, Lauderbaugh mounted it to a wall at a comfortable height and angle. To build the jig, he used a router he owned and commercial hardware costing less than $100.*

Many of my cabinetmaking projects require panels that have dadoes, rabbets, and grooves to allow strong, easy assembly. I've tried lots of ways of cutting these joints and have found that a panel router is the quickest and most accurate tool to use. Unfortunately, the expense of one of the commercial machines (up to $3,500) and the floor space it requires (up to 25 sq. ft.) is more than I can justify. As is often the case, however, once you have tasted using the proper tool for a particular job, using anything else becomes a frustrating compromise.

I had seen other shopmade panel routers, but they lacked features I wanted and seemed complicated. So I set out to design and build my own version of a panel router. By simplifying the guide system and by using common materials and hardware (see the drawing on p. 169), I built a panel router for less than $100 (not including the router, which I already owned). And although this jig easily handles big pieces of plywood and Melamine, the jig folds compactly against the wall when it is not in use.

Designing the panel router

Because the guide rails used in industrial panel routers often get in the way, the rails were the first things I eliminated on my design. The next thing was to orient the machine so that gravity would help feed the router into the work. Big panel routers are oriented horizontally, and they have the capacity to handle 36-in.-wide pieces of plywood. But because shelf dadoes in cabinets and cases are usually less than 3 ft. wide, I scaled things down a bit, and I situated the whole setup vertically. This orientation also saved considerable shop space. Then I came up with a clamp-on router guidance system, so I don't have to do any measuring or marking on a panel. Finally, I devised a router subbase that eliminates depth-of-cut adjustments when changing material thicknesses. To help you understand the abilities of this tool and how it is constructed, I've divided it into six basic components:

1. The workpiece table
2. The router guide system
3. The fence with adjustable stop
4. The upper and lower guide stops
5. The router subbase
6. The router tray

The workpiece table

A panel router requires a flat, stable work surface with a straight edge for mounting the fence. I chose an ordinary 3-ft.-wide hollow core door for the table because it provides those things, and at $15, it cost less than what I could build it for. I mounted the table to a ledger on the wall. A 5-in. space from the wall gives enough clearance for the guide system. Standard door hinges let the table swing out of the way during storage, and side supports hold the table at a 65-degree angle when the table is in use.

The router guide system

Several years ago, I discovered that the aluminum extrusions used in Tru-Grip's Clamp'N Tool® guides interlock when one is inverted. In this configuration, the two pieces slide smoothly back and forth with little side play, like a track.

The fence with adjustable stop

The fence holds the bottom edge of a panel straight, adds a runner for an adjustable stop and measuring system, and gives a place to mount the lower guide stop. Fence construction is partially dictated by the stop you use. I chose a Biesemeyer miter stop because it has two adjustable hairline pointers, which let you set and read both sides of a dado.

For the adjustable stop to work, the fence should be 1½ in. thick and the top edge of the fence has to be 1⅝ in. above the top of the table. My fence is two thicknesses of ¾-in. plywood laminated to form a 1½-in.-thick piece that is 3 in. wide and 96 in. long. The fence is mounted to the bottom edge of the table with 2½-in.-long screws.

The upper and lower guide stops

The upper and lower guide stops allow the Clamp'N Tool guide to be set exactly 90 degrees to the bottom edge of a panel. The lower guide stop is integrated in the fence, and the upper guide stop is fixed to the top of the table. The lower stop is a ⅜-in. bolt threaded into a T-nut inset into a block and glued to a notch in the fence.

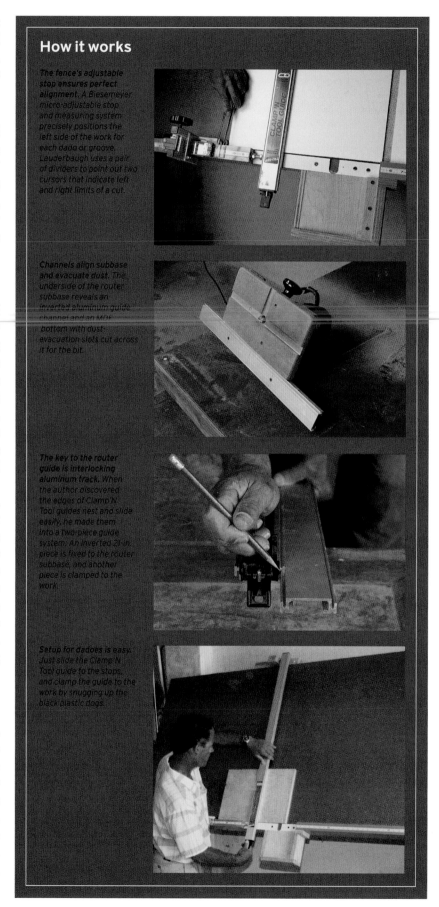

How it works

The fence's adjustable stop ensures perfect alignment. A Biesemeyer micro-adjustable stop and measuring system precisely positions the left side of the work for each dado or groove. Lauderbaugh uses a pair of dividers to point out two cursors that indicate left and right limits of a cut.

Channels align subbase and evacuate dust. The underside of the router subbase reveals an inverted aluminum guide channel and an MDF bottom with dust-evacuation slots cut across it for the bit.

The key to the router guide is interlocking aluminum track. When the author discovered the edges of Clamp'N Tool guides nest and slide easily, he made them into a two-piece guide system. An inverted 2l-in. piece is fixed to the router subbase, and another piece is clamped to the work.

Setup for dadoes is easy. Just slide the Clamp'N Tool guide to the stops, and clamp the guide to the work by snugging up the black plastic dogs.

PANEL-ROUTER ASSEMBLY

Panel router handles common sheet thicknesses, stores flat against wall, folds out for use.

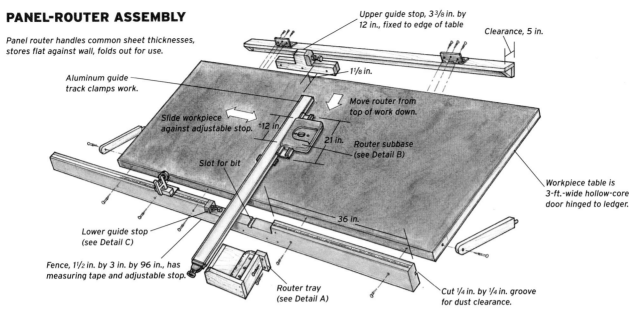

Upper guide stop, 3³/₈ in. by 12 in., fixed to edge of table

Clearance, 5 in.

Aluminum guide track clamps work.

1¹/₈ in.

Slide workpiece against adjustable stop. ±12 in.

Move router from top of work down.

21 in.

Router subbase (see Detail B)

Slot for bit

Lower guide stop (see Detail C)

36 in.

Workpiece table is 3-ft.-wide hollow-core door hinged to ledger.

Fence, 1¹/₂ in. by 3 in. by 96 in., has measuring tape and adjustable stop.

Router tray (see Detail A)

Cut ¹/₄ in. by ¹/₄ in. groove for dust clearance.

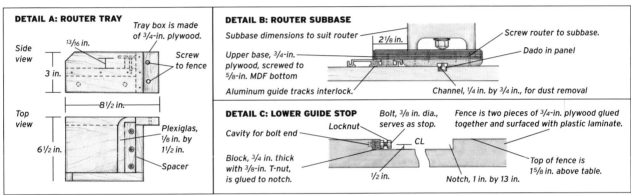

DETAIL A: ROUTER TRAY

Tray box is made of ³/₄-in. plywood.

Side view

¹³/₁₆ in.

3 in.

Screw to fence

8¹/₂ in.

Top view

6¹/₂ in.

Plexiglas, ¹/₈ in. by 1¹/₂ in.

Spacer

DETAIL B: ROUTER SUBBASE

Subbase dimensions to suit router

2¹/₈ in.

Upper base, ³/₄-in. plywood, screwed to ⁵/₈-in. MDF bottom

Aluminum guide tracks interlock.

Screw router to subbase.

Dado in panel

Channel, ¹/₄ in. by ³/₄ in., for dust removal

DETAIL C: LOWER GUIDE STOP

Cavity for bolt end

Locknut

Bolt, ³/₈ in. dia., serves as stop.

CL

Fence is two pieces of ³/₄-in. plywood glued together and surfaced with plastic laminate.

Block, ³/₄ in. thick with ³/₈-in. T-nut, is glued to notch.

¹/₂ in.

Notch, 1 in. by 13 in.

Top of fence is 1⁵/₈ in. above table.

The router subbase

Parts for the router subbase consist of a medium-density fiberboard (MDF) bottom, an upper base made out of ³/₄-in. plywood that mounts to the router, and a piece of upside-down extrusion screwed to the side so it can engage the guide track. Drawing detail B (above) shows the dimensions I used to mount my Porter-Cable® model 690 router. But you could modify the subbase to suit your router. Regardless of the router, the bottom should be ⁵/₈ in. thick so that the extrusions interlock properly.

The router tray

The purpose of the router tray is to give the router a place to rest after it has completed a cut. The tray is mounted to the fence on the back side of the notched-out area. My tray is made out of ³/₄-in. plywood and is screwed to the fence. On the right edge of the tray, a piece of ¹/₈-in. Plexiglas® protrudes into the tray opening. As the router slides down into the tray, the Plexiglas piece fits into a slot cut into the edge of the subbase and prevents the router from lifting out of the tray.

Using the panel router

The panel-router sequence to make a dado goes like this: First, I set the adjustable stop to locate the dado where I want it. Second, I set the panel on the table and slide it up against the adjustable stop. Third, I place the Clamp'N Tool guide on the panel, slide it against the upper and lower guide stops, and clamp it down. In this one step, the guide is squared to the panel and clamped to the table. Fourth, I set the router on the panel with the extrusions interlocked. I hold the router subbase above the top of the panel so the bit clears. Finally, I turn the router on and cut the dado. To make stop dadoes, I insert a spacer block in the bottom of the tray to prevent the router from cutting all the way across a panel. While this setup may not be perfect for a large production shop, it is certainly affordable and conserves space.

Skip Lauderbaugh is a sales representative for Blum hardware and a college woodworking instructor. His shop is in Costa Mesa, California.

CUSTOM-BUILT DOVETAIL JIG

by William H. Page

Shop-built from scraps, these unusual jigs, one for the tails and one for the pins, cut tight-fitting through-dovetails, a task that even many commercial jigs can't handle. Designed for routing dovetails for large carcase construction, the jigs can be built in less than two hours for just pennies.

Layout is simple and can be done as the tail jig is assembled. Fingers screwed to the tail jig guide the router bits; the key is ball bearings. The bits used to cut the joint are guided by bearings the same diameter as the cutter. Pin and tail size and spacing are variable, and jigs can be built to handle any width board.

I start with the tail jig, and in the process of making this jig, I also cut a guide board that precisely locates the pin templates for assembling the pin jig. Using the tail jig to rout the pin-template guide board ensures a perfect match of pins to tails.

The tail jig consists of a collar that surrounds the stock to be joined and a series of fingers screwed to the top of this collar. The fingers serve as a stop when inserting stock into the collar and as a guide for the bearing on the bit. The location of these fingers across the top of the collar determines the spacing of the pins.

With the fingers in place, I run the dovetail bit through the collar of the jig and a scrap piece of stock clamped in the jig. These cuts create the tail piece, or the openings that the pins will fit into, and prepare the jig for use. The collar must be clamped to the stock to avoid any movement that could affect the accuracy of the cut.

The pin jig consists of a collar built around the pin-template guide board, but instead of straight fingers, the pin templates for this jig are wedges with an included angle to match the cut of the dovetail bit, as shown in the figure on the facing page. An outrigger attached to the pin collar provides full support for the router when routing the pins.

With both jigs assembled, I rout a joint in a couple of pieces of scrap clamped firmly in the collars to test the fit and to be sure I like the pattern before proceeding with my good stock.

Minor misfits can be adjusted by shaving the edge of the pin templates or adding masking-tape shims. If you're satisfied with the fit and spacing, slide the appropriate jig over the end of your stock and start cutting. The actual routing of joints takes about five minutes each.

Bill Page is a woodworker in Toledo, Ohio.

To make a tail jig, build a holding fixture that forms a collar around the stock, screw guide fingers to the top edge, and then rout between the fingers to create the sockets.

Precise through-dovetail joints. Refined joints are easy to rout with the aid of a couple of shop-built jigs. Here, the author completes the second part of the joint by routing the pins with a bearing-guided straight bit. The bearing rides against pin templates that have been positioned accurately using a guide board routed with the tail jig, which is the first jig to be built.

MAKING DOVETAIL JIGS

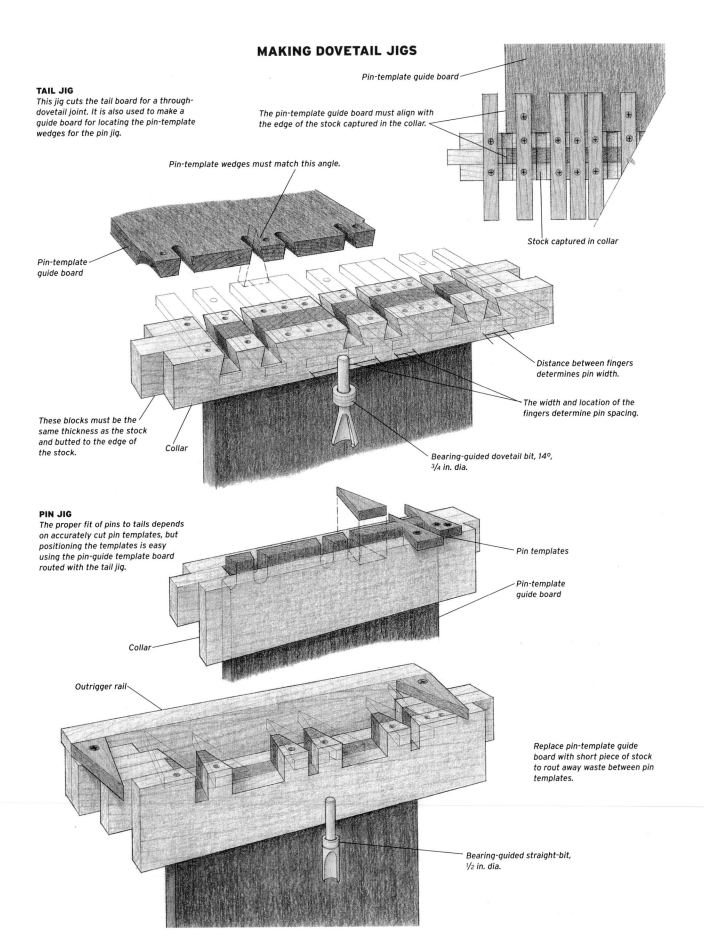

Pin-template guide board

TAIL JIG
This jig cuts the tail board for a through-dovetail joint. It is also used to make a guide board for locating the pin-template wedges for the pin jig.

The pin-template guide board must align with the edge of the stock captured in the collar.

Pin-template wedges must match this angle.

Stock captured in collar

Pin-template guide board

These blocks must be the same thickness as the stock and butted to the edge of the stock.

Collar

Distance between fingers determines pin width.

The width and location of the fingers determine pin spacing.

Bearing-guided dovetail bit, 14°, 3/4 in. dia.

PIN JIG
The proper fit of pins to tails depends on accurately cut pin templates, but positioning the templates is easy using the pin-guide template board routed with the tail jig.

Pin templates

Pin-template guide board

Collar

Outrigger rail

Replace pin-template guide board with short piece of stock to rout away waste between pin templates.

Bearing-guided straight-bit, 1/2 in. dia.

A VERSATILE ROUTER TABLE

By Kevin McLaughlin

Over the years I looked at a lot of router-table designs, but every one I came across lacked one feature or another. Shopmade router tables usually are limited to tabletop routing and fall short if you want to do anything more, like mount the router horizontally or use an overhead pin routing guide. The same is true for most store-bought tables.

My own router-table design combines all of the features I was after. The table I arrived at is easy to build, and it can be made with low-cost materials. Above all, because it accommodates the router in a variety of orientations, it can handle any cut that I could possibly think of making.

With the router mounted horizontally in an adjustable carriage, the table is set up ideally for cutting sliding dovetails or mortise-and-tenons. And shaping the edge of a wide board doesn't require balancing unwieldy material on end.

The adjustable carriage also doubles as a base to mount several overhead attachments. A pin routing

Adjustable carriage adds versatility

An adjustable carriage holds the router in its horizontal cutting position (left) and acts as a base to mount overhead attachments, such as a pin routing guide (right) for template-guided cuts.

A router-table construction

The tabletop and back are Melamine and joined with a miter to provide a smooth, unobstructed surface for routing. The recess in the center of the table allows the router baseplate to sit flush with the tabletop. Size the opening in the top so that the router can be lowered in from above. The measurements in the drawing may need to be modified should you use different hardware.

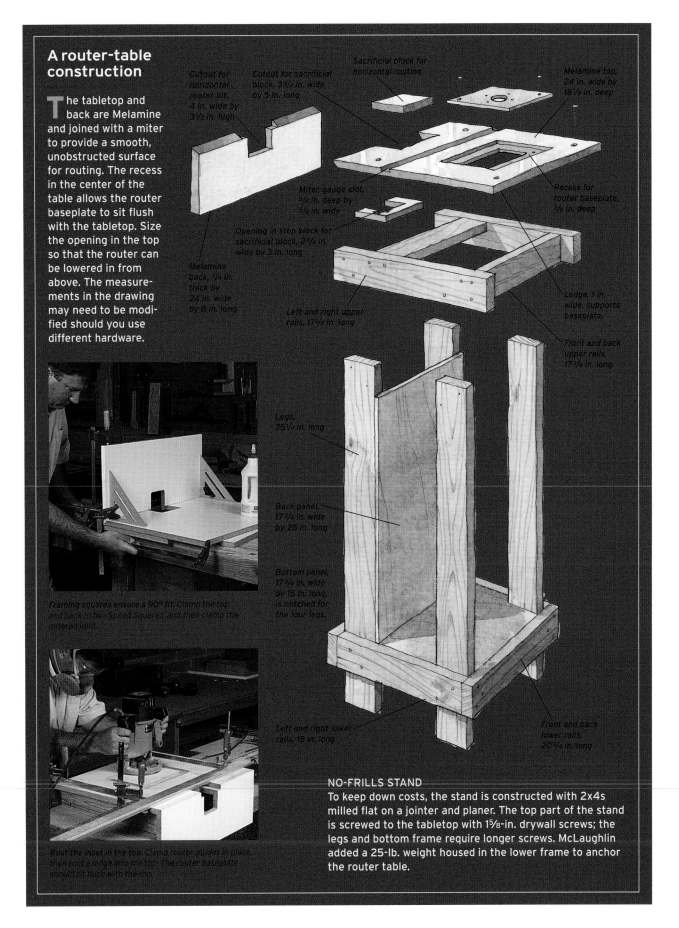

Cutout for horizontal router bit, 4 in. wide by 3½ in. high

Cutout for sacrificial block, 3¾ in. wide by 5 in. long

Sacrificial block for horizontal routing

Melamine top, 24 in. wide by 18⅛ in. deep

Recess for router baseplate, ⅜ in. deep

Miter-gauge slot, ⅜ in. deep by ⅝ in. wide

Opening in stop block for sacrificial block, 2¾ in. wide by 3 in. long

Melamine back, ¾ in. thick by 24 in. wide by 8 in. long

Left and right upper rails, 17½ in. long

Ledge, 1 in. wide, supports baseplate.

Front and back upper rails, 17¾ in. long

Legs, 35¼ in. long

Back panel, 17¾ in. wide by 25 in. long

Bottom panel, 17¾ in. wide by 15 in. long, is notched for the four legs.

Left and right lower rails, 15 in. long

Front and back lower rails, 20¾ in. long

Framing squares ensure a 90° fit. Clamp the top and back to two Speed Squares, and then clamp the mitered joint.

Rout the inset in the top. Clamp router guides in place, then rout a ledge into the top. The router baseplate should sit flush with the top.

NO-FRILLS STAND

To keep down costs, the stand is constructed with 2x4s milled flat on a jointer and planer. The top part of the stand is screwed to the tabletop with 1⅝-in. drywall screws; the legs and bottom frame require longer screws. McLaughlin added a 25-lb. weight housed in the lower frame to anchor the router table.

THE ADJUSTABLE CARRIAGE

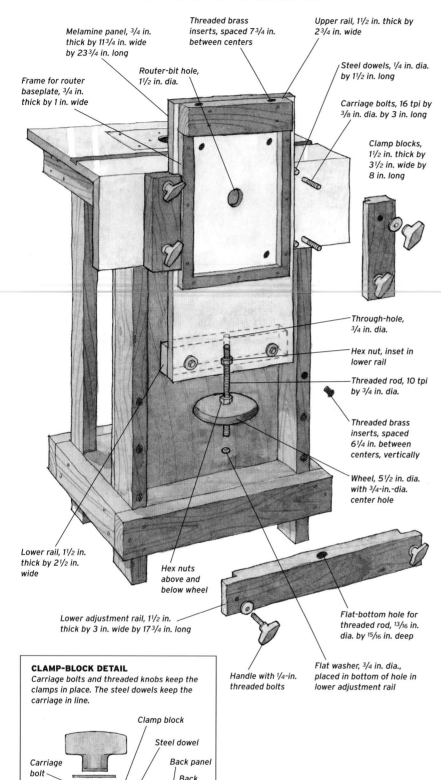

Melamine panel, 3/4 in. thick by 11 3/4 in. wide by 23 3/4 in. long

Threaded brass inserts, spaced 7 3/4 in. between centers

Upper rail, 1 1/2 in. thick by 2 3/4 in. wide

Frame for router baseplate, 3/4 in. thick by 1 in. wide

Router-bit hole, 1 1/2 in. dia.

Steel dowels, 1/4 in. dia. by 1 1/2 in. long

Carriage bolts, 16 tpi by 3/8 in. dia. by 3 in. long

Clamp blocks, 1 1/2 in. thick by 3 1/2 in. wide by 8 in. long

Through-hole, 3/4 in. dia.

Hex nut, inset in lower rail

Threaded rod, 10 tpi by 3/4 in. dia.

Threaded brass inserts, spaced 6 1/4 in. between centers, vertically

Wheel, 5 1/2 in. dia. with 3/4-in.-dia. center hole

Lower rail, 1 1/2 in. thick by 2 1/2 in. wide

Hex nuts above and below wheel

Lower adjustment rail, 1 1/2 in. thick by 3 in. wide by 17 3/4 in. long

Handle with 1/4-in. threaded bolts

Flat-bottom hole for threaded rod, 13/16 in. dia. by 15/16 in. deep

Flat washer, 3/4 in. dia., placed in bottom of hole in lower adjustment rail

CLAMP-BLOCK DETAIL
Carriage bolts and threaded knobs keep the clamps in place. The steel dowels keep the carriage in line.

Clamp block

Steel dowel

Carriage bolt

Back panel

Back of table

guide makes the table useful for template routing. A fence guard is easy to set up for safety. Finally, a horizontal carriage attachment allows the router to be mounted upright above the table surface and the workpiece. In this orientation, you can reference the flat side of the workpiece on the tabletop, which is helpful when removing wide areas of material or when cutting irregular moldings. With such a simple system for mounting attachments, I can build new ones to tackle any tasks I think of down the road.

The adjustable carriage moves in a true vertical line perpendicular to the tabletop, so overhead attachments can rest on top and be moved up and down while remaining parallel to the tabletop, a design that's critical to using the overhead attachments effectively.

The construction of the router table is relatively simple. The stand is made of 2x4s held together with drywall screws. This is a sturdy and inexpensive method that can be modified easily if you want to add drawers or make an enclosed cabinet.

I began by choosing the router table baseplate, then built the tabletop to accommodate it.

For the tabletop and adjustable carriage I used 3/4-in.-thick Melamine. I chose Melamine because it has a slick finish and is extremely flat. The various attachments are constructed with Melamine and 3/4-in.-thick birch plywood.

Kevin McLaughlin is a mechanical designer and machinist by trade living in Helena, Alabama.

Useful accessories

This router table can be modified easily to accommodate various routing tasks. With the router mounted upside down in the table, you can make use of several overhead attachments. For example, a pin guide allows for easy template routing. McLaughlin built four attachments for his router table, shown here. They follow only one standard requirement: They must attach to the top of the adjustable carriage with two threaded bolts with handles that are placed 7¾ in. apart from center to center.

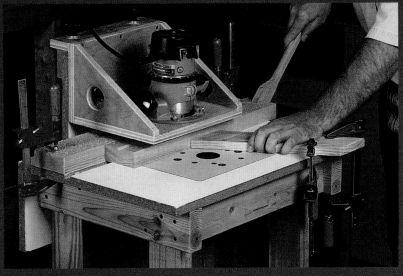

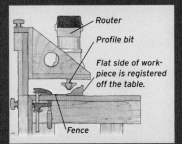

Threaded bolts with handles

Threaded bolts with handles, spaced 6¼ in. between centers

1½-in.-dia. hole for router bit.

Router

Profile bit

Flat side of workpiece is registered off the table.

Fence

An overhead router carriage holds the router upright above the table, allowing the flat side of a workpiece to be referenced on the tabletop.

PIN ROUTING GUIDE

A steel dowel, positioned in line with a nonbearing straight router bit, is used for template-routing. The template is guided along the pin while the router bit cuts the workpiece to match. The pin guide is attached to the adjustable carriage.

FENCE GUARD

A clear plastic shield keeps fingers away from the bit when the router is mounted upside down in the table. A flattened 2x4 clamped to the table makes an adequate fence.

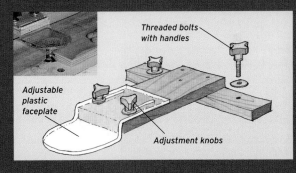

Threaded bolts with handles

Adjustable plastic faceplate

Adjustment knobs

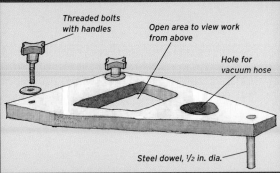

Threaded bolts with handles

Open area to view work from above

Hole for vacuum hose

Steel dowel, ½ in. dia.

VACUUM-HOSE ATTACHMENT

This adjustable overhead attachment places a shop-vacuum hose right where you need it.

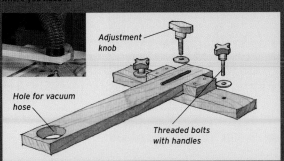

Adjustment knob

Hole for vacuum hose

Threaded bolts with handles

ROUTER TABLE ACCESSORIES

By Patrick Warner

A SIMPLE, EFFECTIVE FENCE

You can get by with a piece of MDF or jointed hardwood as long as it is straight. A pivot point at one end makes fine adjustment easier. The other end is secured with a C-clamp.

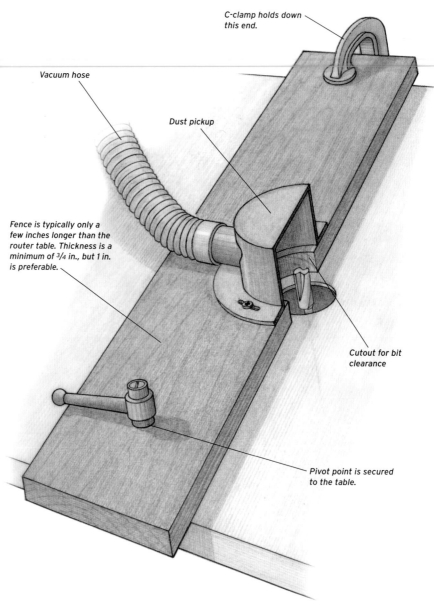

C-clamp holds down this end.

Vacuum hose

Dust pickup

Fence is typically only a few inches longer than the router table. Thickness is a minimum of 3/4 in., but 1 in. is preferable.

Cutout for bit clearance

Pivot point is secured to the table.

Fence and cutter setup. Using a sample with the desired final profile, establish the correct height of the cutter and the final position of the fence (top). Mark this location by clamping a registration block to the table (below).

If you decide to build your own router table, you are welcome to make it as sophisticated as you like. However, the table does not have to be that complex. All that is required for maximum control of the workpiece and highest quality of cut are a flat table that's at a comfortable working height and a good fence. But a quality fence does not have to be complex or difficult to make.

The fence must be straight, flat, and square to the top. Adjustability would be nice, but if it ain't flat and straight, the depths of cut will vary, and there may be some risk to the user. The fence seen here will handle the bulk of the work you perform at the router table.

Like a group of mischievous lads, a router can get where no other tool can. You can enter the edge, the end, or the face of nearly any stick. The cut can be blind, half blind, through, or cut to any fractional depth.

Finish the cut. *Stepped cuts are made by moving the fence back in stages. The final cut will be made with the fence against the registration block*

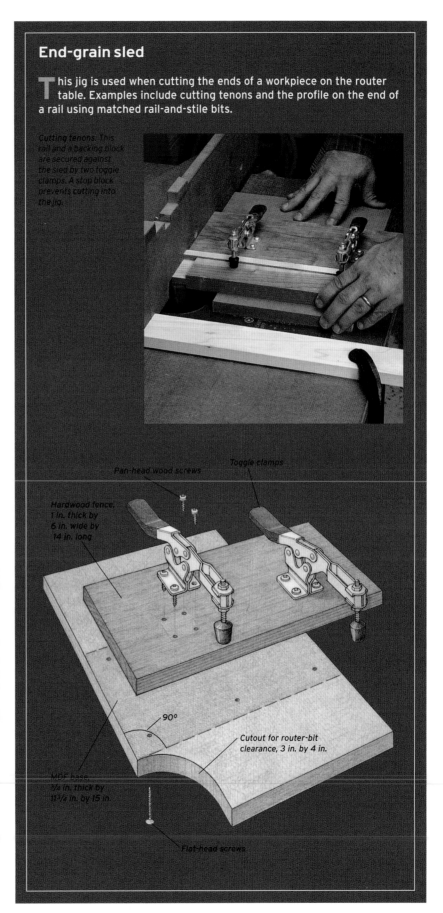

End-grain sled

This jig is used when cutting the ends of a workpiece on the router table. Examples include cutting tenons and the profile on the end of a rail using matched rail-and-stile bits.

Cutting tenons: This rail and a backing block are secured against the sled by two toggle clamps. A stop block prevents cutting into the jig.

Pan-head wood screws

Toggle clamps

Hardwood fence, 1 in. thick by 6 in. wide by 14 in. long

90°

Cutout for router-bit clearance, 3 in. by 4 in.

MDF base, 3/4 in. thick by 11 3/4 in. by 15 in.

Flat-head screws

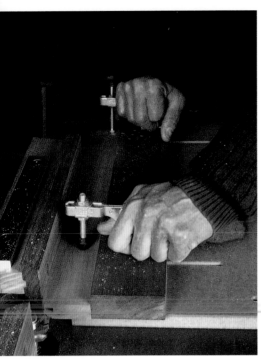

A router bit can't be expected to behave without adversity under all of these conditions. A cutter can chatter the walls and floors of its pathway. It can tear out as it encounters wavy grain. It can burn in cherry and spoil the entry and exit of cross-grain cuts such as dadoes. A bit can break, bend, burn, vibrate, scream, lose its carbide, or go dull in seconds if it's abused.

To combat these problems, it is the accepted practice to use hold-downs, featherboards, and other contrivances to manage difficult cuts on the router table. I don't. In my view, if the operation is a risky one, it requires a proper jig to control the workpiece safely and achieve a quality cut.

Over the years I've also developed numerous jigs for use with a router, but two simple ones will aid many of your cuts on the router table. The first is an end-grain sled on pp. 176–177, used when cutting the end of a workpiece, particularly a narrow one. The work is secured with toggle clamps, and a backup piece of scrap can be placed between the workpiece and the jig's fence to prevent breakout.

The second jig is a long-grain sled (see the photo at left and drawings below) used when routing the face of long, narrow stock, where control by finger-tips alone would be an accident waiting to happen. Stock that is rigidly held, not resonated with a featherboard, will be chatter free.

Patrick Warner is a furniture maker, writer and teacher. He lives in Escondido, California.

Cutting profiles. Warner uses this long-grain sled when routing profiles on long, narrow boards. The toggle clamps are safer and more effective than using fingers to guide the work this close to a cutter.

LONG-GRAIN SLED

This jig is used for running the long side of a workpiece past the cutter. The sled can help cut the long edges of rails and stiles using one cutter from a matched set. It can also aid in cutting decorative profiles and moldings.

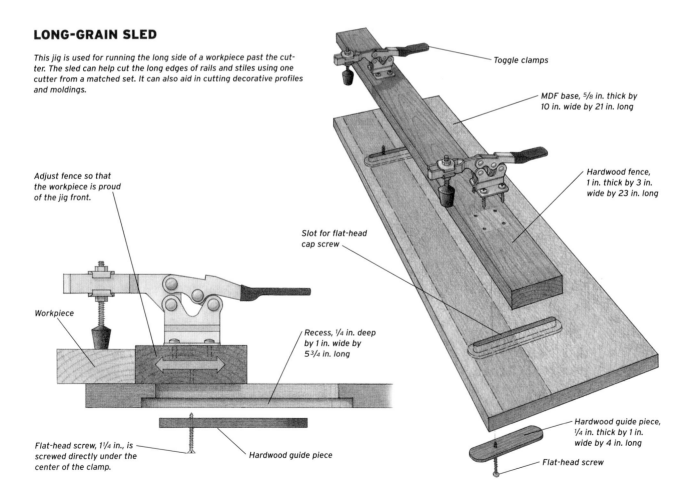

Adjust fence so that the workpiece is proud of the jig front.

Workpiece

Slot for flat-head cap screw

Recess, 1/4 in. deep by 1 in. wide by 5 3/4 in. long

Flat-head screw, 1 1/4 in., is screwed directly under the center of the clamp.

Hardwood guide piece

Toggle clamps

MDF base, 5/8 in. thick by 10 in. wide by 21 in. long

Hardwood fence, 1 in. thick by 3 in. wide by 23 in. long

Hardwood guide piece, 1/4 in. thick by 1 in. wide by 4 in. long

Flat-head screw

VERSATILE SHOP STORAGE SOLUTIONS

by Joseph Beals

During the 10 years I worked in a cellar shop, I installed cabinets, drawers and open shelving wherever room allowed. The results were typical: I knew where to find everything, but there was little order to the method, and junk and dust were a chronic problem.

When I moved to a converted garage building, I left those built-ins behind. I packed tools, hardware, and supplies into dozens of 5-gal. buckets, and I worked out of them for the next year until the new shop was at last functional. To avoid re-creating the past, I designed a new storage system that remedies many of the usual irritations. I resolved to minimize any sort of generic storage that invites accretions of dust and junk. This meant little or no open shelving, no big drawers under the bench and no casual boxes or bins.

Finally, with the agony of moving so close behind me, I wanted a fully portable storage system. And I wanted a system that could be moved around easily.

Mobile cabinet

With these goals in mind, I built a set of floor and wall cabinets, as shown in the photo above, which offer exceptional utility in concert with a pleasing, traditional appearance; I also built special wall storage racks, as discussed in the sidebar on p. 182. The floor cabinets are mounted on casters and incorporate a series of guide rails for shelves or drawers. The wall cabinets hang from simple wall-mounted cleats (see the photo on p. 181) and include integral dadoes to allow any combination of plain or purpose-built shelving. To cut costs, I built the cabinets from a

Storage A-plenty. *These movable cabinets keep tools stored, on slide out shelves or in drawers, neat and dust free. Casters make the base cabinets mobile while a cleat-mounting system allows the wall cabinets to be easily rearranged.*

variety of wood species using leftover stock and cutoffs, including quartersawn white oak, black walnut, mahogany, elm, and cherry. All cabinets include paneled doors, ½-in.-thick birch plywood backs and straightforward joinery.

I used molded frames, raised panels, and a polished finish to create a display for clients visiting my shop, but there are many simpler options. Pine frames made on the tablesaw, router table, or entirely by hand, together with ¼-in.-thick plywood panels and a paint finish are attractive and require no special tooling. A solid, flat panel, rabbeted around the perimeter to fit the frame grooves, is fully traditional and easy to make. If you are new to frame-and-panel work, these alternatives are a practical and satisfying introduction.

For a contemporary appearance, substitute plywood for frame-and-panel construction. Plywood cabinet sides can be grooved to house shelving or drawers, eliminating the guide rails required by a frame-and-panel carcase.

Base cabinets

I built all the cabinets in multiples for maximum benefit of bench and machine time. I began with the frame-and-panel sides (see figure 1 on p. 180). The stiles are equal in length to the height of the frame, but stile and rail widths and the length of the rails, are determined according to personal preference and the method of joinery. Mortise-and-tenon joinery, for example, requires additional length on the rails for the tenons.

I used a matched set of cope-and-pattern cutters on the shaper to machine the frame, but there are many other equally suitable methods.

FIG. 1: BASE STORAGE CABINET

Mobile storage cabinets make it easy to rearrange your shop layout. Uniform spacing of drawer guides makes all drawers and shelves interchangeable.

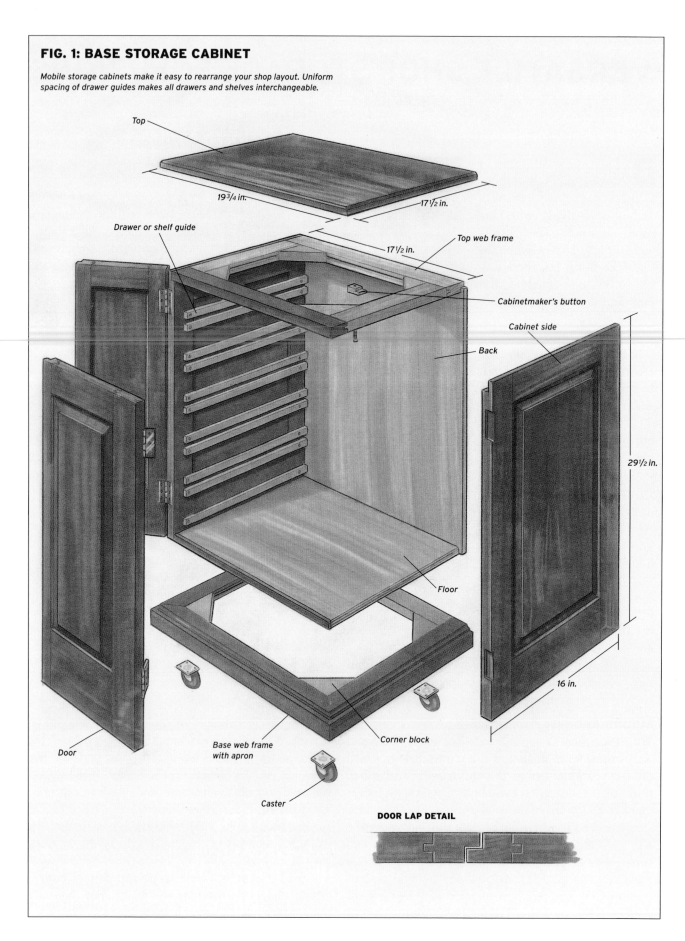

Top

Drawer or shelf guide

19³/₄ in.

17¹/₂ in.

17¹/₂ in.

Top web frame

Cabinetmaker's button

Cabinet side

Back

29¹/₂ in.

Floor

16 in.

Door

Base web frame with apron

Corner block

Caster

DOOR LAP DETAIL

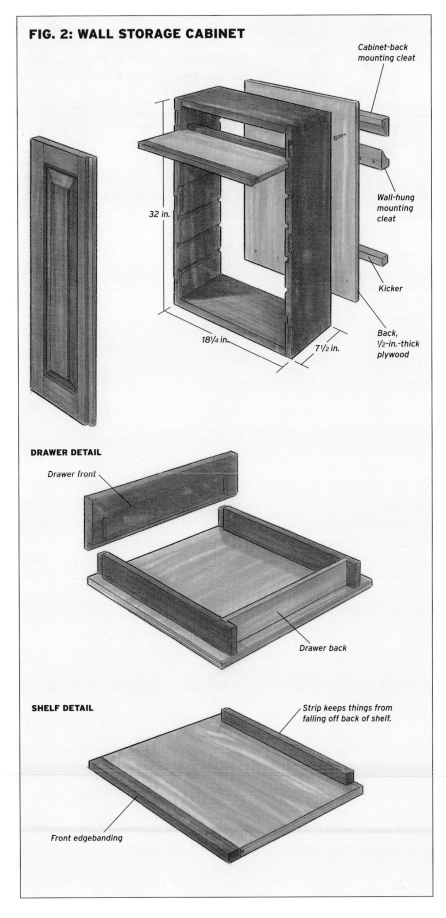

FIG. 2: WALL STORAGE CABINET

Cabinet-back mounting cleat

Wall-hung mounting cleat

Kicker

Back, ½-in.-thick plywood

32 in.

18¼ in.

7½ in.

DRAWER DETAIL

Drawer front

Drawer back

SHELF DETAIL

Strip keeps things from falling off back of shelf.

Front edgebanding

All the cabinet components are screwed together, so assembling the cabinet is quick and easy. The two sides are fastened to the lower web frame with screws driven up from below, just inside the skirt. The upper web frame is screwed down into the sides from the top, and the plywood back is screwed into the rabbets that house it. I used no glue in the assembly, which makes it possible to take the carcase apart for any reason. I used shop-grade elm for a serviceable top on all floor cabinets. The tops are given a half-round profile on the front and sides, and they're fastened to the upper web frame with traditional buttons (see figure 1 on the facing page).

The cabinet shelves can be solid stock or sheet goods, as preference dictates. I used ½-in.-thick birch plywood, banded on the front to match the cabinet wood. The shelves pull out easily on the guides, and thin cleats glued to the back keep things from falling off the back edge.

Cleats allow cabinets to be moved. Strips ripped at 45 degrees, one screwed to the wall and one to the cabinet back, make it easy to rearrange cabinets. A kicker screwed to the cabinet back near the bottom makes the cabinet hang plumb.

To keep the design simple, I built the drawers as a box fastened to a shelf, as shown in the detail on p. 181. The two sides engage the front with sliding dovetail joints, and the front of the shelf fits in a rabbet on the drawer front. I screwed the sides and back to the bottom from below. The cabinet will hold six shallow drawers, but deeper drawers can be made by doubling or tripling the spacing module.

Building wall cabinets

Construction of the wall cabinets is simplicity itself (see figure 2 on p. 181). The solid carcase can be assembled in a variety of ways, but through-dovetails offer the strongest and best-looking joint. I cut all dovetails by hand, which took less than an hour for each cabinet. Before the carcase was assembled, I used a dado set on the radial-arm saw to cut six shelf dadoes in each side.

Frame-and-panel doors

All cabinets are provided with a pair of narrow, paneled doors. A single-wide door might seem simpler, but the sweep can be awkward, especially on a floor cabinet in a restricted space. The doors are constructed like the floor cabinet sides and for appearance, have the same dimensional proportions of stiles and rails.

I used aniline dye to stain all but the cherry cabinet. Because cherry darkens so rapidly and dramatically, it is generally better not to color the wood under the finish. All cabinets received a half dozen coats of shellac, and after the last coat is well rubbed out, I applied a beeswax polish for a soft, lustrous finish.

Joseph Beals is a builder and custom wood-worker who lives in Marshfield, Massachusetts.

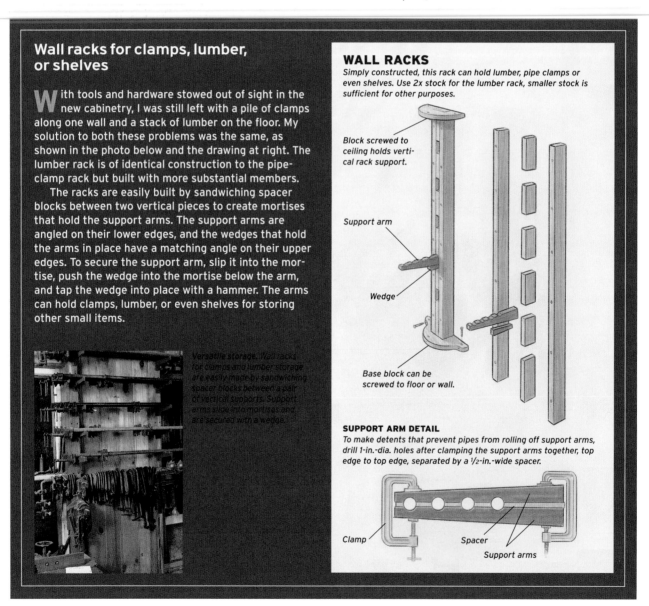

Wall racks for clamps, lumber, or shelves

With tools and hardware stowed out of sight in the new cabinetry, I was still left with a pile of clamps along one wall and a stack of lumber on the floor. My solution to both these problems was the same, as shown in the photo below and the drawing at right. The lumber rack is of identical construction to the pipe-clamp rack but built with more substantial members.

The racks are easily built by sandwiching spacer blocks between two vertical pieces to create mortises that hold the support arms. The support arms are angled on their lower edges, and the wedges that hold the arms in place have a matching angle on their upper edges. To secure the support arm, slip it into the mortise, push the wedge into the mortise below the arm, and tap the wedge into place with a hammer. The arms can hold clamps, lumber, or even shelves for storing other small items.

Versatile storage. Wall racks for clamps and lumber storage are easily made by sandwiching spacer blocks between a pair of vertical supports. Support arms slide into mortises and are secured with a wedge.

WALL RACKS

Simply constructed, this rack can hold lumber, pipe clamps or even shelves. Use 2x stock for the lumber rack, smaller stock is sufficient for other purposes.

Block screwed to ceiling holds vertical rack support.

Support arm

Wedge

Base block can be screwed to floor or wall.

SUPPORT ARM DETAIL

To make detents that prevent pipes from rolling off support arms, drill 1-in.-dia. holes after clamping the support arms together, top edge to top edge, separated by a 1/2-in.-wide spacer.

Clamp

Spacer

Support arms

WALL PANELS ORGANIZE HAND TOOLS

By Jerry H. Lyons

Like many woodworkers, I have lots of hand tools, and I want to be able to find a tool when I need it. I would rather spend my time working than looking. To organize my hand-tool collection, I built four tool panels near my workbenches. Each tool, regardless of its size, fits into its own space within one of these panels. The panel backs are made of ¾-in.-thick seven-ply oak plywood. The edging is solid oak rabbeted to receive the plywood and mitered at the corners.

To accommodate the needs of several students at once, all panels include common tools such as handsaws and planes. Whenever possible, I grouped tools—such as those for measuring, layout, and cutting—according to use.

I used a bandsaw, handplanes, and sanders to shape and mold each tool holder's unique configuration. I glued the tool holders in place and used screws and dowels for reinforcement.

Jerry H. Lyons, who taught furniture making for 21 years, recently built his dream shop near Glasgow, Kentucky.

Designs on display. *Lyons finds it helpful to keep plans for his current project displayed so that he can reference them easily but not get them damaged.*

Tools are grouped according to use. *Layout tools and clamps are gathered on this tool panel.*

A place for everything. *Wall panels display hand tools, making them easy to find and access.*

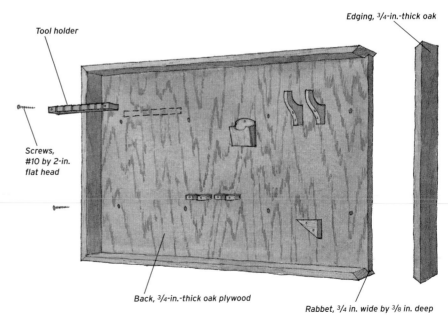

Tool holder

Screws, #10 by 2-in. flat head

Edging, ¾-in.-thick oak

Back, ¾-in.-thick oak plywood

Rabbet, ¾ in. wide by ⅜ in. deep

HEIRLOOM TOOL CHEST

By Chris Gochnour

A COMFORTABLE HOME FOR TOOLS

Made of cherry and constructed entirely with hand tools, the tool chest incorporates dovetail joinery, frame-and-panel construction, and applied molding.

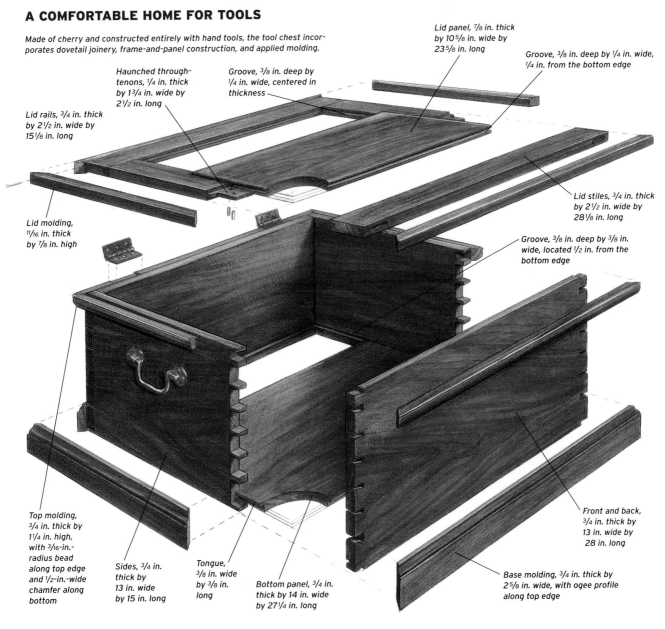

Lid panel, 7/8 in. thick by 10 5/8 in. wide by 23 5/8 in. long

Groove, 3/8 in. deep by 1/4 in. wide, 1/4 in. from the bottom edge

Haunched through-tenons, 1/4 in. thick by 1 3/4 in. wide by 2 1/2 in. long

Groove, 3/8 in. deep by 1/4 in. wide, centered in thickness

Lid rails, 3/4 in. thick by 2 1/2 in. wide by 15 1/8 in. long

Lid stiles, 3/4 in. thick by 2 1/2 in. wide by 28 1/8 in. long

Lid molding, 11/16 in. thick by 7/8 in. high

Groove, 3/8 in. deep by 3/8 in. wide, located 1/2 in. from the bottom edge

Top molding, 3/4 in. thick by 1 1/4 in. high, with 3/16-in.-radius bead along top edge and 1/2-in.-wide chamfer along bottom

Sides, 3/4 in. thick by 13 in. wide by 15 in. long

Tongue, 3/8 in. wide by 3/8 in. long

Bottom panel, 3/4 in. thick by 14 in. wide by 27 1/4 in. long

Front and back, 3/4 in. thick by 13 in. wide by 28 in. long

Base molding, 3/4 in. thick by 2 5/8 in. wide, with ogee profile along top edge

14 in.

29 1/2 in.

16 1/2 in.

A cabinetmaker's tool chest embodies a certain nostalgia and charm for modern woodworkers. It speaks of a time when craftsmen had few tools but an abundance of skill. Tool chests often served as a calling card to display a craftsman's talents. However, some were utilitarian, built simply to house tools.

This tool chest is of the latter kind—practical, enduring, and simple. But in a time when woodworkers have an abundance of power tools at every turn, making this tool chest with traditional hand-tool techniques can be a bridge to an era past. I recommend using this project as a hand-tool exercise, though power tools could be substituted for any of the operations. Practicing the techniques involved in the

chest's construction will make you more confident with hand tools, and you may find them an indispensable resource in your day-to-day shop tasks.

Because the tool chest is intended to be carried, choose wood that is lightweight yet durable. For this box I chose cherry, which is easy to work and attractive; however, woods such as red alder, poplar, and white pine also are appropriate.

VERSATILE TOOL TRAYS

The interior tool trays slide along cleats attached to the carcase sides. The sides and bottoms of the trays are 1/4 in. thick. The ends of the small trays are 1/2 in. thick. The ends of the saw box are 3/4 in. thick and notched to fit the cleat.

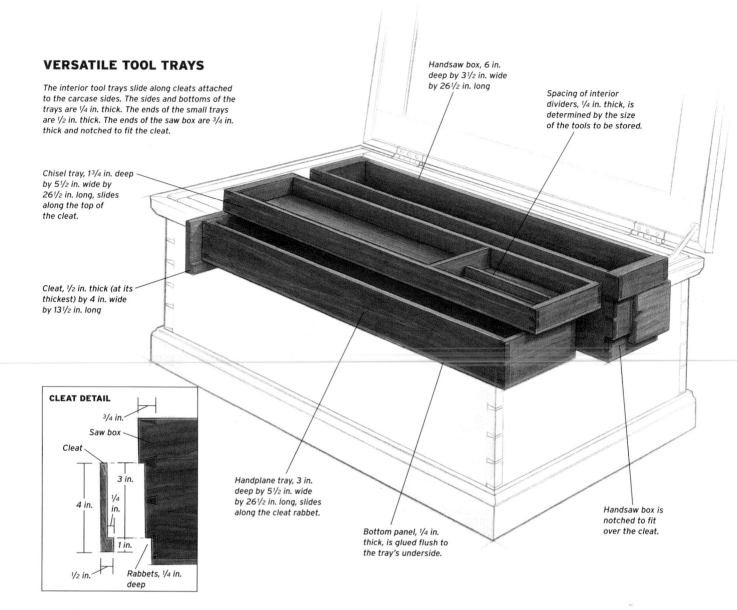

Handsaw box, 6 in. deep by 3 1/2 in. wide by 26 1/2 in. long

Spacing of interior dividers, 1/4 in. thick, is determined by the size of the tools to be stored.

Chisel tray, 1 3/4 in. deep by 5 1/2 in. wide by 26 1/2 in. long, slides along the top of the cleat.

Cleat, 1/2 in. thick (at its thickest) by 4 in. wide by 13 1/2 in. long

Handplane tray, 3 in. deep by 5 1/2 in. wide by 26 1/2 in. long, slides along the cleat rabbet.

Bottom panel, 1/4 in. thick, is glued flush to the tray's underside.

Handsaw box is notched to fit over the cleat.

CLEAT DETAIL

3/4 in.

Saw box

Cleat

3 in.

4 in.

1/4 in.

1 in.

1/2 in.

Rabbets, 1/4 in. deep

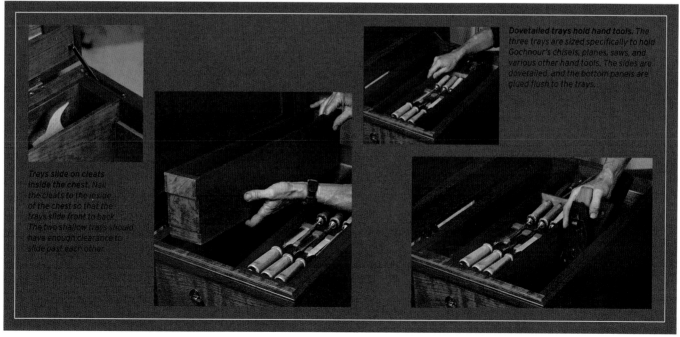

Trays slide on cleats inside the chest. Nail the cleats to the inside of the chest so that the trays slide front to back. The two shallow trays should have enough clearance to slide past each other.

Dovetailed trays hold hand tools. The three trays are sized specifically to hold Gochnour's chisels, planes, saws, and various other hand tools. The sides are dovetailed, and the bottom panels are glued flush to the trays.

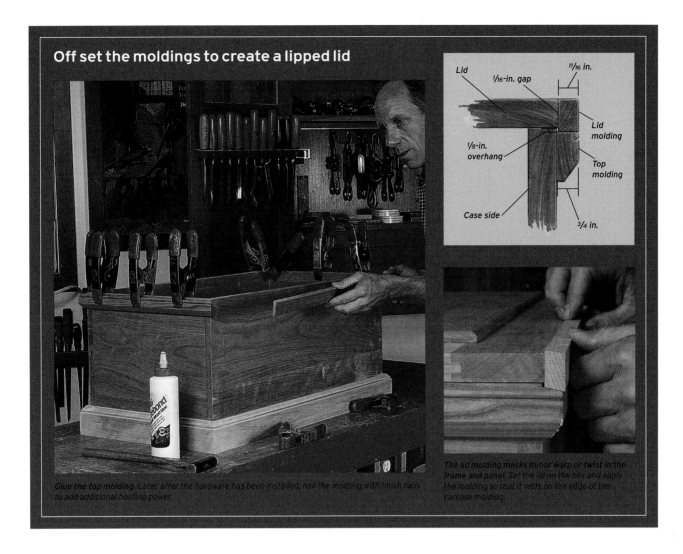

Off set the moldings to create a lipped lid

Lid

1/16-in. gap

11/16 in.

Lid molding

1/8-in. overhang

Top molding

Case side

3/4 in.

Glue the top molding. Later, after the hardware has been installed, nail the molding with finish nails to add additional holding power.

The lid molding masks minor warp or twist in the frame and panel. Set the lid on the box and apply the molding so that it rests on the edge of the carcase molding.

To reduce the likelihood of warp and twist, select clear, straight-grained wood for the lid frame. This type of wood also is good for the moldings because it will make them easier to work with molding planes. Knots are fine on panels, but keep them away from the edges so that they will be out of the way of the joinery.

Once you've dimensioned the lumber for each part, follow a sequential pattern of construction: Join the box using dovetails, build the frame-and-panel lid with mortise-and-tenon joinery, shape and apply moldings, and install the hardware.

Because this tool chest is such a personal item, the inner tray system can be personalized, too. I designed mine with three removable sliding trays, which hold saws, chisels, handplanes, and a host of other hand tools. The tray boxes are dovetailed, and the bottom of each tray is glued flush in place. Two stepped cleats tacked onto the inner sides of the chest support the trays, allowing them to slide forward and backward on different planes.

Finish off the tool chest by installing the brass hardware, which consists of two 90-degree stopped handles, two mortised hinges, and a lid stay. The hinges are screwed onto the molding, which is why it's a good idea to reinforce the molding with a few finish nails once the hardware has been installed.

I finished the chest with three coats of Tried and True® oil/varnish blend applied over several days, scuff-sanding between coats. Tool chests often get abused, so I avoid built-up finishes such as shellac or lacquer, which are prone to scratching and scuffing. But painting the chest would not be out of character with traditional tool chests. Use a flat acrylic latex paint, which imparts a look similar to milk paint, and top it off with a thin shellac topcoat.

Chris Gochnour makes custom furniture in Salt Lake City, Utah.

TOOL CABINET FOR A WORKBENCH

By Lon Schleining

The workbench is maple, with walnut wedges in the trestle joinery. I like the visual contrast between these two woods, so I chose maple plywood for the carcases, and solid walnut for the drawer fronts.

To make sure the carcases would stand up to heavy use, I splined the miter joints and glued a full ¾-in.-thick panel into a rabbet in the back of each carcase. On the front and back edges of each box, I glued solid edgebanding to cover the plywood edges and splines.

I measured the heights of the tools I wanted to keep in the cabinet and discovered I needed more small drawers than large ones. I standardized the drawer sizes as much as I could so that I could make several parts of the same size. Your tools differ from mine, so size the drawers accordingly.

One sheet of ¾-in. maple plywood is plenty for the carcases. I used three 5x5 sheets of Baltic birch plywood for the drawers, one ½ in. thick for the drawer sides and two ¼ in. thick for the bottoms.

Heavy-duty, ball-bearing drawer slides offer smooth action and full extension, so they were an easy choice. I used Accuride 3832 slides rated at 100 lb., which should be plenty strong, even when I pull out a drawer slightly to help support a wide board or panel held on edge in the front vise.

For drawer pulls, I chose inset brass ring pulls, which match the brass bench dogs and won't catch on cords.

Lon Schleining makes furniture and stairs in Long Beach, California, and teaches woodworking throughout the United States.

It's exasperating when I can't find a tool. Usually I know it's in a pile somewhere, or on a shelf, or over there where I think I saw it last. . .

Well, all that frustration is behind me now. After 27 years as a professional woodworker, I finally have a real tool chest.

When the editors and I designed "The Essential Workbench" (see pp. 56–57), we deliberately positioned the stretchers to accommodate a tool cabinet as large as 24 in. deep by 44 in. wide by 16 in. tall. The idea was to follow up the bench project with this one on how to build a complementary tool cabinet.

As with all of my projects, I first drew the cabinet full scale in three views, including all the construction details I could think of.

I like the look of mitered corners and made that basic decision early on. Then I realized I wasn't very comfortable mitering an edge on a plywood panel nearly 4 ft. wide by only about 2 ft. long, so I decided to break the cabinet into two separate boxes. This makes the parts smaller and easier to handle, especially on the tablesaw. I also like the idea that if you have to break down your bench to move your shop, the two boxes will be manageable.

BUILD TWO OF THESE

The fact that this is a shop cabinet influenced many of the construction choices. Two separate boxes are easier to make than one big one. Plywood cabinets are joined with miters and splines and dressed up with solid-wood edgebanding and drawer fronts. Plywood drawer boxes get quick box joints, applied fronts, and commercial slides.

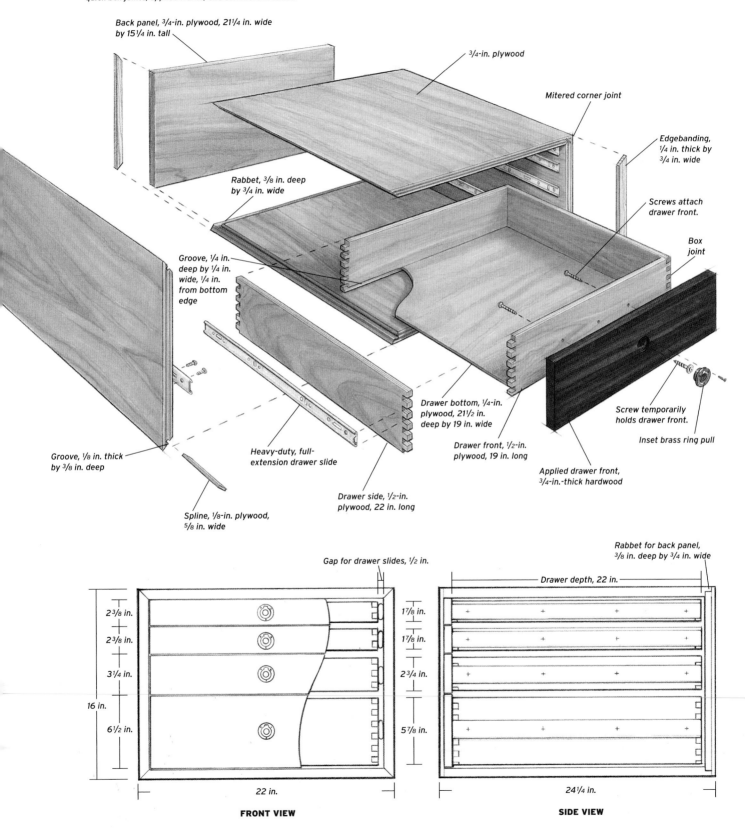

Back panel, ³/₄-in. plywood, 21¹/₄ in. wide by 15¹/₄ in. tall

³/₄-in. plywood

Mitered corner joint

Edgebanding, ¹/₄ in. thick by ³/₄ in. wide

Rabbet, ³/₈ in. deep by ³/₄ in. wide

Screws attach drawer front.

Box joint

Groove, ¹/₄ in. deep by ¹/₄ in. wide, ¹/₄ in. from bottom edge

Groove, ¹/₈ in. thick by ³/₈ in. deep

Spline, ¹/₈-in. plywood, ⁵/₈ in. wide

Heavy-duty, full-extension drawer slide

Drawer bottom, ¹/₄-in. plywood, 21¹/₂ in. deep by 19 in. wide

Drawer side, ¹/₂-in. plywood, 22 in. long

Drawer front, ¹/₂-in. plywood, 19 in. long

Applied drawer front, ³/₄-in.-thick hardwood

Screw temporarily holds drawer front.

Inset brass ring pull

Gap for drawer slides, ¹/₂ in.

Rabbet for back panel, ³/₈ in. deep by ³/₄ in. wide

Drawer depth, 22 in.

2³/₈ in.

2³/₈ in.

3¹/₄ in.

16 in.

6¹/₂ in.

1⁷/₈ in.

1⁷/₈ in.

2³/₄ in.

5⁷/₈ in.

22 in.

24¹/₄ in.

FRONT VIEW

SIDE VIEW

AN INSPIRED TOOL CHEST

By Bill Crozier

Between my freshman and sophomore years at the Rhode Island School of Design, I was looking ahead to the fall when I would begin studying woodworking under Tage Frid. That same summer, my father mounted a show of illustration at the New York Historical Society. The exhibition was a pretty big deal—but with precious little relevance, you might think, to woodworking. However, one evening as my father entered the Historical Society by the usual after-hours route—through a basement area stuffed with holdings in storage—he stumbled upon an extraordinary find: the tool chest of Duncan Phyfe, the New York City cabinetmaker who gave his name to an elegant style of furniture in the first decades of the 19th century. My father said he'd try to get permission for me to see it. A week later, I got my chance.

One fine chest leads to another. *Bill Crozier found an idea worth emulating when he came across Duncan Phyfe's tool chest (above) in a museum. Scottish-born Phyfe (1768-1854) established himself in New York as the preeminent cabinetmaker. Almost synonymous with the Federal style, Phyfe's furniture was typically made of mahogany and often finely carved with lyres, reeding, and swags. Phyfe left an estate of a half million dollars—a sum that testifies to his popularity, his craftsmanship, and his business acumen.*

If I had seen the chest closed, I might have walked right by it. Typical of an Old World–style joiner's tool chests, it was essentially a ruggedly built blanket chest with drawers and compartments inside for tools. This box had the usual simple, scuffed exterior, but when the lid was lifted, I was in for a treat. The drawer box, or till, had rows of shallow, beautifully proportioned drawers veneered with crotch Cuban mahogany and filled with scores of exquisite tools, with handles of bone or ebony or rosewood, all well used but in superb condition. The drawers were joined with flawless, tiny dovetails and sported pulls turned from elephant ivory. Below the drawers, dozens of molding planes were nested in neat compartments.

I wasn't permitted to touch the chest or the tools, but the curator who agreed to let me see them said that if I wanted anything moved I could ask the guard on duty nearby. Well, I gave the poor guy a workout. I was there the better part of a day, absorbing and drawing every detail. After sketching the cabinet construction and layout, I noted which tools were contained in each of the drawers. I took particularly careful notes because I knew that the first project in Tage Frid's curriculum was to build a tool chest, and I figured I had found a pretty good starting place for the design of mine.

In the following weeks, I worked to design my own tool chest, using Duncan Phyfe's as inspiration. What appealed to me most about his chest was the drawer till, with its pleasingly slim and perfectly proportioned drawers. I decided to make a fairly direct copy of it, adding one row of drawers. But I didn't like the idea of having to bend over to fetch my tools, and I didn't want to have to root around in a dark box, moving one tool to get to another. So for my design, I essentially lifted Phyfe's drawer till out of the big blanket chest and put it on an open stand at a comfortable height.

I followed Phyfe's lead again in turning drawer pulls in a range of sizes—larger ones for the bigger bottom drawers and smaller ones to suit the smaller drawers. I turned mine from rosewood instead of ivory. And although I loved the way the crotch

ARTICULATED DOORS FOLD QUIETLY AWAY

Triple-hinged accordion doors fold up at the ends of the case during use and can be pulled across to lock it shut. The author built deep doors to accommodate hanging tool storage, but hasn't used them that way.

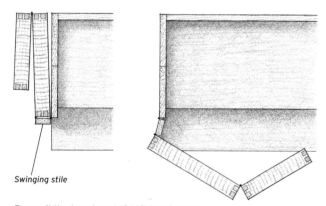

Swinging stile

To permit the deep doors to fold flat against the cabinet, the author hinged a narrow strip of wood to the cabinet side, creating a swinging stile.

mahogany looked on his drawer fronts, I chose to have solid fronts on my drawers and made them from a mixture of bird's-eye maple and tiger maple.

I admired the way Phyfe used his chest as well as the way he made it. He arranged things so tools with similar functions were in adjacent drawers. I did the same thing: I keep layout and marking tools in the first row of drawers, with squares in one drawer, marking knives and pencils in another, compasses and dividers in a third. The second row is reserved for chisels, with paring chisels in one drawer, mortising chisels in the one beside it and Japanese chisels in the next. This has made it easy to remember where things are even in a bank of 20 drawers. To protect the tools, I lined the top two rows of drawers with upholstery velvet. For the bottom three rows, I glued sheet cork in the bottoms.

I still wanted to be able to lock the chest, so I gave it a lid and built accordion-style doors that fold out of the way at the ends of the drawer box but can be pulled across to engage the lid and lock the whole thing shut. As it turns out, I never close them. But I suppose when you design something like this you are just guessing how the future will go, and you are not always right. I also left cavities below the bottom drawers for trays I envisioned as holding the day's tools. They would be easily removable so I could take them to the bench or wherever I was working. That still sounds like a good idea, but I've never made the trays. I also left a space on the stand below the drawer box because I intended to build a case of larger drawers for power tools. Maybe I'll build it next year.

So far, I've gotten two decades of service from my tool chest. But it would have served me well even if I'd never used it, because making it was like a double apprenticeship—one in joinery and the other in design—under a pair of masters. We were asked to build our boxes using either all mortise-and-tenon joinery or all dovetails. I chose dovetails because I'd never cut them and was eager to try. Cutting all the dovetails in the stand, the doors, the drawer box and the drawers themselves with Tage Frid's guidance was a real dovetail apprenticeship. And as I made my way through my first attempt to design and build a major piece, I was also serving a design apprenticeship under the eye of Duncan Phyfe.

Bill Crozier designs and builds furniture in Providence, Rhode Island.

HOW BIG ARE ELEGANT DRAWERS?

The author based the layout of drawers in his chest on Duncan Phyfe's, but added a fifth row of drawers. Phyfe jumped from six drawers in the top row to four in the second. The author made rows of six, five, four, three and two. As Phyfe did, the author turned pulls that graduate in size to suit the drawers.

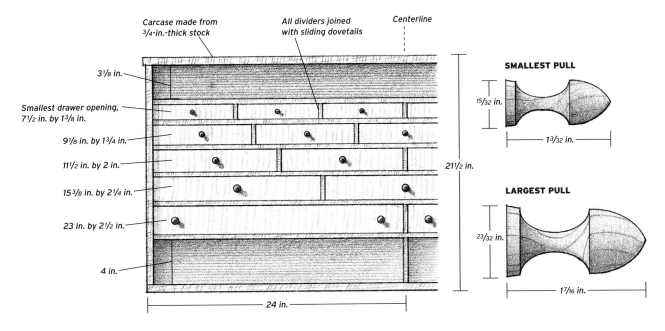

Carcase made from ³/₄-in.-thick stock

All dividers joined with sliding dovetails

Centerline

3¹/₈ in.

Smallest drawer opening, 7¹/₂ in. by 1³/₈ in.

9¹/₈ in. by 1³/₄ in.

11¹/₂ in. by 2 in.

15³/₈ in. by 2¹/₄ in.

23 in. by 2¹/₂ in.

4 in.

21¹/₂ in.

24 in.

SMALLEST PULL

15/32 in.

1³/₃₂ in.

LARGEST PULL

23/32 in.

1⁷/₁₆ in.

MOBILE CLAMP CART

By David DiRanna

I took up woodworking 22 years ago when I received a radial-arm saw as a present. For most of that time, I had to share shop space with two cars in a three-car garage. But about five years ago, I kicked out the cars, reorganized the layout of the shop and built storage cabinets along many of the walls.

The end result gave me a lot more floor space to work in, and so when the time came to figure out how to store my small clamp collection, I decided a mobile cart was the best solution for me. I put most of the machinery on casters for the same reason—I like the freedom of being able to move things around. On one end, two casters are fixed, while the other two are swivel— that combination works best.

My main problem with clamps is that I keep buying more. When I first started building this clamp-storage cart, I didn't have the master design for it as it now looks, because I had many fewer clamps than I do now. The design of the cart has undergone a sort of organic evolutionary process.

The purchase of every new batch of clamps has turned this into a modular construction project. I just keep finding ways to add onto the cart to accommodate my most recent clamp purchases. The cart got so heavy at one point that I found it necessary to replace the original 3-in. casters with a heavier-duty 5-in. ball-bearing style. I figured out recently that I'm storing more than $2,000 worth of clamps on the cart. I just hope I don't find it necessary to buy any more.

David DiRanna taught college-level business courses for many years before switching careers to a business-management position.

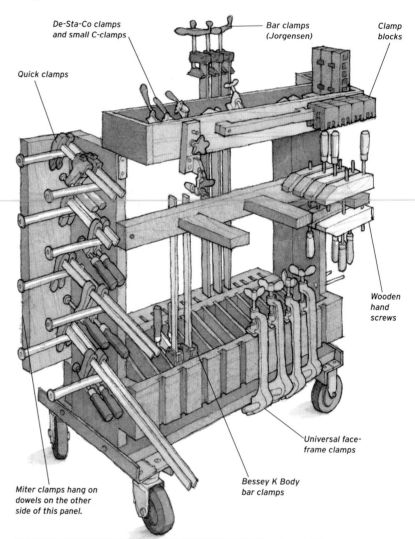

De-Sta-Co clamps and small C-clamps

Quick clamps

Bar clamps (Jorgensen)

Clamp blocks

Wooden hand screws

Universal face-frame clamps

Miter clamps hang on dowels on the other side of this panel.

Bessey K Body bar clamps

Have clamps, will travel. *Blessed with plenty of floor space, DiRanna chose to put all of his many clamps on a rolling cart.*

CLAMP-CART UTILITY

DiRanna's clamp cart, made mostly from scrap framing lumber, keeps getting bigger. As he buys more clamps and different kinds of clamps, he figures out a way to make them fit. At some point, he found it necessary to beef up the underside with welded steel angle irons and larger casters to carry the increased weight.

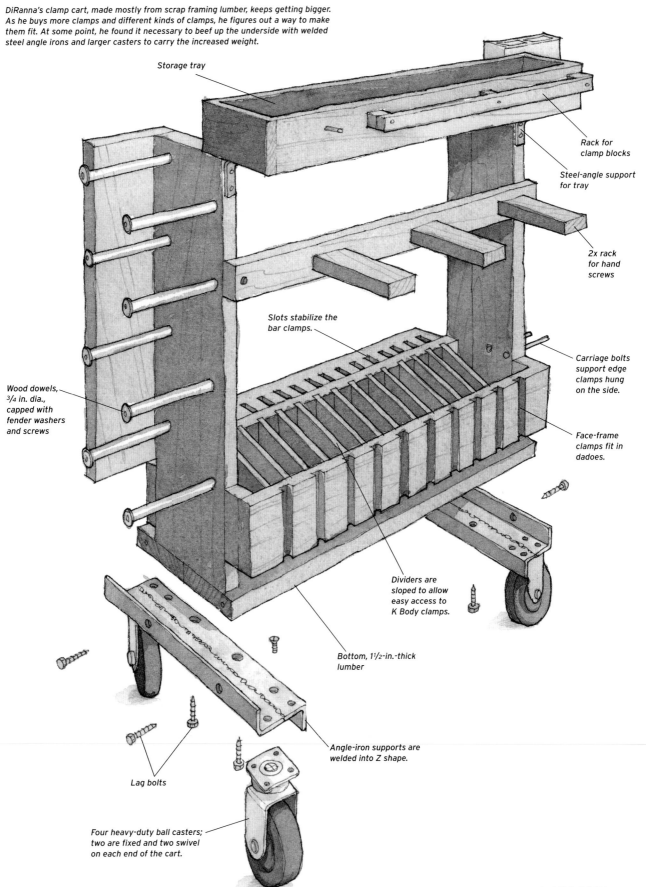

Storage tray

Rack for clamp blocks

Steel-angle support for tray

2x rack for hand screws

Slots stabilize the bar clamps.

Carriage bolts support edge clamps hung on the side.

Wood dowels, 3/4 in. dia., capped with fender washers and screws

Face-frame clamps fit in dadoes.

Dividers are sloped to allow easy access to K Body clamps.

Bottom, 1 1/2-in.-thick lumber

Angle-iron supports are welded into Z shape.

Lag bolts

Four heavy-duty ball casters; two are fixed and two swivel on each end of the cart.

STACK AND SAW LUMBER ON THE SAME RACK

By Chris Gochnour

A BENCH FOR A COMPOUND-MITER SAW

This bench is built for its strength and utility rather than for its looks. Hardwood is used for the posts, the main structural arms, the fence and the drawer runners. Plywood (3/4 in. thick) is used for the remainder of the carcase, and 3/4-in.-thick MDF for the top. Construction is mainly dadoes and pocket screws.

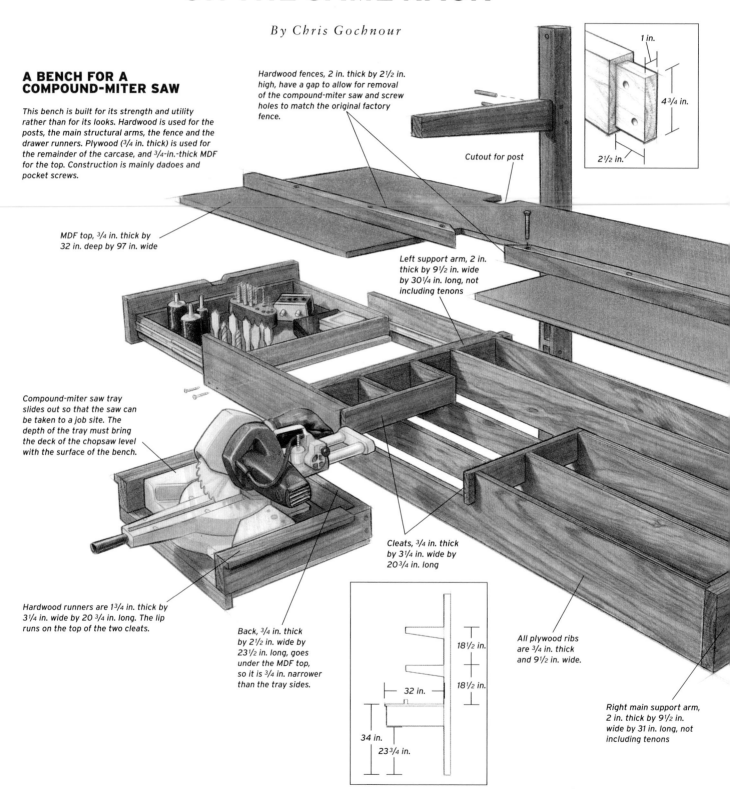

Hardwood fences, 2 in. thick by 2 1/2 in. high, have a gap to allow for removal of the compound-miter saw and screw holes to match the original factory fence.

1 in.

4 3/4 in.

2 1/2 in.

Cutout for post

MDF top, 3/4 in. thick by 32 in. deep by 97 in. wide

Left support arm, 2 in. thick by 9 1/2 in. wide by 30 1/4 in. long, not including tenons

Compound-miter saw tray slides out so that the saw can be taken to a job site. The depth of the tray must bring the deck of the chopsaw level with the surface of the bench.

Cleats, 3/4 in. thick by 3 1/4 in. wide by 20 3/4 in. long

Hardwood runners are 1 3/4 in. thick by 3 1/4 in. wide by 20 3/4 in. long. The lip runs on the top of the two cleats.

Back, 3/4 in. thick by 2 1/2 in. wide by 23 1/2 in. long, goes under the MDF top, so it is 3/4 in. narrower than the tray sides.

18 1/2 in.

18 1/2 in.

32 in.

34 in.

23 3/4 in.

All plywood ribs are 3/4 in. thick and 9 1/2 in. wide.

Right main support arm, 2 in. thick by 9 1/2 in. wide by 31 in. long, not including tenons

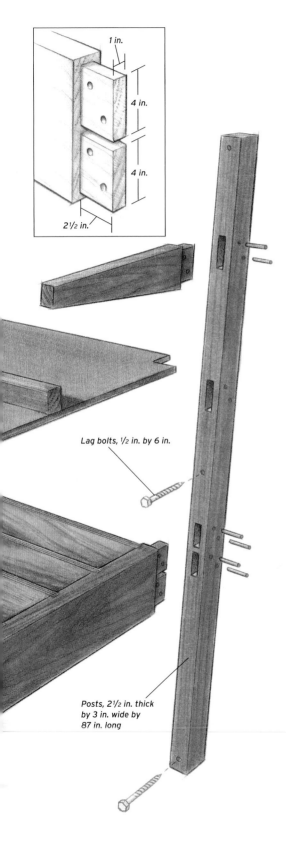

1 in.

4 in.

4 in.

2½ in.

Lag bolts, ½ in. by 6 in.

Posts, 2½ in. thick by 3 in. wide by 87 in. long

Storing lumber effectively is a challenge in any shop, but it's especially challenging in a small shop. When I designed my current lumber rack, the efficient use of space was a priority. I wanted my lumber to be accessible and close to the compound-miter saw, where I cut it to rough length.

The rack's framework consists of two hardwood posts and a series of cantilevered arms that hold the lumber and support the crosscutting table. The posts are lag-bolted to the stud wall. I chose bolts long enough to give me 3 in. of threads in the studs, and I mounted the posts 6 ft. apart to correspond with the wall studs.

The arms, also hardwood, are tenoned into the posts and secured with glue and draw-bored pegs. I chose to taper the arms so that I could have the strength of a large tenon mounted into the posts but more room for lumber on the outside. For ease of assembly, I glued the arms into the posts before bolting the posts to the wall.

The arms that support the crosscutting table are almost twice the width of the others and are not tapered. I modified the joinery for these arms, stacking two tenons for each arm rather than making a very wide one. This improves the joint because less material is removed from the post, which minimizes the risk of splitting. It also avoids wood-movement problems that can occur with wide tenons.

The arms for the compound-miter saw table have a series of dadoes cut on the inside faces to accept plywood ribs that support the tabletop. I made the top of the table out of medium-density fiberboard (MDF), because it is very flat and a good utility work surface. I also built a hardwood fence with stops for repetitive cutoff work.

The compound-miter saw is mounted on a small tray that slides into place and is secured with two screws. With this setup, I can remove the two bolts and take the saw with me.

In the shop, my fence replaces the factory fence. But when I take the saw on the road, I remount the factory fence.

My drill press is just a few feet away from the table, so I installed a drawer at one end to hold drill bits and drill-press accessories.

My rack is just inside the large door I use for bringing lumber into the shop. I simply back in my truck and unload lumber right onto the rack. Let the work begin.

Chris Gochnour is a furniture maker in Salt Lake City, Utah.

A MACHINIST-STYLE TOOL CHEST

by Ronald Young

FIG. 1: A MACHINIST-STYLE TOOL BOX

Using the simplified construction techniques illustrated here, you can build this tool chest in a weekend.

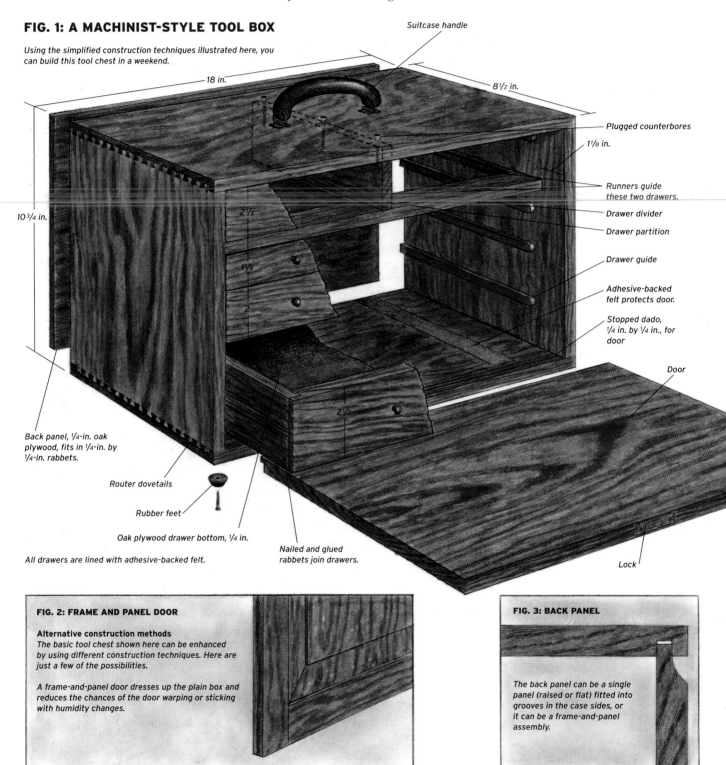

Suitcase handle

18 in.

8¹⁄₂ in.

Plugged counterbores

1¹⁄₈ in.

Runners guide these two drawers.

Drawer divider

Drawer partition

Drawer guide

Adhesive-backed felt protects door.

Stopped dado, ¹⁄₄ in. by ¹⁄₄ in., for door

10³⁄₄ in.

2¹⁄₂

1¹⁄₄

2

2¹⁄₂

Door

Back panel, ¹⁄₄-in. oak plywood, fits in ¹⁄₄-in. by ¹⁄₄-in. rabbets.

Router dovetails

Rubber feet

Oak plywood drawer bottom, ¹⁄₄ in.

All drawers are lined with adhesive-backed felt.

Nailed and glued rabbets join drawers.

Lock

FIG. 2: FRAME AND PANEL DOOR

Alternative construction methods
The basic tool chest shown here can be enhanced by using different construction techniques. Here are just a few of the possibilities.

A frame-and-panel door dresses up the plain box and reduces the chances of the door warping or sticking with humidity changes.

FIG. 3: BACK PANEL

The back panel can be a single panel (raised or flat) fitted into grooves in the case sides, or it can be a frame-and-panel assembly.

ashioned after the old-style machinists' boxes, this small tool chest provides convenient, portable storage for your finest tools, instruments, rules, and other small items. The original machinists' chests were traditionally made of walnut or fumed oak. I made mine of oak and stained it to match the rich brown tone the old-timers achieved through the chemical reaction that occurs when oak is exposed to ammonia fumes. The stack of graduated drawers helps prevent small objects from being inextricably buried at the bottom of the box. A separate door can be locked covering the drawers for security during storage. The door also keeps the drawers from falling out when you're carrying the box from job to job. When you're using the box, the door slides neatly into the chest under the bottom drawer, as shown in the photo at right.

My 18-in.-wide by 10¾-in.-high tool chest suits my space and storage requirements, but you should modify these dimensions and the drawer configuration to suit your particular needs. I used ⁹⁄₁₆-in.-thick oak for most of the chest. The drawer backs and sides are ⁵⁄₁₆-in.-thick poplar, and the back panel and drawer bottoms are ¼-in.-thick oak-veneer plywood. I suggest buying your hardware before you begin construction, so you can be sure you've dimensioned the chest appropriately.

The main body of the chest is a dovetailed box, which I constructed using a commercial dovetail jig and ¼-in.-dia. dovetail bit.

Tool box turns to woodworking. *A machinist-style tool chest is a perennial favorite for storage of treasured tools because the stack of felt-lined drawers provides easy access and a safe haven.*

Drawer construction is straightforward with simple butt and rabbet joints, as shown in figure 1. I cut the drawer-slide grooves slightly oversize to allow for smooth movement. To finish the chest, I rubbed on two coats of Watco Danish oil and then sprayed two coats of Deft® spray polyurethane on the exposed surfaces. And to protect my finest tools, I lined the drawers with adhesive-backed felt.

Because of the simple construction shown in figure 1, I was able to build this chest in a couple of days. If you would prefer less of a plain-vanilla chest, you might want to consider using some alternate construction methods, as shown from in figures 2 to 4. These techniques will probably take you a little longer and call for a little more material.

Ron Young is a woodworker in Decatur, Alabama.

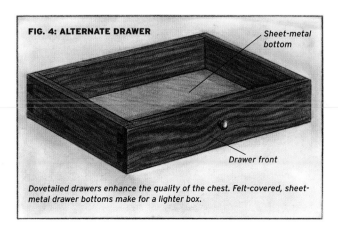

FIG. 4: ALTERNATE DRAWER

Sheet-metal bottom

Drawer front

Dovetailed drawers enhance the quality of the chest. Felt-covered, sheet-metal drawer bottoms make for a lighter box.

CLAMP RACKS FOR CEILINGS AND WALLS

By Brook Duerr

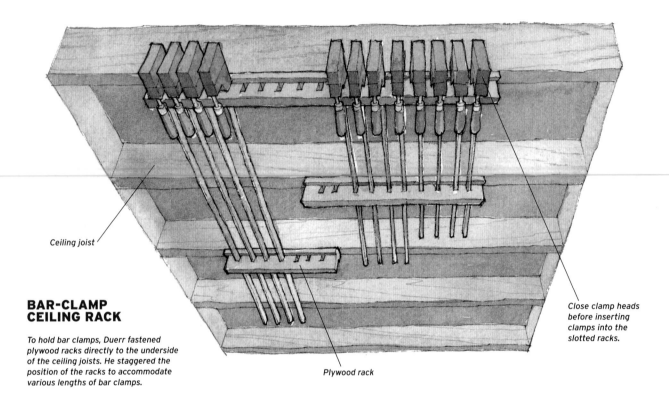

BAR-CLAMP CEILING RACK

To hold bar clamps, Duerr fastened plywood racks directly to the underside of the ceiling joists. He staggered the position of the racks to accommodate various lengths of bar clamps.

Ceiling joist

Close clamp heads before inserting clamps into the slotted racks.

Plywood rack

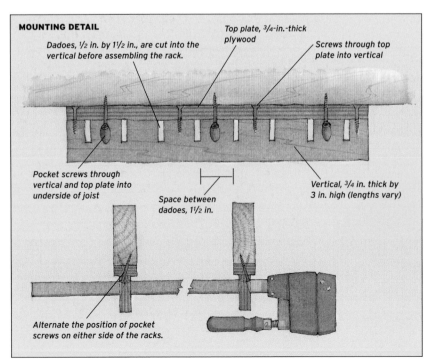

MOUNTING DETAIL

Dadoes, 1/2 in. by 11/2 in., are cut into the vertical before assembling the rack.

Top plate, 3/4-in.-thick plywood

Screws through top plate into vertical

Pocket screws through vertical and top plate into underside of joist

Space between dadoes, 11/2 in.

Vertical, 3/4 in. thick by 3 in. high (lengths vary)

Alternate the position of pocket screws on either side of the racks.

In my basement shop, wall space and open floor space are scarce. Faced with a growing collection of all kinds of clamps, I didn't know where to store them. One day it dawned on me that I could make use of the unfinished ceiling, with its exposed joists, and one wall alcove to store clamps out of the way. I designed and built several different racks, basing the design on the dimensions of each type of clamp.

For my bar clamps, I constructed each rack with two strips of 3/4-in.-thick Baltic birch plywood, fastened together into a T shape with screws driven through the top plate. Before assembling the two pieces, I used a dado blade to cut a series of 1/2-in. by 11/2-in.

dadoes to serve as slots for sliding the clamps into the racks. I put the clamps into the closed position and slip them into the racks with the bottom end first.

For all of my Quick-Grip® clamps, I made a rack out of a single piece of plywood screwed into a joist from below. I cut a series of dadoes on one side only for hanging each clamp. I also used the dado blade to cut a groove in the top surface that runs the length of that edge. The rivets on the bottoms of the clamps sit in that groove and keep the clamps from falling out.

For my pipe clamps I arrived at a solution similar to the ceiling racks for my bar clamps. I drilled a series of 1½-in.-dia. holes in matching pairs of ¾-in.-thick material and mounted them onto a plywood back, which in turn was screwed to studs against a wall. With this design, it's important that one end is on the outside corner of the wall so that the clamp handles don't bind against the wall as you place the pipe clamps into the rack; then you'll have easy access to them when you need them.

Brook Duerr is a research scientist for a medical-device manufacturer. He does woodworking in his basement shop in a suburb of St. Paul, Minnesota.

QUICK-CLAMP CEILING RACK

After running out of room on a wall rack, Duerr added this ceiling rack. He routed a groove into the top to stabilize the hanging clamps and keep them from falling out.

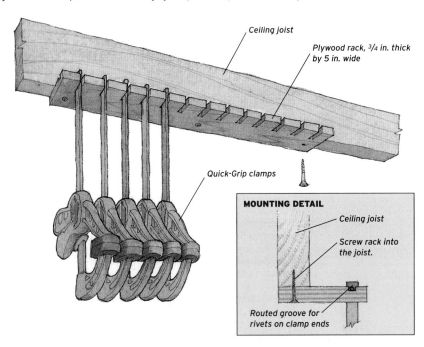

Ceiling joist

Plywood rack, ³/₄ in. thick by 5 in. wide

Quick-Grip clamps

MOUNTING DETAIL

Ceiling joist

Screw rack into the joist.

Routed groove for rivets on clamp ends

PIPE-CLAMP WALL RACK

A small alcove near a dust collector became a perfect spot to install this rack.

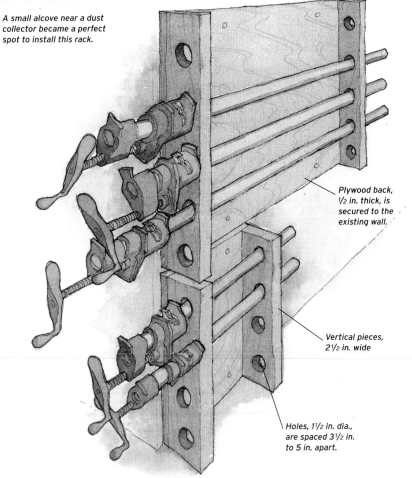

Plywood back, ½ in. thick, is secured to the existing wall.

Vertical pieces, 2½ in. wide

Holes, 1½ in. dia., are spaced 3½ in. to 5 in. apart.

A CLEVER TOOL CASE

By Yeung Chan

Starting when I was a boy in China, making hand tools became second nature to me. Most of the hand tools I use today are ones I have made. My tools are the extensions of my hands, helping me work faster, safer, and with better results. So I treat them with care, keeping them sharp and well tuned.

It's not a good idea to store cutting tools in a box without separating each one; tools hitting one another will cause damage and dull the cutting edges. When I went into business as a furniture maker, my first solution for tool storage was a large tool board mounted on the shop wall. However, I soon found that I needed my tools with me when I did installation jobs or taught classes. It became a big job to remove all of the tools from the tool board and arrange them in good order for travel.

So I made a toolbox with the following mission in mind: to carry and protect an essential group of hand tools, big enough to handle most situations but not too heavy to carry. My toolbox may be small, but it's efficient.

To keep the tools from tumbling out when the box is closed, I made a retainer panel from ¼-in.-thick Baltic birch plywood for each half of the box. The panels also double as a knockdown for the box.

I used shopmade plywood for the top and bottom of the toolbox, allowing me to glue it into its rabbet and strengthen the case.

Two straps hold the case together. I decided against hinges because the weight of each box would rip them off the thin walls. Plus, I like having the two parts separate so I can put them where I need them.

I was very happy that the idea worked perfectly: The tools stay in place when the box is closed, and the two halves stand up side by side, good for use in the shop or in the classroom. When I give seminars and demos, my handmade tool kit becomes an exhibit, always generating lots of interest and questions.

Yeung Chan is a woodworker and teacher in Millbrae, California.

BOX LAYOUT AND CONSTRUCTION

The top section of the box holds chisels, gouges, knives, spokeshaves, and marking gauges. The bottom section holds handplanes, sharpening stones, saws, a hand drill, and a pencil box.

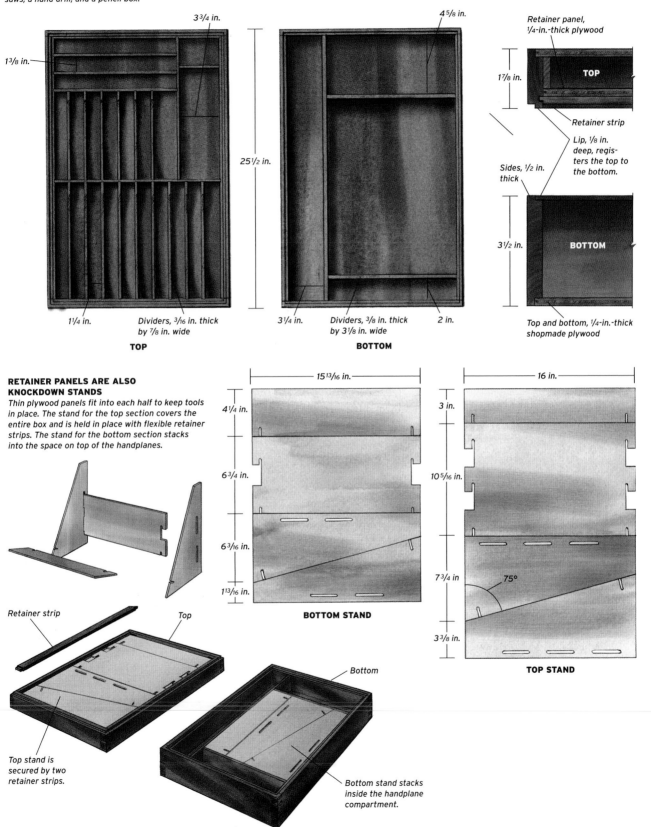

TOP

3³⁄₄ in.

1³⁄₈ in.

25¹⁄₂ in.

1¹⁄₄ in.

Dividers, ³⁄₁₆ in. thick by ⁷⁄₈ in. wide

BOTTOM

4⁵⁄₈ in.

3¹⁄₄ in.

Dividers, ³⁄₈ in. thick by 3¹⁄₈ in. wide

2 in.

Retainer panel, ¹⁄₄-in.-thick plywood

TOP

Retainer strip

1⁷⁄₈ in.

Lip, ¹⁄₈ in. deep, registers the top to the bottom.

Sides, ¹⁄₂ in. thick

3¹⁄₂ in.

BOTTOM

Top and bottom, ¹⁄₄-in.-thick shopmade plywood

RETAINER PANELS ARE ALSO KNOCKDOWN STANDS

Thin plywood panels fit into each half to keep tools in place. The stand for the top section covers the entire box and is held in place with flexible retainer strips. The stand for the bottom section stacks into the space on top of the handplanes.

15¹³⁄₁₆ in.

4¹⁄₄ in.

6³⁄₄ in.

6³⁄₁₆ in.

1¹³⁄₁₆ in.

BOTTOM STAND

16 in.

3 in.

10⁵⁄₁₆ in.

7³⁄₄ in.

75°

3³⁄₈ in.

TOP STAND

Retainer strip

Top

Top stand is secured by two retainer strips.

Bottom

Bottom stand stacks inside the handplane compartment.

WALL RACK FOR CLAMPS

By John West

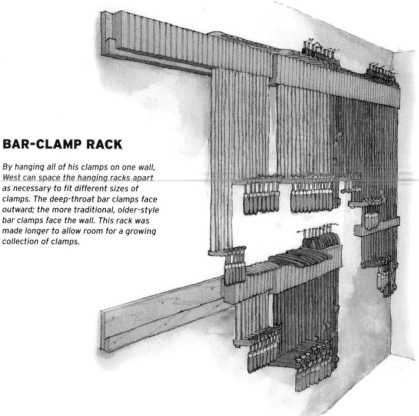

BAR-CLAMP RACK

By hanging all of his clamps on one wall, West can space the hanging racks apart as necessary to fit different sizes of clamps. The deep-throat bar clamps face outward; the more traditional, older-style bar clamps face the wall. This rack was made longer to allow room for a growing collection of clamps.

Having recently moved to a smaller shop, I had to find somewhere to store my fairly large collection of bar clamps and hand clamps. When considering where to put them, I decided against a fancy rack that rolls around the shop on casters because the floor space it would require is too dear. I wanted my clamps near the area where large glue-up projects will be done, but I also wanted to keep them out of the way when they're not needed. The solution was to hang the clamps on the outside wall of a lumber-storage rack. (In the business world, they call this "multitasking.")

The racks I designed are quite simple, and they can be used to store a variety of different-size clamps. Depending on the type of clamps, they will hang better facing in or out, because of how the weight is balanced. On the 12-ft. wall shown here, I currently store 108 clamps, and there's room for more.

John West owns and operates Cope and Mould Millwork in Ridgefield, Connecticut.

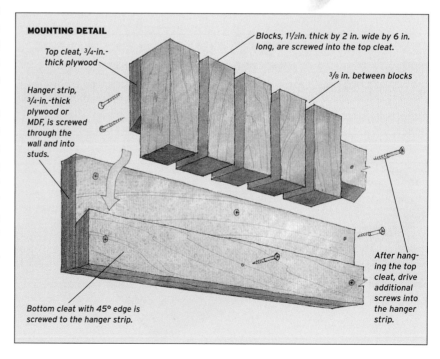

MOUNTING DETAIL

Top cleat, 3/4-in.-thick plywood

Hanger strip, 3/4-in.-thick plywood or MDF, is screwed through the wall and into studs.

Blocks, 1½ in. thick by 2 in. wide by 6 in. long, are screwed into the top cleat.

3/8 in. between blocks

After hanging the top cleat, drive additional screws into the hanger strip.

Bottom cleat with 45° edge is screwed to the hanger strip.

FINE FURNITURE FOR TOOLS

by Steven Thomas Bunn

I wanted a toolbox that was both visually striking and had a lot of storage space. Appearance was a prime consideration because as a one-man shop, I can't afford to keep finished work around as showpieces, and piles of wood or half-finished parts are not impressive to a drop-in client who isn't familiar with cabinet-making. I needed a toolbox that, like the journeyman's boxes of old, was an advertisement and demonstration of my capabilities.

I like the European-style toolbox that hangs on the wall with tools hung neatly inside. However, I don't like the large volume of wasted space behind the closed doors. In addition, the sheer number and weight of tools I possess ruled out a box that could be hung on the wall. I like the out-of-sight storage of drawers, similar to a mechanic's toolbox. I also

Fit for a showroom. *Because the author doesn't have a display of finished furniture, he built this toolbox to advertise his capabilities to drop-in customers. It also offers lots of convenient storage with 20 removable drawers that can be carried to the workbench.*

Shop or home furniture? *This tool chest could be equally at home in the parlor with just minor changes to the interior to accommodate china, silver or even stereo equipment.*

TOOL CHEST AND BASE

All stock is 3/4 in. thick unless otherwise noted.

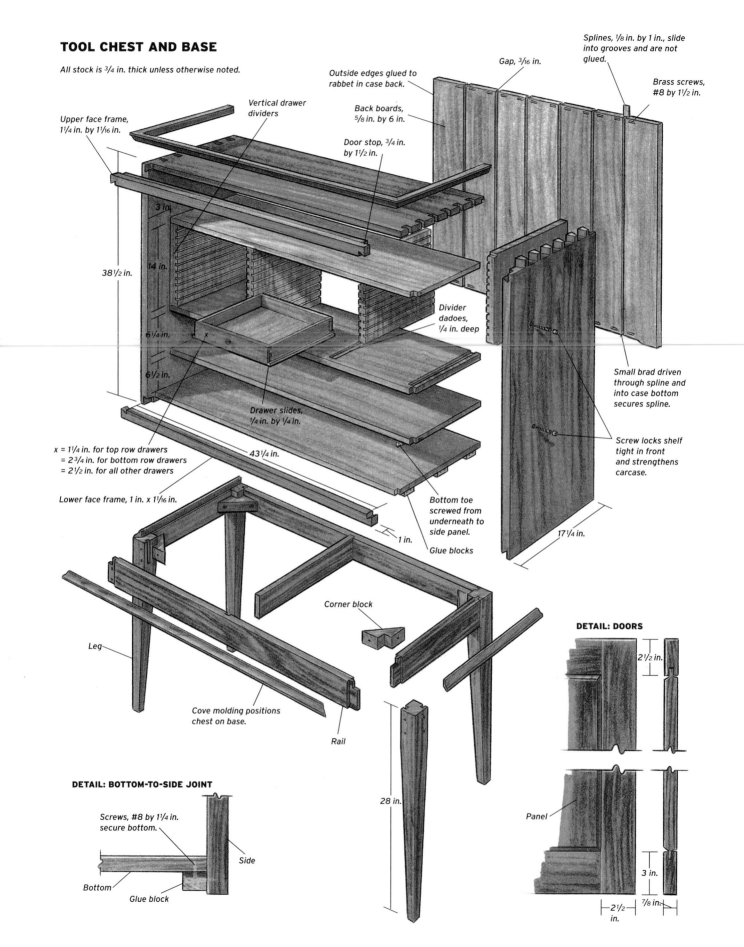

Upper face frame, 1 1/4 in. by 1 1/16 in.

Vertical drawer dividers

Outside edges glued to rabbet in case back.

Back boards, 5/8 in. by 6 in.

Gap, 3/16 in.

Splines, 1/8 in. by 1 in., slide into grooves and are not glued.

Brass screws, #8 by 1 1/2 in.

Door stop, 3/4 in. by 1 1/2 in.

38 1/2 in.

3 in.

14 in.

6 1/4 in.

6 1/2 in.

Divider dadoes, 1/4 in. deep

Small brad driven through spline and into case bottom secures spline.

x

Drawer slides, 1/4 in. by 1/4 in.

43 1/4 in.

Screw locks shelf tight in front and strengthens carcase.

x = 1 1/4 in. for top row drawers
  = 2 3/4 in. for bottom row drawers
  = 2 1/2 in. for all other drawers

Lower face frame, 1 in. x 1 1/16 in.

Bottom toe screwed from underneath to side panel.

Glue blocks

1 in.

17 1/4 in.

Leg

Corner block

Cove molding positions chest on base.

Rail

28 in.

DETAIL: DOORS

2 1/2 in.

Panel

3 in.

2 1/2 in.

7/8 in.

DETAIL: BOTTOM-TO-SIDE JOINT

Screws, #8 by 1 1/4 in. secure bottom.

Side

Bottom

Glue block

like the idea of grouping similar tools in a single drawer so that I can pull out a drawer of chisels or gouges, set it on my bench, and then go to work. Also, drawers keep sawdust and wood chips from accumulating over my tools.

Incorporating drawers meant the cabinet needed to be relatively deep: I calculated about 17 in. deep to be effective. For both design and practical reasons, I decided to put the tool chest on its own stand, as shown in the photo on p. 205. The cabinet and stand offer exceptional storage capacity for fine hand tools at a height that keeps me from having to reach up or bend down to get to anything. But with some slight modifications of the interior storage arrangements, the tool chest could easily house linens, china or electronic equipment. In fact, my tool chest is an interpretation of the Gate's sewing cabinet shown in *Measured Shop Drawings for American Furniture* by Thomas Moser (Sterling, 1985).

Building the carcase

The solid panels of the case top, sides, shelves, and bottom are all made of ¾-in.-thick stock.

The chest sits on the rails, and cove molding glued to the top edge of the rails hides the joint between the chest and base. The chest is not screwed to the frame; its weight is sufficient to keep it from moving. The legs were tapered on a bandsaw and cleaned up on the jointer. Corner blocks strengthen the base and add support for the tool chest, as shown in the bottom photo at right.

I have been using this chest for the past 6½ years and am very pleased with it. The only thing I would change is the excessive number of drawer slide grooves in the drawer dividers. I also have considered replacing the stand with a lower case for storing items like routers and drills. But this one looks just too nice to change.

Steven Bunn is a woodworker in Bowdoinham, Maine.

Preventing door sag. Legs screwed to the doors' lock stiles help support the heavy tools hung on the doors and prevent the hinge screws from pulling out.

Oversize storage holds big items. This two-drawer box slides into place between the shelves to hold long items that don't fit in the smaller drawers.

Supporting heavy loads. Corner braces reinforce the mortised-and-tenoned rail-to-leg joint and enable this elegant base to support the heavy tool chest.

LUMBER-STORAGE SOLUTIONS

by Andy Beasley

Anyone who ever has tried to create a functional shop knows that fitting it into a finite space is a far more challenging proposition. Once all of the necessary tools, materials, and that last bottle of glue have been shoehorned into the workshop, you can find yourself on the outside looking in.

When building my shop several years ago, I experimented with different layouts until I found the one that worked best for me. I've been happy with the result, largely because the lumber-storage system I developed added considerably to the efficiency of my shop while taking up little of its finite space.

Wall rack handles the long stuff

The centerpiece of my storage system is a horizontal rack along one wall. The rack is exceptionally stable, and the various levels hold a lot of material within a small footprint. The design is straightforward, the materials are relatively inexpensive, and the construction time is short.

I frequently store 16-ft. lengths of molding, so I decided to install six vertical stanchions to provide the necessary horizontal space. The 2×6 studs in the shop wall are on 16-in. centers; I installed a stanchion on every other one, or 32 in. on center. These stanchions are merely lengths of 1x4 pine, glued and nailed to 2×4 spacers. The spacers add stiffness, create pockets for the support arms, and provide a solid attachment point for the lag screws that mount the assembly to the wall.

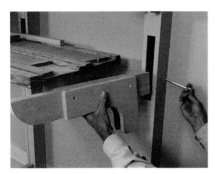

Lumber at the ready. *A wall-mounted rack keeps lumber organized and accessible without taking up valuable floor space.*

Simple mounting system. *Lumber rests on a series of support arms that are bolted to stanchions.*

WALL RACK FOR LUMBER

With stanchions spaced 32 in. on center, the rack can be made to fit a wall of any length and height.

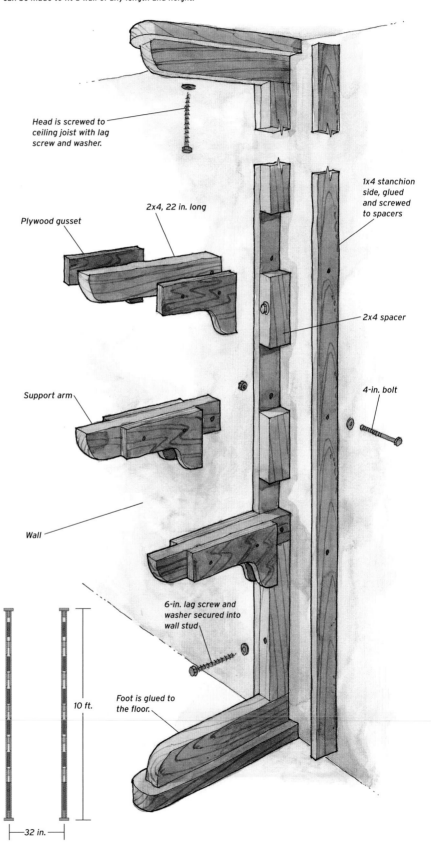

Head is screwed to ceiling joist with lag screw and washer.

Plywood gusset

2x4, 22 in. long

1x4 stanchion side, glued and screwed to spacers

2x4 spacer

Support arm

4-in. bolt

Wall

6-in. lag screw and washer secured into wall stud

10 ft.

Foot is glued to the floor.

32 in.

Although the stanchion assembly is simple to build, it helps to choose stock that is straight, without bow or twist. Gluing and nailing the pieces together on a level floor is an easy way to keep them true.

This rack is designed to support considerable weight if it is mounted securely to a sturdy wall. To attach the stanchions to the shop wall, I first marked the locations of the electrical wires in the wall so that I could give them a wide berth. Then I secured the stanchions with 6-in. lag screws through the spacer blocks and into the wall studs.

This rack can be attached equally well to a concrete wall as long as heavy-duty masonry anchors are used. The small, plastic expanding

Rolling cart adds convenience. A framed plywood box on wheels provides the perfect place to store offcuts. [Photo by Tom Begnal]

CART FOR LUMBER OFFCUTS

Simplified frame-and-panel construction means the cart assembles without much fuss, yet has plenty of strength.

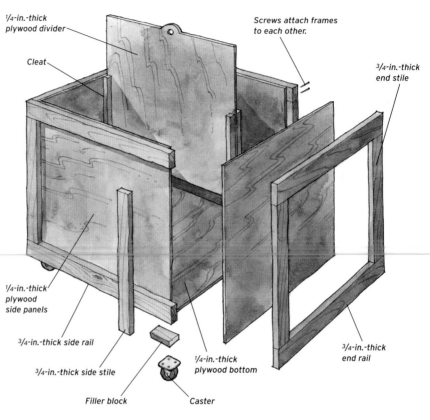

1/4-in.-thick plywood divider

Cleat

Screws attach frames to each other.

3/4-in.-thick end stile

1/4-in.-thick plywood side panels

3/4-in.-thick side rail

3/4-in.-thick side stile

Filler block

1/4-in.-thick plywood bottom

Caster

3/4-in.-thick end rail

anchors used to hang pictures on cinderblock walls won't provide the necessary pull-out resistance. For similar reasons, don't mount this rack to a hollow gypsum or paneled wall.

The head and foot of each stanchion help prevent twisting, stabilizing the rack when it's under load. The head is screwed to a ceiling truss, while the matching foot is glued securely to the floor.

The horizontal support arms do the hard work. They're made of 2×4s with 3/4-in.-thick plywood gussets screwed to each side. I angled the arms upward 2 degrees to keep material from sliding off, and I rounded the protruding ends to soften any inadvertent collision between my head and one of the arms. My wife painted most of the rack before installation. However, to prevent lumber from picking up unwanted stains, the top edge of each arm was left unpainted.

I started at the top row and installed each arm by drilling a hole through the stanchions and the inner end of the arm. A 1/2-in.-

dia., 4-in.-long bolt secures each arm. In the future, though, should I decide to change the elevation of the arms, the oversize pockets in the stanchions give me the ability to drill a new bolt hole and shift each arm to a new location.

Roll-around cart for short pieces

Besides death, taxes, and slivers, I think the accumulation of lumber offcuts is about the only thing woodworkers can take for granted. The woodstove can handle just so much; and besides, that peanut-size chunk of walnut may come in handy someday. Owning up to my pack-rat tendencies, I built three storage carts for offcuts that fit in the unused area under the bottom shelf of the wall rack. I left the rest of that area open for future storage needs.

The carts are simple boxes on casters. To stave off the chaos that would ensue if I just threw scrap into the carts, I installed removable dividers, which allow for a rough sort of organization. By adding a removable plywood top to one of the carts, I immediately had a mobile workbench.

Vertical box stores sheet goods in minimal space

I'd initially planned to store sheet goods flat or on some sort of horizontal cart, but I discarded those ideas because they ate up too much floor space. The obvious answer was vertical storage. Holding 15 to 20 sheets, the rack I constructed is little more than a doubled-up plywood bottom, a few 2×4 posts, and a plywood top.

Because there's little outward pressure on this type of rack, it can

RACK FOR SHEET GOODS

Stored vertically in this rack, sheet goods like plywood and medium-density fiberboard (MDF) can be accessed with relative ease.

Plywood top

Plywood gusset

2x4 post

2x4 spacer

Plexiglas covers the plywood bottom.

Base end

Pull-out pad covered with a carpet scrap

Choose and use. *This vertical rack makes it easy to flip through the sheets and pull one out without damaging it.*

Protective pad. *The outside bottom corner of sheet goods gets some protection from damage, thanks to a pull-out pad.*

be attached to a wall with either nails or wood screws. To this simple structure, I added a few user-friendly features. The 2×4 spacers on the side walls of the rack give me some finger room when I want to withdraw a sheet that's located near the edge. A layer of Plexiglas covering the plywood bottom makes sliding even the heaviest sheet a breeze. And because I don't relish the idea of dinging the corner of an expensive sheet, I installed a pull-out pad to protect the pivoting corner as I load or unload material. To squeeze the last bit of utility from the rack, I use the outer frame as a place to hang levels, squares, and cutting jigs.

A storage system works only if you use it

Just as a closet won't pick up that shirt you've thrown over a chair, a lumber rack won't do you any good if you don't use it. I've developed habits to keep the shop both uncluttered and efficient. At the end of each day, I select the offcuts I intend to keep. Any boards shorter than 24 in. go into the roll-around lumber cart; longer pieces are stored on the horizontal rack. When I return plywood or sheet goods to the vertical rack, I always write the new width on the exposed edge. That prevents miscalculations

when I'm reviewing the material I have on hand for a project, and I don't have to slide out a piece to check its width.

This storage system works exceptionally well. Now, when work is going smoothly and all my materials are stowed neatly away, I sometimes let my mind wander to those minor problems of infinity.

Andy Beasley works on his unfinished house near Hillside, Colorado.

A DOVETAILED TOOL CABINET

by Carl Dorsch

A study in dovetails. For practice cutting dovetails, this cabinet with drawers is a great project. Through dovetails join the carcase while tapered, sliding dovetails secure the shelves and vertical dividers. The banks of graduated drawers include lots of through and half-blind dovetails.

When I needed a tool cabinet, I saw it as a great opportunity to practice cutting dovetails. The cabinet I designed features through dovetails, half-blind dovetails and tapered, sliding dovetails. All of these joints can be cut either by hand or by machine; I cut mine by hand except for the tapered, sliding dovetails, which I cut with a router.

Because my cabinet has doors, it protects the tools from dust and curious visitors, yet it leaves them readily available. The upper portion of the cabinet displays my antique planes. The shelves are spaced to hold the handplanes upright, and the cabinet is deep enough so that two planes fit side by side. The bottom of the cabinet contains several drawer banks for storing accessories and other tools.

The carcase sides are joined to the top and bottom with through dovetails. I cut the dovetails with the tails on the sides and the pins on the top and bottom so that the mechanical lock of the joint resists the weight of the cabinet and its contents. I used stopped, tapered, sliding dovetails for the shelves and drawer dividers because I prefer them functionally and aesthetically.

The drawers have through dovetails at the back and half-blind dovetails up front. Instead of installing the bottom in grooves in the sides and in the front, they're screwed to the assembled drawers and extend past the sides to create slides that ride in dadoes routed in the carcase sides and dividers, as shown in the drawing on the facing page.

The doors are typical frame-and-panel construction and overlap where they meet at the cabinet's center.

Because the knife hinges that I used to mount the doors have no provision for adjusting the doors' fit, they must be accurately mortised in place. I've found that by mounting the hinges to the doors first and leaving the hinge mortises in the carcase slightly short, I can chisel out the mortises to sneak up on a perfect fit.

The cabinet can be set on a bench or hung on the wall. I hung mine on the wall using beveled cleats, one on the rear of the cabinet and one on the wall.

Carl Dorsch is a woodworker in Pittsburgh, Pennsylvania.

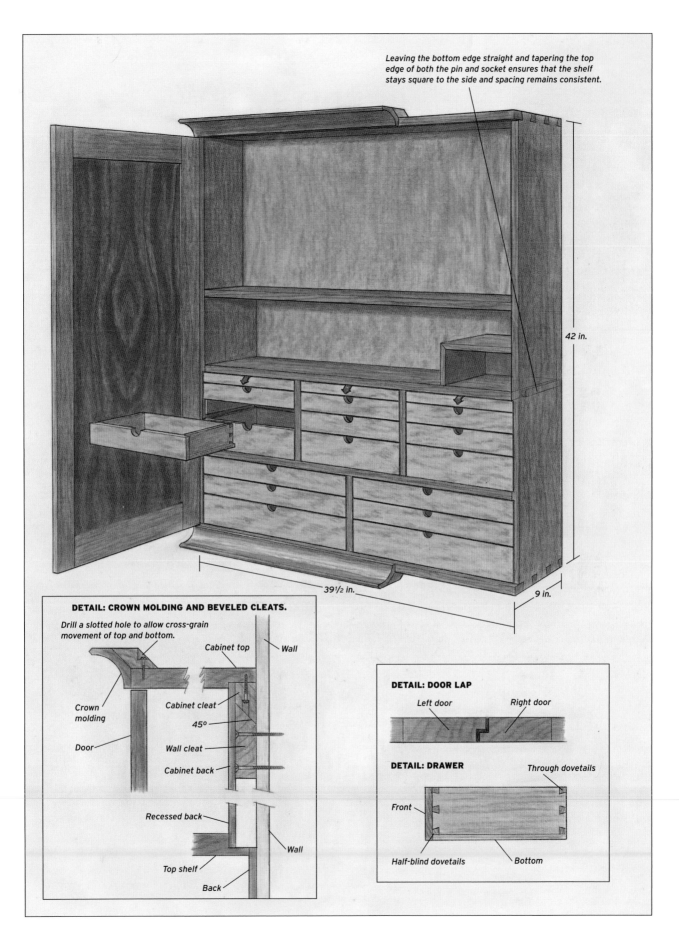

Leaving the bottom edge straight and tapering the top edge of both the pin and socket ensures that the shelf stays square to the side and spacing remains consistent.

42 in.

39½ in.

9 in.

DETAIL: CROWN MOLDING AND BEVELED CLEATS.

Drill a slotted hole to allow cross-grain movement of top and bottom.

Crown molding

Door

Cabinet top

Wall

Cabinet cleat

45°

Wall cleat

Cabinet back

Recessed back

Top shelf

Back

Wall

DETAIL: DOOR LAP

Left door

Right door

DETAIL: DRAWER

Through dovetails

Front

Half-blind dovetails

Bottom

CREDITS

The articles in this book appeared in the following issues of Fine Woodworking:

p. 4: A Tilt-Top Shop Cart Handles Plywood by Fred Sotcher, issue 160. Photos by Anatole Burkin, © The Taunton Press, Inc.; Drawings by Melanie Powell, © The Taunton Press, Inc.

p. 6: Rolling Compound-Miter Saw Stand Saves Space by Charles Jacoby, issue 98. Photo by Charles Jacoby, © The Taunton Press, Inc.; Drawing by David Dann, © The Taunton Press, Inc.

p. 8: Sawhorses for the Shop by Christian Becksvoort, issue 161. Photos by Michael Pekovich, © The Taunton Press, Inc., except for photo on p. 8 by Tim Sam, © The Taunton Press, Inc.; Drawing by Heather Lambert, © The Taunton Press, Inc.

p. 14: Low Assembly Bench Puts Work at the Right Height by Bill Nyberg, issue 118. Photos by Aime Fraser, © The Taunton Press, Inc.; Drawing by Heather Lambert, © The Taunton Press, Inc.

p. 16: Dovetailer's Bench and Carcase Press by Charles Durham Jr, issue 105. Photos by Vincent Laurence, © The Taunton Press, Inc.; Drawing by David Dann, © The Taunton Press, Inc.

p. 19: Assembly Cart Raises Work by Jerry H. Lyons, issue 170. Photo by Mark Schofield, © The Taunton Press, Inc.; Drawing by Jim Richey, © The Taunton Press, Inc.

p. 20: Shop Drafting Table Folds Away by Dwayne Intveld, issue 179. Photos by Tom Begnal, © The Taunton Press, Inc.; Drawing by Vince Babak, © The Taunton Press, Inc.

p. 24: Vacuum Hold-Down Table by Mike M. McCallum, issue 102. Photos by Mike M. McCallum, © The Taunton Press, Inc.; Drawings by Matthew Wells, © The Taunton Press, Inc.

p. 26: A Downdraft Sanding Table by Peter Brown, issue 153. Photos by William Duckworth, © The Taunton Press, Inc.; Drawing by Bob La Pointe, © The Taunton Press, Inc.

p. 28: Fold-Down Sanding Table Collects Dust by David DiRanna, issue 174. Photos by Tom Begnal, © The Taunton Press, Inc.; Drawing by Jim Richey, © The Taunton Press, Inc.

p. 30: Shooting Board by Ed Speas, issue 174. Photos by Alec Waters, © The Taunton Press, Inc.; Drawing by Bob La Pointe, © The Taunton Press, Inc.

p. 31: Rolling Tool Cabinets Save Space by Bill Endress, issue 167. Photos by Matt Berger, © The Taunton Press, Inc.; Drawing by Brian Jensen, © The Taunton Press, Inc.

p. 34: Vertical Press Simplifies Panel Glue-Ups by Jim Tolpin, issue 112. Photos by Vincent Laurence, © The Taunton Press, Inc.; Drawing by Dan Thorton, © The Taunton Press, Inc.

p. 36: Convertible Clamping Workstation by Gary B. Foster, issue 174. Photos by Matt Berger, © The Taunton Press, Inc.; Drawing by Melanie Powell, © The Taunton Press, Inc.

p. 40: A Bench Built to Last by Dick McDonough, issue 149. Photos by Tom Begnal, © The Taunton Press, Inc.; Drawing by Vince Babak, © The Taunton Press, Inc.

p. 44: Rock-Solid Plywood Bench by Cecil Braeden, issue 181. Photos by Mark Schofield, © The Taunton Press, Inc.; Drawings by Chuck Lockhart, © The Taunton Press, Inc.

p. 47: Multipurpose Support Stand by John White, issue 166. Photos by Mark Schofield, © The Taunton Press, Inc.; Drawings by Jim Richey, © The Taunton Press, Inc.

p. 48: Hefty Workbench With All the Frills by Jon Leppo, issue 162. Photos by Tom Begnal, © The Taunton Press, Inc. Drawings by Bob La Pointe, © The Taunton Press, Inc.

p. 53: Mobile Table Serves Many Needs by Jerry H. Lyons, issue 170. Photos by Mark Schofield, © The Taunton Press, Inc.; Drawings by Jim Richey, © The Taunton Press, Inc.

p. 54: Power-Tool Workbench by Lars Mikkelsen, issue 101. Photo by Sandor Nagyszalanczy, © The Taunton Press, Inc.; Drawings by Mario Ferro, © The Taunton Press, Inc.

p. 56: The Essential Workbench by Lon Schleining, issue 167. Drawings by Bob La Pointe, © The Taunton Press, Inc.

p. 58: Heavy-Duty Bench With A Knockdown Base by Mike Dunbar, issue 153. Photo by Michael Pekovich, © The Taunton Press, Inc.; Drawings by Bob La Pointe, © The Taunton Press, Inc.

p. 62: A Benchtop Bench by Jeff Miller, issue 176. Photos by Tom Begnal, © The Taunton Press, Inc.; Drawings by Stephen Hutchings, © The Taunton Press, Inc.

p. 65: Clamping Table by Jerry H. Lyons, issue 170. Photos by Mark Scofield, © The Taunton Press, Inc.; Drawings by Jim Richey, © The Taunton Press, Inc.

p. 66: Versatile and Affordable Workbench by John White, issue 139. Photos by Jefferson Kolle, © The Taunton Press, Inc.; Drawings by Jim Richey, © The Taunton Press, Inc.

p. 69: Sliding Drill Press Table for Mortising by Gary Rogowski, issue 140. Photo by Anatole Burkin, © The Taunton Press, Inc.; Drawings by Vince Babak, © The Taunton Press, Inc.

p. 70: Auxiliary Drill Press Table for Mortising by Roland Johnson, issue 182. Photos by Asa Christiana, © The Taunton Press, Inc.; Drawings by Jim Richey, © The Taunton Press, Inc.

p. 72: Adjustable End-Boring Jig for the Drill Press by Jeff Greef, issue 102. Photo by Jeff Greef, © The Taunton Press, Inc.; Drawings by Lee Hov, © The Taunton Press, Inc.

p. 74: Vertical Boring Jig for the Drill Press by Gary Rogowski, issue 140. Photo by Anatole Burkin, © The Taunton Press, Inc.; Drawings by Vince Babak, © The Taunton Press, Inc.

p. 75: Folding Extension Tables Save Space by Dwayne J. Intveld, issue 163. Photos by Tom Begnal, © The Taunton Press, Inc.; Drawings by Bob La Pointe, © The Taunton Press, Inc.

p. 78: Picture Framer's Miter Jig by Robert Hamon, issue 176. Photos by Mark Scofield, © The Taunton Press, Inc.; Drawings by John Hartman, © The Taunton Press, Inc.

p. 80: Sliding Miter Guage Fence Lends Accuracy by Tim Hanson, issue 118. Photos by Aime Fraser, © The Taunton Press, Inc.; Drawings by Christopher Clapp, © The Taunton Press, Inc.

p. 82: One-Stop Cutting Station by Ken Picou, issue 107. Photos by Vincent Laurence, © The Taunton Press, Inc.; Drawing by Michael Gellatly, © The Taunton Press, Inc.

p. 84: Tablesaw Sled for Precision Crosscutting by Lon Schleining, issue 128. Photos by Strother Purdy, © The Taunton Press, Inc.; Drawing by Michael Pekovich, © The Taunton Press, Inc.

p. 86: Tablesaw Sled Cuts Box Joints by Lon Schleining, issue 148. Photos by Matthew Teague, © The Taunton Press, Inc.; Drawings by Vince Babak, © The Taunton Press, Inc.

p. 89: Tenoning Jig for the Tablesaw by Brad Schilling, issue 154. Photos by Tom Begnal, © The Taunton Press, Inc.; Drawings by Jim Richey, © The Taunton Press, Inc.

p. 92: Angled Tenons on the Tablesaw by William Krase, issue 99. Photos by Vincent Laurence, © The Taunton Press, Inc.; Drawings by Maria Melesching, © The Taunton Press, Inc.

p. 94: Dovetailing Sled for the Tablesaw by Jeff Miller, issue 120. Photos by Aime Fraser, © The Taunton Press, Inc.; Drawings by Vince Babak, © The Taunton Press, Inc.

p. 98: Tablesaw Jig Cuts Slip Joint by Frank Klaus, issue 115. Photos by William Duckworth, © The Taunton Press, Inc., except p. 98 by Boyd Hagen, © The Taunton Press, Inc.; Drawings by Heather Lambert, © The Taunton Press, Inc.

p. 100: Shop-Built Roller Extension Table by Bob Gabor, issue 112. Photos by Charley Robinson, © The Taunton Press, Inc.; Drawings by Bob La Pointe, © The Taunton Press, Inc.

p. 102: Tablesaw Dovetail Jig by Mark Duginske, issue 296. Photos by Sandor Nagyszalanczy, © The Taunton Press, Inc.; Drawings by David Dann, © The Taunton Press, Inc.

INDEX